CARING ABOUT MORALITY

CARING ABOUT MORALITY

Philosophical Perspectives in Moral Psychology

Thomas E. Wren

London

First published 1991
by Routledge
11 New Fetter Lane, London EC4P 4EE

© 1991 Thomas E. Wren

Typeset in 10/12pt Palatino by
Ponting–Green Publishing Services, London
Printed in England by Clays Ltd, St Ives plc

British Library Cataloguing in Publication Data
Wren, Thomas E.
Caring about morality : philosophical perspectives in
moral psychology.
1. Moral development
I. Title
155.25

ISBN 0 415 06259 4

To Carol, Kathy, and Michael

CONTENTS

CONTENTS

PREFACE

This book began as a critical study of the rationalism in recent psychological studies of morality. It is therefore ironic that its main conclusion is that if psychology is to explain the motivational force of conscience it must first do justice to the cognitive dimension of experience. I have come to appreciate this fact after discussing the matter with a number of very different thinkers, whose courtesy and good advice I acknowledge here. Richard Brandt first showed me how a serious philosopher can make use of the empirical literature on altruism, and introduced me to his colleague Martin Hoffman, who showed me how philosophically sensitive a psychologist can be. Hence the present book is much more influenced by these two men than its conclusions might suggest. Also, despite their own misgivings about the cognitive development approach, they directed me to that literature, which struck me as egregiously rationalistic even though I could not deny the importance it ascribed to human subjectivity. My efforts at clarifying the conative and affective aspects of that subjectivity without losing sight of the cognitive aspects were further helped by several philosophers who had published work on the concept of motivation that proved decisive in my thinking. These authors, Philippa Foot, Harry Frankfurt, Rom Harré, Richard Peters, and Charles Taylor, were as personally gracious as they were philosophically instructive. Later, when I became more familiar with the paradigm of Lawrence Kohlberg, I realized that his rationalism was largely a reaction to the anti-structuralism and anti-cognitivism of his fellow psychologists, and that his delphic remarks about moral motivation can be interpreted more generously than I had originally thought.

That the cognitive development paradigm need not be a

rationalistic system is clear from the work of Carol Gilligan, who has gone far beyond the Piagetian limits that Kohlberg set on his own views. She has made 'care' and 'responsibility' two of the most frequently used nouns in contemporary moral psychology, and quite correctly points out that being a woman is not irrelevant to her use of this language. What she means by these terms is not quite the same as what I am investigating here, which is the way psychologists have charted the experience of 'ought' – an experience which seems to me to be gender neutral as far as its conative structure is concerned. However, if I am correct in thinking that the next major task of moral psychology is the integration of the cognitive, conative, and affective dimensions, then the voice (or better, voices) of feminist psychology and philosophy must be heeded by everyone in the field.

My intellectual and personal debts are too numerous for me even to try to acknowledge them all. Several friend-scholars read and commented on portions of this manuscript or one of its earlier versions: John Broughton, Gus Blasi, Helen Haste, Georg Lind, and Patricia Werhane. Priscilla Murphy's extraordinary copy-editing is especially appreciated, as is the help of all those whose names are not mentioned here.

I also wish to thank the University of Chicago Press for permission to use parts of my article 'Social Learning Theory, Self-Regulation, and Morality,' which appeared in *Ethics* (1982), and the MIT Press for permission to use parts of my chapter 'The Possibility of Convergence between Moral Psychology and Meta-ethics,' in *The Moral Domain: Essays in the Ongoing Discussion between Philosophy and the Social Sciences* (1990). I am especially indebted to the Spencer Foundation, not only for the grants which enabled me to work on this book but also for what was 'moral support' in all senses of that term.

I have also received financial and moral support from my university, which I acknowledge with great pleasure. But my greatest pleasure is in acknowledging the support of my wife and best critic Carol, and our two children Kathy and Michael, to whom this book is lovingly dedicated.

1

MORAL MOTIVES AND MORAL MOTIVATION

For all its burdens and ambiguities, morality is nonetheless something people care about in a very personal way. Our private and public lives might be appallingly banal, but at some deep level most of us want to do good and act rightly, and to raise our children to be like us in at least this one respect – even if we do not think of ourselves as moral exemplars. The widespread tendency to care about morality is, I believe, a psychological and sociological fact, albeit a general one that allows for many counterinstances; despite those counterinstances its factuality (and rather less often, its justifiability) is taken for granted by theorists as well as by ordinary moral folk. I see no strong reason to challenge its factual status in this study, nor even to ask (except indirectly) whether moral care is a good thing. For this is mainly a 'second level' sort of enquiry, whose aim is to tease out some of the structures of moral care by asking how it has been represented in moral philosophy and, especially, recent moral psychology.

To open the inquiry we may consider what two great eighteenth-century moral philosophers, Joseph Butler and Immanuel Kant, said about what I have called *moral care* and they called *conscience*. Each of these otherwise very different philosophers described conscience as an instinct that was also a kind of judicial process. For Butler conscience was 'a superior principle of reflection' that 'magisterially exerts itself.' Thus he declared in the second of his *Sermons upon Human Nature*:

> It is by this faculty, natural to man, that he is a moral agent, that he is a law to himself; by this faculty, I say, not to be considered merely as a principle in his heart, which is to have some influence as well as others, but considered as a

1

faculty in kind and in nature supreme over all others, and which bears its own authority of being so.

(1726/1983, pp. 37–8)

Echoing this view a few years later but avoiding its reference to faculty psychology, Kant wrote in an important early work, *Lectures on Ethics*, that we find in ourselves

> an instinct, an involuntary and irresistible impulse in our nature, which compels us to pass a judgment with the force of law upon our actions, visiting us with an inner pain when we do evil and an inner pleasure when we do good, in accordance with the relation our actions bear to the law. This is the conscience, the instinct to judge and pass sentence upon our actions....If it is to be an inner tribunal it must have the power to compel us to bring our actions involuntarily to judgment and to pass sentence in our hearts, condemning or acquitting ourselves.

(1775–80/1963)

Butler and Kant's metaphors have fallen out of favor among many contemporary moral philosophers, and their use of the term 'conscience' is only one of several which that term has enjoyed over the years. For moral thinkers and actors like Augustine and Luther, conscience is an aspect of a more primal religious concern. For others, including not only heroes of existentialist novels and dramas but probably most of the philosophers, psychologists, and others for whom this book is written, conscience is understood as a secular moral concern but not as a British or Prussian courtroom. Some secular moralities center on the common good, whereas others center on human rights, the call of duty, self-realization, love, or some other value. However, Butler and Kant's basic idea that we have a profound tendency to care about morality still stands, shaping our attitudes toward others as well as the way we judge ourselves.

It is surely because most of us (except pure cynics, who are a separate story) so naturally and confidently expect people to care about rightness and goodness – and indeed to care quite seriously – that we are unnerved, if not knocked completely off balance, if an interlocutor suddenly blocks our ethical discourse by remorseless 'I-don't-give-a-damn' rhetoric. In general, scholars are as ready as ordinary folk to believe that people seriously care about

2

their moralities: a theoretical postulate that this pretheoretical belief is factually and normatively correct can be found between the lines of virtually every scholarly study of moral experience, as well as in the empirical data collected on the topic. The people I am talking about are, of course, ordinary moral agents. The theoretical postulate in question does not directly refer to the many philosophers, psychologists, and other theorists who have investigated morality or moral agency – though since scholars are people too, it follows from this postulate that caring about morality is also a standard feature of their personal lives, regardless of how imperceptible it might be in their theorizings.

The place psychological theorizing tacitly assigns to moral care is not always obvious, as we shall see in the following chapters. For the most part they deal with the writings of social and behavioral scientists rather than with the work of moralists or philosophers, for two reasons. The first is that what I have just called 'moral care' is a mode of human motivation and hence constitutes a proper theme for psychological research. The second reason for the focus on these scientists is my conviction that their research on morality is in considerable disarray, largely because so many of these authors fail to appreciate the philosophical dimensions of the psychological positions they have argued for (and from).

But before we take up the literature of contemporary moral psychology, we need to get straight on several philosophical matters, to which this chapter and the next are devoted. It is not my intention to develop here a systematic philosophy of morality – that would be a book in itself, or better, a small library of books, as anyone who has tried to develop such a philosophy knows to his or her own dismay. Rather I shall introduce certain broad-scale philosophical concepts and distinctions that will come into play in the later chapters, such as the open-texturedness of moral psychology, the concept of a moral domain, and several interrelated distinctions having to do with morality and motivation. To begin, then, let us consider how the design of the present study relates to the way philosophers and psychologists have discussed the familiar but elusive experience of conscience or moral care.

Moral philosophy and moral psychology

In both the classical view of moral care and that of present-day common sense, it has seemed truistic (i.e., logically redundant or tautological) to say that a moral agent finds his or her morality to be motivating. But this standard expectation ceased to be truistic – though it did not cease to be standard – in the eighteenth century, when it was thematized in a moral sense theory of psychology that not only construed conscience as a faculty but went on to separate it into what Francis Hutcheson and others of that time called its 'discriminatory' and 'exciting' functions. Ever since then psychologies of morality have had difficulty reconnecting these two functions of conscience, despite the fact that psychologists, like other theoreticians as well as layfolk, continue to assume that people take their moralities seriously. Lacking any theoretical warrant, they nonetheless continue to assume that people tend to regard their own moral discriminations as inherently 'exciting' in the eighteenth-century sense of that term, namely, as having intrinsic motivational import.

It is somewhat surprising that this assumption is seldom if ever examined in its own right. As we shall see in our discussion of modern moral psychologies, a tension arises from the fact that in our own time the two functions are typically conceptualized as more or less distinct from each other. In general, persons who take their scholarship seriously feel a need to bring their theorizing and their pretheoretical beliefs or intuitions into alignment. In the present case the intuition at stake – viz., that moral judgments are motivating – is a belief whose theoretical expression has been lost in the psycho-philosophical shuffles that go back to the exciting-versus-discriminating distinction of the eighteenth-century moral sense theorists.

However, I shall not pursue this last claim since this book is not a historical study but rather a discussion of the shuffles going on in contemporary psychological research on morality. The topic is psychological research since, paradoxically, it is there that the motivational features specific to morality *per se* have been most neglected. But I shall try to speak with a predominantly philosophical voice, even though I doubt that it is possible or even desirable to establish any exact borders between the two disciplines – especially when the topic is morality. My references to psychologists and their theories will be intertwined with technical but, I hope, not arcane philosophical references and arguments. Furthermore, within the philosophical domain I shall pass to and from such subdomains as moral philosophy, metaethics, logic, and epistemology without remark, just as I shall often blithely ignore the balkanization of psychology into personality theory, cognitive science, developmental theory, social psychology, and so on.[1] Of course such categorizing has its uses, and I would not want to give the impression that I think the standard subdivisions of either philosophy or psychology are purely arbitrary gerrymanderings. However, in this study I shall try to transcend those divisions and so avoid the conceptual mischief they can cause. Thus I have dusted off the neoclassical term 'moral psychology,' using it in a fairly loose way to denote those portions of psychology (and, indirectly, ethics and the philosophy of mind) that concentrate on moral behaviors and their psychic origins, especially the cognitive and motivational processes associated with moral judgments. Accordingly, the term covers a variety of radically different theoretical approaches, which we shall later consider along a spectrum of *cognitive* and *noncognitive* ways of investigating the moral workings of human nature.

I said above that the motivational dimension of morality has been neglected in modern psychology, even while it remains part of our pretheoretical notion of conscience. The matter is somewhat different in modern moral philosophy, which has not so much neglected the study of motivation as transmuted it into a formalistic analysis of the meaning of valuational utterances and the logical nature of 'good reasons.' However, it is significant that even in the 1950s, when ethical formalism was most abstract, philosophers generally stuck by their intuitions that moral beliefs are inherently motivational, forging their commonsense notions about conscience into metaethical theories to the effect that action tendencies are implicit in judgments about what one ought morally to do. The subsequent dominance of these theories in the literature of metaethics reflects the general readiness of philosophers, especially moral philosophers, to take as their default assumptions the constructs and paradigms of folk psychology. Unlike behavioral and social scientists, philosophers (at least those philosophers who develop ethical theories) are not typically ready to map human experience in ways contrary to settled intuitions, introspections, and linguistic practice. However one accounts for this difference in intellectual styles, it seems safe to say that a little intellectual conservativism on a theorist's part is not always a bad thing, especially regarding moral phenomenology.

Between nominalism and realism

On the other hand, it would be logically fallacious and scientifically irresponsible to jump to the opposite conclusion, i.e., that since the lack of theoretical chutzpah just mentioned is not always a bad thing, it is perforce always a good thing. The truth is otherwise: a student of human behavior needs to be on constant guard against the temptation to absorb into one's psychological paradigms an ordinary-language construct such as 'conscience' solely because it is a familiar term. In short, it does not automatically follow from the everyday currency of 'conscience' or any similar category that it is necessarily useful for scholarly investigations. Still less does it follow that such categories or conceptualizations correspond to some power or property 'really present' in the moral agent, even though there is no shortage of philosophers, be they classical or contemporary, religious or secular, academic or crackerbarrel, who assume that people really do have *epikeia,* a moral faculty, an inborn sense of right and wrong, or some other sort of wee small voice built in as part of their intrapsychic makeup. No contemporary psychologist would subscribe to that sort of naïve psychological realism, which is only a small step away from the Jiminy Cricket picture of conscience as a moralizing homunculus. The consensus is quite to the contrary. Although Anglo-American psychologists are considerably more willing now than they were a few years ago to use mentalistic categories, many if not most still keep their fingers crossed when they use a cognitively loaded word like 'conscience.' If pressed, they would eschew psychological realism in favor of the nominalism of those classically tough-minded theorists of the last generation typified by the British psychologist H. J. Eysenck (1970, 1976), who rejected the notion of conscience as a basic fact, phenomenon, power, or unitary process. Combining classical nominalism with reinforcement theory, he argued that the phenomena collectively denoted by the term 'conscience' are a loose array of conditioned reflexes for avoiding acts that have been punished by society. He agreed that it may be useful to take a single term like 'conscience' as a shorthand designation for that particular group of learned inhibitions, just as labeling a set of actions as 'evil' streamlines the moral educator's task by encouraging the child 'to react in the future with anxiety to everything thus labeled' (1976, p. 109). But for Eysenck and those who followed him in Britain and elsewhere, such usefulness is purely instrumental: in their view a term such as 'conscience' has no objective status or cognitive reality. Supposedly, even its convenience is unaccompanied by any heuristic significance, in the sense of helping us discover something about how morality itself really is.

I have called this general approach to psychological matters nominalistic because it follows that well-known British tradition in regarding abstract terms as more or less arbitrary designations or 'names' rather than as categories that, so to speak, carve reality at its joints. To be sure, Eysenck is hardly the first British theorist to take a nominalist line toward conscience. Over a century earlier, Jeremy Bentham tried to demythologize moral sense theory by calling conscience 'a thing of fictitious existence, supposed to occupy a seat in the mind' (1834/1983, p. 9). The notion of conscience is thereby reduced to what Bertrand Russell later called a 'logical construction,' such that meaningful statements about conscience are supposedly translatable without residue into statements about more fundamental entities of another sort, e.g., the conditioned reflexes mentioned by Eysenck.[2] But that view shares the weakness of all nominalisms, viz., its silence about why these and only these fundamental entities (or reflexes or whatever) are gathered under a single name. For these and probably other reasons as well, the actual practice of most psychologists who discuss both morality and motivation stops short of the nominalist extreme just mentioned. As Eysenck's definition of conscience as a socially specified and socially conditioned set of inhibitions shows, when psychologists do discuss these topics, the Russellian, logical-construction approach to conscience is complemented – or rather diluted – by an unspoken but supposedly reality-based consensus on the criteria for inclusion in the class 'moral.' Like most nominalisms actually subscribed to, theirs stops short of the Humpty-Dumptean conclusion[3] that there is really nothing in common among things bearing the same name other than that they are called by the same name. Whatever other criticisms we might have concerning a theoretical view that reduces conscience to a loose set of disparate psychological events or dispositions deemed 'moral,' we would be wrong to make too much of that view's seeming nominalism regarding the label 'moral' and, by extension, the labels 'conscience' and 'moral motivation.' I know of no moral psychologist who actually holds that there is *no* way of specifying how a moral domain or subdomain is established; noncognitivists such as Eysenck only insist (wrongly, I think) that any such specification must consist exclusively of some distinct and readily identifiable set of nonmoral terms, which may or may not be nonmentalistic ones as well.

The functions of conscience

Let us turn then to the question of whether an intermediate position can be found between these two extremes of reifying conscience as a wee small voice and dismissing it as nothing more than an incidentally useful but basically arbitrary labeling device. The history of moral philosophy suggests it can be found. True, there are enormous substantive differences in the ways philosophers have conceptualized conscience, one of the most crucial being the shift from the Greek notion of an intellectual virtue (*phronesis*) to the recent emotivist notion recognizing only the affective features of conscience. But by and large the philosophical history of 'conscience' has revolved around the *role* conscience is thought to play, from which has arisen a conception that is not so much substantive as function-oriented.[4] Since Plato's *Euthyphro*, conscience has been thought of as an internalized conduct control that commends, blames, and otherwise regulates one's overt and covert behavior by means of self-monitoring evaluative cognition. This idea is eminently compatible with western theologies, as Augustine's *Confessions* and even Butler's *Sermons* demonstrate. However, it is also quite compatible with naturalistic theories of human behavior, as Justin Aronfreed tried to show in the opening pages of his watershed theoretical study *Conduct and Conscience* (1968b). This function-oriented notion retains the valid insight of the old moral sense theorists and others who have reified conscience – that there really *is* something special about moral cognition, even if that something is not a general feeling tone, a specific kind of behavioral output, or any other empirical feature of conscience.

In the following pages I shall try to show how that insight is present in the work of various moral psychologists, and I shall do so by considering the function of conscience as itself having two aspects or sub-functions. The first can be thought of as the tendency or set of tendencies to act in conformity with one's moral judgments. These compliance tendencies include other-oriented motives such as love or gratitude and self-oriented ones such as the need for acceptance and approval. I shall refer to them as *moral motives*. The second role of conscience can be thought of as an underlying sense of conscientiousness or moral care, which for lack of a more perspicuous term I shall call *moral motivation*. Whether it is best thought of as distinct from the first role of conscience remains to be seen, but what I have in mind here is a general disposition or metamotivation, cutting across the historical and conceptual manifold of moral situations with their diverse sorts of actions and moral principles, in such a way that the deliverances of moral judgment are understood by the agent as exciting as well as discriminating reasons for action.

The interrelation between the two aspects or roles of conscience is complex, but it can be articulated in a matrix formed by combining the two pairs of contrasting terms already mentioned. The upper part of the matrix is formed by the intersection of two rows, representing moral motives and moral motivation, and two columns, representing the above-mentioned contrast between noncognitivist and cognitivist ways of regarding the subject matter of psychology. The four cells generated by the intersection of these rows and columns refer to the epistemological and metaethical views that can be taken toward each of the two main motivational concepts. In the next few pages I shall briefly describe these views under the headings of the *summary* and *constitutive* conceptions (of moral motivation) and the *externalist* and *internalist* perspectives (on moral motives). However, what is especially distinctive about these two rows is their common reference to the *moral domain*. This is hardly a simple concept, and so beneath these I have added a third row, whose two cells refer to alternative ways of conceiving the moral domain. As we shall see at the end of this chapter, these ways are not so much theories as definition-generating views, oriented respectively toward either the *contents* or the *core features* of the moral domain. Thus the full picture of our matrix looks like this:

9

	NONCOGNITIVISM	COGNITIVISM
MORAL MOTIVATION:	Summary view	Constitutive view
MORAL MOTIVES:	Externalist view	Internalist view
MORAL DOMAIN:	Contents view	Core features view

There are, of course, many other philosophical categories and distinctions that could be mentioned in connection with morality and motivation. Some of these will surface in the course of our subsequent analysis of moral psychology. But the ones I have singled out here show the general philosophical framework within which the psychological audit in the present study will be carried out.

Moral motives and moral motivation

In the rest of this chapter I shall discuss the views represented by the six cells of our matrix. But let us begin with a closer look at the pivotal distinction that structures the top part of the matrix. As I have already indicated, the first of my two terms of art, 'moral motives,' refers in this study to a loosely linked set of relatively distinct conative dispositions, many of which bear the same names as the virtuous action patterns they generate, such as kindness, courage, fidelity, and piety. Since they function as mediators between thought and action, they are sometimes characterized as dispositions a moral person 'acts out of' (e.g., charity, loyalty, or gratitude).[5] The second term, 'moral motivation,' refers to their conative foundation or (to borrow a phrase from linguistics) a *deep structure* whose function is much like that which Butler and Kant assigned to the so-called 'natural faculty,' 'irresistible impulse,' or 'instinct' of conscience. I have already characterized this function, whose very existence is indeed disputable, as moral care. It can also be characterized as the disposition to take a moral point of view, from which other action tendencies present themselves as moral motives, all charged with moral significance and overriding urgency for the agent as well as for any evaluating onlookers.

By calling the two terms of this distinction 'terms of art' I mean (to put it less elegantly) that to some extent they have been cooked up especially for this study.[6] As *ad hoc* stipulations they are not really subject to debate: however, it remains to be seen just how useful the distinction they portray is to moral psychology – or, more exactly, to our understanding of what moral psychologists are up to. Bearing in mind what was said above about the tendency of psychologists to take a nominalist approach toward folk categories such as 'conscience,' one may well ask whether from their perspective the proposed distinction between moral motives and moral motivation could possibly be a meaningful one. Furthermore, even if it is allowed as meaningful, one may nonetheless ask how sharply the distinction can or should be made, as well as whether the meaning of one of the two terms of the distinction is parasitical on that of the other. Predictably, how one answers such questions will depend on one's other theoretical commitments, sympathies, and orientations. The most important of these is the cognitive or noncognitive orientation from which one theorizes, which for most psychologists is a matter of degree and not an a priori rule or methodological principle.

I have already suggested that even relatively noncognitive moral psychologists (e.g., Eysenck) assume that there are grounds for grouping certain psychological processes or phenomena under certain labels, and that these grounds amount to something more than merely *ad hoc* convenience for the theorist. In the present context, this means that, allowing for differences of idiom, among moral psychologists it is generally recognized that to some extent a moral agent 'really has' certain dispositions – i.e., moral motives – such as a tendency to engage in helping behavior, a readiness to stand by friends or to tell the truth, and so on.[7]

This is not to deny that among psychologists the motivational dimension of morality is frequently construed quite nominalistically. For instance, in the recent controversy over cross-situational personality constructs (one species of which would be moral dispositions), what was really under attack was not the idea that people have more or less robust and stable tendencies to comply with moral norms (moral motives) but rather the idea of what Mischel (1976, p. 103) called 'a unitary intrapsychic moral agency like the superego or ... a unitary trait entity of conscience' – what I am here calling 'moral motivation.' The point social learning theorists such as Mischel would surely make about this latter term is not that it has no reference whatever but rather that what it refers to in the singular is the very same thing that is referred to in the plural by my other term, 'moral motives.'

11

Moral motivation: its summary and constitutive conceptions

In other words, hard-headed moral psychologists like Mischel and Eysenck, as well as Bentham and their other philosophical forebears, would not be very impressed by the way I am parsing the motivational dimension of morality, assuming that they would even allow the terminology I have introduced. Nor would they be alone in their reaction. My proposal of 'moral motivation' as a psychological construct is sure to raise eyebrows, if not hackles, among most behavioral scientists, and with good reason. After all, to suppose that a construct is isomorphic or even indirectly correspondent with reality exposes a researcher to the risks of violating the principle of parsimony and, ultimately, of having nothing to show for one's efforts. Hence inquiry into 'the' structure of moral motivation might very well turn out to be a snipe hunt, or, to borrow a well-known characterization of metaphysics, a search by a blind man in a dark room for a black cat that isn't there.

To avoid these risks without giving up the convenience of using singular terms such as 'moral motivation' (not to mention more familiar terms such as 'conscience' and 'conscientiousness'), one might interpret them along the lines of Russell's aforementioned 'logical construction,' namely, as having no content or meaning beyond that of the individual entities to which the term collectively refers. Such a move would drastically weaken the notion of moral motivation I had in mind when I introduced it above, changing it from a real albeit functional property of moral consciousness to a purely *summary conception*. Since in that case the 'individual entities' that are gathered up are moral motives, the summary conception of moral motivation could be characterized as verbally different but not really distinct from the conception of moral motive. However, it is worth noting that this distinction has also been collapsed in at least one non-summary conception of moral motivation, that found in classic psychoanalytic theory. Freud's general conception of conscience as an intrapsychic agency (the superego) is just the opposite of social learning theory's summary conception, in that for him the role of moral motives is absorbed into that of moral motivation rather than the other way around. However, the net effect is the same as in the case of social learning theory: the contrast I have set up between moral motives and moral motivation again turns out to be a distinction without a difference.

For a motivational account in which this contrast can be a distinction *with* a difference, we shall look to still more cognitive forms of moral psychology, of which the most prominent are the cognitive developmental theories of Jean Piaget and Lawrence Kohlberg. We shall see in their accounts that the function of what I am calling moral motivation is often (though not always) understood 'top-down,' i.e., as a determining factor or regulative disposition that somehow constitutes the stage on which more specific motives play themselves out. Hence I have called this the *constitutive conception* of moral motivation. To recall my earlier comparison with linguistic theory, one could say that cognitive moral psychologists see moral motivation as a deep structure, without which there would be no determinate, specifically moral inclinations. They are therefore in sharp contrast to noncognitivists, who understand the role of moral motivation 'bottom up,' which is to say as a purely summary concept, an aggregate of prosocial or other typically moral (whatever 'typically' might mean) action tendencies. It is surely no coincidence that as our discussion moves toward the cognitive end of the spectrum of moral psychologies, we shall see nominalism fade into realism, much as in linguistic theory one finds Chomsky and others at the mentalistic end of that spectrum arguing for innate structures that in some distinctive sense 'are really there.' However, the contrast between the summary and constitutive conceptions can also be illustrated by a comparison that does not involve a cognitive–noncognitive spectrum. The comparison is between moral psychology and existentialism, which around the middle of this century featured an intense internal debate over the notion of a 'fundamental project.' Jean-Paul Sartre, who brought that term into currency, regarded day-to-day choices as governed by some sort of super-choice, operating in the wings so to speak and endowing specific projects with value and intelligibility. In contrast, other existentialists such as Maurice Merleau-Ponty used the term to refer to the aftermath of more specific choices, which is to say as the resultant of one's more concrete projects rather than their cause. As in the case of those relatively noncognitive moral psychologists who have a purely summary notion of conscience, they said the distinction in question is only verbal: there is no real difference.

The plausibility of a real difference

It should be clear from the way I originally introduced the distinction between moral motives and motivation that this study favors the top-down or 'constitutive' conception of moral motivation. However, it should be equally clear that its extreme form is just as untenable as the naïve realist pictures of conscience dismissed above. When drawn along lines analogous to Sartre's picture of a super-choice, the picture of a master motivation holds little promise, though if we regard moral motivation more as a structure (Chomsky's approach) than as a choice, it may be possible to stay within the limits of plausibility. Here as with so many metatheoretical questions, the proof of the pudding is in the eating. The best way to argue that there really is a difference between the concepts of moral motive and moral motivation, and that this difference is important for psychological theorizing about morality, is to take a look at some moral psychologies and see whether these two concepts or their functional equivalents can be found there in some guise or other. In this book we shall take that way, following it for its own sake but also to see whether moral psychology would be better off if it paid more attention to the moral motives–motivation distinction.

Moral motives: internalist and externalist perspectives

The distinction I have drawn between moral motivation and moral motives ought not to be confused with the distinction between moral judgments and moral actions. Judgments about moral right and wrong or moral good and evil are cognitions that arise as a result of one's having taken a moral point of view, which is itself not a moral cognition but rather an interpretive tendency, a readiness to process reality in moral terms. Furthermore, from the simple fact that one is disposed to cognize reality from a moral point of view nothing follows as to whether that person will act morally, either in general or on specific occasions. There is considerable debate among philosophers concerning the logical structure and other formal features of the passage from moral thought to action, just as there is considerable debate among psychologists concerning its more concrete structures. Among philosophers, the debate takes the form of an argument over whether any motivational component is built into the very notion that a given cognition is a moral judgment. Among psychologists, the debate takes the form of an argument over whether moral cognitions are intrinsically motivating. The two sorts of debate do not map perfectly onto each other, but they share many of the same basic concerns, such that the position a person takes in the first debate usually determines the position he or she takes in the second, and vice versa. Thus, philosophers and psychologists can be of some use to each other, notwithstanding the enormous differences in their jargons, methodologies, and ways of carving up human experience.

The philosophical debate – essentially a metaethical one – has been held in Anglo-American circles under the billing *Internalism vs. Externalism*. As the second row of our matrix indicates, these terms represent two alternative views of moral motives, or more exactly, two ways of understanding the relationship between moral motives and their cognitive counterparts, moral judgments. The views in question are metaethical, not normative, in that they are views about how ethical thinking itself works. Presumably they have existed implicitly as long as ethical theories have been around, but the distinction between them was not explicitly formulated until this century, first in Falk (1947–8) and a few years later in a well-known article by Frankena (1958). Externalism, Frankena has told us, is the view that it is not especially odd 'for an agent to have, or to see that he has, an obligation, even if he has no motivation, actual or dispositional, for doing the action in question' (1958, p. 40). Internalism, by contrast, is the view that this would be paradoxical, anomalous, or even logically impossible. This description was subsequently picked up and refined by Thomas Nagel, who defined internalism as the view that in moral action 'the necessary motivation is supplied by ethical principles and judgments themselves,' and externalism as the view that 'an additional psychological sanction is required to motivate our compliance' (1970, p. 7).

In the present study I shall use the terms in the spirit of Nagel's definitions. However, the contrast is more easily seen by putting the matter schematically as follows. We may think of internalist theories of morality as those which hold that a proposition like

P1: 'Eve believes that abortion is wrong'

15

entails assertions of the form

P2: 'Eve is at least somewhat motivated to oppose abortion.'

Or more simply, the thesis of internalism is: P1 entails P2. Externalist theories, in turn, are those which implicitly or explicitly deny this entailment, no matter how much importance they otherwise attach to the motivational features of moral living.

Most philosophers who discuss the issue turn out to be internalists, and I am no exception. Some take what I have elsewhere called the 'causal internalist' view, since they ascribe causal efficacy to the intellectual component of moral judgment (P1). Others take the 'expressive internalist' view, believing that the moral judgment articulates motivational structures (P2) already in place within the agent. Still others, including myself, combine these two versions of internalism in various ways (Wren, 1990, pp. 18–28; see Nagel, 1970, pp. 7–8, and Sytsma, 1990). However, this is not the place to ring the changes on the internalism–externalism debate. I shall only observe that externalist theories rely on a conception of moral discourse and moral cognition that is proper to *observers*, e.g., visiting anthropologists trying to catalogue a tribe's mores, whereas internalist theories employ a conception of moral discourse and moral cognition characteristic of the *participants* themselves. It seems to me that the externalist puts scare quotes or inverted commas around moral terms, in much the same way that R. M. Hare (1952) did when he allowed that the word 'good' could sometimes be used sarcastically or in some other non-commendatory way. Because the inverted commas sense of a term is meaningful only after its straightforward sense is known, externalism is logically parasitical on internalism. This conclusion suggests in turn that the latter is the more suitable metaethical perspective for conducting a study of the motivational dimension of morality – which after all is an inquiry into the psychology of moral *agents*, not moral anthropologists.

Until now the internalism-externalism issue has remained undiscussed outside the ranks of professional philosophers. Not a single psychological study of morality has explicitly referred to it, though such studies proceed, usually unwittingly, from one or the other of these metaethical perspectives, as we shall see. The perspective favored by most moral psychologists is (regrettably, in my view) the externalist one, about which I shall have more to say in the next chapter.

The moral domain: contents and core features

What I have said so far about the motivational dimension of morality presupposes some general linguistic intuitions about the referential range of terms such as 'moral.' This is a favorite philosophical theme, which I shall only touch on here so that my deliberately broad use of those terms in the following chapters will not seem mere carelessness. Philosophers have written so extensively and divergently on this topic that it is sometimes difficult for them to realize most people do not regard the term as especially ambiguous. On the other hand, most moral psychologists share the general public's confidence that the basic meaning of 'moral' is self-evident. This confidence has led social learning theorists and other relatively noncognitive psychologists who investigate the moral domain to ignore its formal properties and instead to understand it only in terms of its *contents*. Not surprisingly, the more noncognitive a moral psychology is, the more strictly is its research confined to those moral contents that either are overt behaviors or, in the case of covert behaviors and attitudes, can be operationalized and measured. In general, these contents are prosocial acts or attitudes, e.g., beneficence or obedience, whose prosociality is itself usually assessed by looking at the objective consequences of such deeds rather than at their subjective intentionality. I say 'usually assessed' because as the third row of our matrix suggests, some moral psychologists – the more cognitively oriented ones – do look at the intentionality of the behaviors in question, as provided by interviews or direct self-reports. In doing so they begin to move from a content orientation toward a more formal understanding of morality, or as I prefer to put it, toward an increasingly definite appreciation of the *core features* constituting its conceptual structure. Eventually, when our discussion gets to the far cognitive end of the spectrum, we shall find psychologists such as Lawrence Kohlberg explicitly concerned with the way subjects understand the formal features of morality and not just with those other-regarding attitudes and values that, when operationalized as prosocial actions, form the standard contents of the moral domain.

Both sorts of approaches have their philosophical problems. As I noted a few lines back, philosophers are divided among themselves as to what a consistent and otherwise adequate formal definition of the term 'morality' should look like. But it seems impossible to do without any formal definition at all, since otherwise there would be no way of bringing new actions, attitudes, or situations under the rubric of morality. What usually happens, of course, is that resemblances are noted thanks to which new cases are assigned the same moral labels that older ones already wear. But sometimes new cases are too novel, or their moral salience too weak, for the case-by-case method of labeling to work. When that happens general, non-nominalistic principles of classification come into play, though they usually do so without being formulated very clearly or systematically in the minds of the classifiers. Thus moral worth is conventionally assigned to both virginity and conjugal sexuality, to prudent self-restraint as well as courageous intervention, and so on, not because these practices exhibit a single quality or essence called 'morality' but because they are perceived to be members of a domain of human activity that has features counted by our linguistic community as more or less necessary conditions for the application of terms such as 'moral.' Following the lead of so-called neorealist philosophers who have written about the meaning of meaning (see Putnam, 1975), I have identified a few of the more salient features as stereotypical marks of the moral domain. These core features (there may also be others), which I shall describe here in the briefest possible terms, are three: the executive character of morality, the value it places on impartial reasoning, and the seriousness with which it is taken by those who practice it.[8] These three core features are embodied in prosocial behaviors and other standard contents of morality, but they are of a very different conceptual order owing to their implicit reference to an 'inner' aspect of morality, in particular the reasons for which moral actions are performed.

The first of these features has already been alluded to, when we noted that morality involves self-regulation: this feature is summed up in the notion of morality as an *executive* function. It falls under the category of what some philosophers have called 'higher level motivation' (Alston, 1977) or 'second-order desire' (Frankfurt, 1988a; Taylor, 1976, 1989). In contrast to the nonreflective desires and aversions we have for things 'out there,' its objects are themselves intentional states, i.e., first-order desires, affections, and other psychic states that cause a person to act in and with the world. Thus I may have envy, anger, and other sorts of hostile attitudes toward you, and at the same time take a point of view on them from a higher, second-order perspective. In doing so I evaluate my own conscious life and hence shape or *regulate* it, not mechanically as in homeostatic self-regulating systems (e.g., thermostats) but rationally, by means of evaluative cognitions or reasons.

The fruits of these cognitions are moral judgments, formed according to criteria that are themselves part of our moral heritage. Of these the most important and least culture-specific is probably the criterion that moral judgments must be acceptable from perspectives other than one's own, which in our own time means they must be fair, just, etc. This leads us to the second feature of the moral domain, its emphasis on *objective reasoning*. It is true that deep personal commitments can have moral weight and even overriding seriousness, but it seems impossible to deny that part of the stereotypical meaning of 'morality' is the impersonal perspective from which one recognizes situations where everyone's claims have equal weight and no one is more important than anyone else. It may well be that, as Nagel claims, 'transcendence of one's own point of view in action is the most creative force in ethics' (1986, p. 8). Exactly how this perspective is related to the subjective perspective from which one says 'I' and 'you' is a complex philosophical matter we cannot examine here, though I cannot resist qualifying Nagel's comment with two observations. The first is that the impulse toward objective thinking originates deep within our subjectivity; the second is that objective thinking is not a bringing of the mind into correspondence with an external reality, as crude moral realists would hold, but rather bringing it into conformity with the demands of its own external view of itself (see Nagel, 1986, p. 148). Some philosophers have chosen to limit the very word 'moral' exclusively to the impersonal realm of duties and rights, e.g., impartial considerations of justice and fairness, and to let 'ethical' denote the answer to the general question of how one should live. However, that terminology seems not only forced but of little use to the present study. Suffice it here to note that regardless of what we call the well-lived life, in western moral discourse impartial concepts such as 'fair' or 'just' are stereotypically (and, some would add, regrettably) associated with such a life as far as most persons and most moral psychologies are concerned.

The third and last core feature of morality I shall mention is *seriousness*. The philosopher Mary Midgley has captured my point a bit differently but to the same end: 'Moral,' she tells us, is the superlative of 'seriousness,' and a serious matter is defined as one 'that affects us deeply' (1981, pp. 124–5). Seriousness is what other contemporary philosophers (following Parfit, 1984) call an agent-relative concept, although it is not an inherently agent-regarding one. (I can also take another person's interests seriously.) That is, a moral issue deals with things perceived as central among our hopes, needs, and so on – our web of purposes. Some of these purposes are unique to the individual, but many are common, either because of our shared genetic endowment and overlapping cultures, or because (to speak commonsensically, though the same point could be made in the post-Kantian language of 'transcendental conditions of possibility') they are just things that *anyone* would have to take seriously. For example, we may think of how important it is to sustain conditions of fellowship and mobility and, inversely, how drastically serious it would be to find oneself in utter solitude or complete physical paralysis. The task of discerning what are truly serious matters is, of course, problematic, and requires cognitive skills that are seldom discussed in the literature of moral psychology, e.g., analogical thinking, responsibility judgments, and autobiographical interpretation. Although I cannot fill this gap myself, at the end of our journey I shall try to show that self-interpretation of this sort is *the* moral dilemma, one that moral agents and moral theorists alike must reckon with if the rest of their moral reasoning is to matter.

This quick tour of the moral domain is just that, a tour, and not a philosophical demonstration. It is not meant to advance, much less settle, the ongoing debate among philosophers over where the boundaries of morality should be drawn. In fact, it is not even meant to delimit the subject matter of the present study. My intention here is essentially negative as well as fairly modest: I want to distance myself from the idea that morality is any single, sharply specified set of behaviors, attitudes, or principles. To be sure, there are philosophical arenas in which a very sharp definition of morality is essential, but this book is not one of them. Our interest is in how psychologists who address topics lying within a somewhat loosely defined moral domain go about their business, especially the business of investigating motivational questions associated with those topics.

Conclusion

In the foregoing pages I have tried to set forth a number of philosophical ideas that will come up in the course of our inquiry into the way moral psychologies treat motivation. Since much of what I have said may have seemed inhospitably arid to non-philosophers, it may be useful to close this introductory chapter on a less formal note. At the risk of repeating what was said above, I shall cite a few common-sense reasons for my belief that the 'exciting function' of conscience includes a general posture of concern for the moral point of view (moral motivation) as well as compliance tendencies (moral motives).

First of all, I am struck by the fact that in our everyday discourse about morality we can and often do separate moral agents of all types from those otherwise normal persons who we say 'have no conscience.' Furthermore, we can speak of the former as having consciences that are weak, strict, tender, and so on, all without regard to the contents or deliverances of those consciences. It is even possible, though often difficult, for us to esteem and commend people for being faithful to consciences that are radically different from our own. Moral tolerance is a special hallmark of today's libertarian ethic of living and letting live. However, it is of a piece with the more general expectation, standard throughout the whole history of our western moral tradition, that the truly conscientious person, i.e., anyone with a well-developed conscience, will be solicitous, committed – in a word, motivated – not only to pursue whatever he or she descries as the moral course, but also to take the trouble to descry it.

With this observation we are taken back to the basic point of the passages I cited from Butler and Kant. Once again, that point – whose validity transcends the legal metaphor they used to make it – is that conscience is not an ability we implement whenever we choose to. On the contrary: in Kant's words, it is *ein Instinkt*, 'an involuntary and irresistible impulse in our nature' that makes the continual, often very intrusive demand that we judge not only our actions but also the dispositions leading up to them. Butler and Kant may have gone too far when they regarded this so-called impulse as a universally distributed part of human nature as such. However, it seems clear that part of what it means to have a 'moral nature' is that one takes one's morality seriously. That idea, with which I opened this chapter,

21

shows up in ordinary life in various versions. One always takes morality seriously when one hauls oneself up for judgment, as Kant remarked. One takes morality seriously by undertaking the task of morally educating one's child. One takes morality seriously when one concedes, however grudgingly, that other persons sincerely following a different moral drummer have moral worth because 'it is better to have some principles, even if they sometimes lead to decisions which we regret, than to be morally adrift' (Hare, 1952, p. 73). Each of these versions of the general idea of taking morality seriously is relatively open-textured or content-free and can be considered as illustrations of the concept 'moral motivation.' To them we can add those innumerable content-specific instances of moral concern in which an agent takes morality seriously simply by heeding his or her conscience in times of temptation, which of course illustrate the concept that I have labeled 'moral motive.'

In other words, the question 'Why do people care about being moral?' can be focused through a wide-angle lens or a narrow-focus one. In the first case, it is asked in some broad, open-ended sense. Thus I have represented it as a query about the constitutive conditions of that common experience which Kant called feeling 'compelled' to pass moral judgments on ourselves. In the second case, the question is asked in a narrow, content-specific sense involving passages from moral judgments to actions. For instance, it could be asked why someone not usually active in social issues has decided to protest against apartheid, or why certain members of Greenpeace take their beliefs in the rights of animals or other environmental considerations so seriously that they are prepared to act on them at great personal risk. In the next chapter we shall consider the deleterious effect on moral psychology in general when its theorists focus through the second of these two sorts of lens from an externalist perspective and without regard for the cognitive conditions that make their own inquiry possible. These considerations will set the stage for an examination in subsequent chapters of how specific psychological theories try to make sense of the motivational structures of moral experience.

2

THE PRINCIPLE OF UNIVERSAL HETERONOMY

In this chapter I shall lay the broad philosophical foundations for the next chapter's more detailed psychological discussion of the large overlap between moral psychology and the part of social psychology that deals with socialization. Most socialization theories rest on a postulate of dubious philosophical worth, as I shall try to show in the following pages. This postulate, tacitly accepted by most of the psychologists over the last half century who have investigated the socialization of moral norms and behavior,[1] is that a person cares about being moral for the same fundamental reason that he or she cares about anything else: the likelihood of rewards and punishments.

Thus the conscientiousness of conscience becomes a purely summary conception. There is no room in their writings for the separate, constitutive conception of moral care proposed in the previous chapter under the rubric 'moral motivation.' For these socialization theorists the fact of moral care is accounted for by the concept of contingent incentives and reinforcements, by means of which specific moral motives are thought to be fully explainable in noncognitive terms.[2] To be sure, there are other moral psychologists, especially cognitive developmentalists and certain personality theorists, who tend to regard moral motives as inherently cognitive and moral cognitions as intrinsically motivating. Such a view is tantamount to the internalist metaethical perspective described above, which currently dominates Anglo-American philosophy. But it is externalism, not internalism, that until now has dominated Anglo-American psychology. None of the standard, reinforcement-oriented views of the general psychological relation between cognition, motivation, and behavior supposes

23

or even hints at any prior conceptual linkage between belief propositions and motive propositions.

This psychological externalism is very different from the externalist perspective from which so-called 'moral realists' argue on epistemological grounds that the truth of moral judgments is utterly independent of the subjective psychological constitution of the individual who makes them. To be sure, many moral philosophers from Plato on have held that epistemological view of moral judgments (cf. Brink, 1989, as well as most of the essays in Gillespie, 1986). But among contemporary socialization theorists concerned with morality, the reason no necessary connection is posited between moral judgments and moral motives is not that these theorists are committed to an epistemology of moral realism. Rather, the reason is that they are fundamentally committed to the reinforcement paradigm. In that paradigm, all human action – and therefore all moral action – is regarded as a response to arbitrary contingencies, whose features as rewards or punishments are logically disconnected from the propositional content of whatever moral beliefs are 'learned,' i.e., acquired and internalized in the course of one's socialization. This conception of human action is not limited to mainline social learning theory: it also operates more or less explicitly in other psychological approaches to morality (e.g., cognitive dissonance theorists such as J. W. Brehm (1960); equity theorists such as Walster, Walster, and Berscheid (1978); and just-world theorists such as Lerner (1970)). But it is most basic, and most striking, in social learning theories of morality.

True, among social learning theorists influenced by W. Mischel (1976) and Bandura (1977, 1986), it has now become acceptable, even fashionable, to employ cognitive categories in psychological explanations. This 'cognitive turn' may eventually lead to a whole new paradigm within which psychological research will be carried out, as was predicted nearly twenty years ago (Heckhausen and Weiner, 1972; Dember, 1974). But as with most attempts to forecast paradigm shifts, the very fact that the shift has not yet taken place makes it difficult if not impossible to know what such a prediction really means. What we *can* say, though, is that, however laudable it might be in itself, the present tendency to appeal to cognitive processes is not easily reconciled with the historical foundations of socialization theory or its prevailing methodologies. Those foundations have been shaped by the behaviorist conception of learning, which replaces the idea of cognitive growth with that of a measurable increase in the probability of certain kinds of (observable) responses to certain kinds of stimuli. Similarly, the methods used by most socialization theorists, even those who claim to have made a cognitive turn in their theorizing, presuppose that what is under investigation is a congeries of separately identifiable occurrences (some of which happen to be covert), whose relationships with each other can be mapped quantitatively and without appeal to the phenomenological deliverances of experience.[3]

In my own view, the current enthusiasm of socialization theorists for cognitive categories is better regarded as the prelude to a conceptual revolution than its actual beginning. That is, the much-vaunted cognitive turn is not really much more than a new twist, but it has provided a climate of readiness for more fundamental changes. Indeed, conditions in psychology have never been so promising for the emergence of a moral psychology that is both mature and truly cognitive. The present chapter and the next are critical of the externalism that characterizes so many psychological studies of moral socialization. But the underlying hope is that these criticisms, along with the more constructive analysis proposed later in this study, can contribute to a true revolution, one which I would prefer to call a 'motivational turn' because it would restore the missing link between cognition and conation. Such a revolution would liberate, not oppress, social learning theory and other reinforcement-oriented theories of moral socialization and moral behavior, for it would enable them to explain morality without destroying it for the theorists themselves. This book attempts to contribute to this grand goal by looking for a metaethical framework within which psychologists can better interpret the enormous amount of data already gathered about moral behavior and thereby deepen the insights they already have concerning the nature of moral experience.

Socialization and heteronomy

To hook these ideas into the internalism–externalism distinction described in the last chapter, let us recall how that debate looks at purportedly descriptive statements such as 'Eve believes that abortion is wrong,' which I represented above as P1. As their choice of grammatical subjects makes clear, these statements are primarily biographical assertions or (in some cases) auto-biographical ones; they are not themselves moral judgments although some such judgment is embedded in them, such as Eve's judgment 'Abortion is wrong.' Furthermore, assertions such as P1 are not themselves theoretical claims, in the sense of their being part of a specific theoretical system. However, how they are understood by a psychological theorist will have relatively specific underpinnings, whose nature depends on the motiva-tional paradigm he or she subscribes to. In a reinforcement-based moral psychology, the main theoretical underpinning of P1 is the postulate that the ontogenesis of the moral judgment embedded in P1 can always be explained entirely in terms of externally imposed rewards and punishments, i.e., by conditioning. I shall refer to this postulate as the *Principle of Universal Heteronomy*, drawing on Kant's distinction between a will that is ruled from without (heteronomy) and one ruled from within (autonomy).

At first sight, it might seem that the Principle of Universal Heteronomy takes (or just *is*) an internalist metaethical per-spective. After all, one might ask, does it not follow from the very definition of 'conditioning' that if someone who believes that an action is wrong has that belief solely because of social conditioning, that person will necessarily be averse to doing the action he or she judges to be wrong? So put, it would seem that P1 logically entails P2 (the proposition about Eve's aversive disposition toward abortion), which is of course the very entail-ment postulated by internalism.

But it is by no means clear in reinforcement-oriented accounts just what it is that the subject is assumed to believe when he or she thinks that something 'is wrong.' Is it really assumed that the primary object of a moral judgment such as 'Abortion is wrong' is the social sanction itself? The question is seldom raised, much less answered, in the writings of even the most cognitively oriented socialization theorists. In general, their use of such constructs as 'anticipatory guilt,' 'internalized behavioral suppression,' and 'evaluative cognition' carefully avoids postu-lating anything so semantically deep as a propositional belief in a moral principle, even though the so-called 'social cognitive theory' recently put forth by Bandura (1986, pp. 497–8) and others recognizes that moral agents regulate their conduct by internalized norms as well as by social expectations.

26

It is not clear how semantically demanding our analysis should be at this point. We may recall the claim made above, that where there is no genuinely propositional moral judgment (P1), there can be neither an affirmation nor a denial of the internalist thesis that it entails any motivational propositions (P2). But to understand all reinforcement-based theories of moral socialization in this way seems unduly strict, since in it the contrast between internalism and externalism does not even get started. It seems more in line with the intentions of such influential socialization theorists as Bandura, W. Mischel, and Aronfreed to take a more generous view of the cognitive dimension of their theories, rather than to regard them as having no semantic depth whatsoever. That is, it seems reasonable to regard these theories as cognitive not only in the minimal sense of employing expectancy constructs but also in this somewhat more significant one: the sense of employing in their accounts of moral learning certain notions of moral belief (or moral judgment or moral reasons) that are primarily informational and to that extent genuinely propositional. Thus P. Rushton (1980) has characterized the work done on altruism by himself and others working within the social learning theory tradition as follows:

> These studies of the reinforcement of altruism were more to increase the frequency of behavior that already had been acquired than to produce new behavioral repertoires. In this sense, reinforcement, although it may have some direct response-strengthening properties, *functions primarily in terms of its informational and incentive value. From information about what is likely to be valued socially, people construct norms of appropriate social behavior.* According to this formulation, if people see others valuing altruistic considerations for others, then this will become internalized as an appropriate standard of behavior. If the reinforcement contingencies change and altruism becomes socially devalued, then the norms might be expected to alter.
>
> (p. 93, italics added)

So regarded, the metaethical perspective of social learning theorists and other psychologists of moral behavior is thoroughly externalist concerning moral motives. It is a latter day version of the perspective from which Bentham viewed moral motives as responses to the expected sanctions of the 'sovereign masters'

Pleasure and Pain. In both of these perspectives the central content of the moral belief about action A being wrong is thought to be an unambiguously descriptive, factual proposition, viz., that there are certain sorts of socially established sanctions attached to doing A. As has been pointed out by the late H. L. A. Hart, a philosopher whose own philosophy of law and morality was deeply influenced by Bentham, since this external, observer's point of view is not positioned to give an account of how members of the socialized group view their own behavior, its description of their life cannot be in terms of rules at all, but only observable regularities of conduct.[4] Hart uses this point to criticize what he calls 'the predicative theory of obligation,' but it would not be regarded as an objection at all by the moral psychologists under discussion here. Committed as they are to the reinforcement paradigm, they maintain that action-determining moral dispositions are acquired and maintained solely by the expectation on the part of the subject that deviations from the social-moral code will lead to negative affect. Moral beliefs are fundamentally pieces of information about the prevailing social code and the likely costs of breaking it, although once they are associated with the prospect of negative or positive affect they are transformed from theoretical beliefs into evaluative cognitions that are indeed motivational.

This seems to be what Aronfreed (1968b, p. 278) had in mind when he recommended that socialization theorists conceive of evaluative thought as

> a set of classificatory operations which employ a representational cognitive base that is both constructed and imposed upon the flow of information from a social environment. The representational base may be regarded as having structural properties to the extent that it has dimensions along which acts or events may be ordered, categories which are assigned by classification on more than one dimension, and other features which introduce sequence and hierarchy into evaluative operations.

Even so, it is not because of their 'representational base' that evaluations engage behavior, but rather because in another, conceptually distinct phase of the socialization process they have been vested with positive or negative affect. Thus Aronfreed follows up his recommendation with a qualification that could just as well have been written by Bentham (or Hobbes, though not by Butler or Kant):

> However, an evaluative structure is not merely a cognitive scheme for the economical coding of information. It is the quality and magnitude of the affectivity that becomes associated with the particular classifications which permit the structure to enter into the operations of value and to exercise some control over behavior.

When this conception of evaluative cognition is applied to morality, it divorces the motivational dimension of moral evaluation from specifically moral *meanings* – by which I mean the propositional or semantic content of a moral belief (or, more simply, that which makes a consideration count from the moral point of view as a 'good reason'). Because of this divorce, moral socialization theory finds itself constrained by a motivational postulate much more radical than any general claim to the effect that many or even virtually all people are motivated only by external sanctions and not by the intrinsic contents of such familiar moral principles as the Golden Rule. That claim would be a strictly empirical proposition, which for all its generality and all its cynicism[5] about Everyman's moral motivation still leaves conceptual room for the possibility of discovering some not-so-ordinary persons who find morality intrinsically motivating. However, that possibility is foreclosed in any psychology of moral socialization that assumes, both as a metaethical viewpoint and also as the scientific perspective from which all psychological theories must be developed, what I have called the Principle of Universal Heteronomy. It can now be stated more carefully, as the principle that all moral actions are molded by sanctions arising neither from an objective order of moral reasons nor from a subjective order of one's own desires and self-interpretations but rather solely from an environment populated by objectified 'socializers,' be they individual persons or institutions and other sorts of collectives. At first glance this appears to be an astonishing thing to say, especially about oneself. To anyone whose intellectual socialization has taken place entirely outside the academic walls of Anglo-American psychology, it will seem odd that the heteronomous aspect of the Principle of Universal Heteronomy has gone unremarked or, when noticed, has been accepted without demur by so many moral psychologists whose professional interest in morality is, presumably, not unrelated to their personal experiences of trying to do the right thing, feeling sincere, etc. – in short, their own experiences of being a moral agent. How is this blithe acceptance on their parts of the Principle of Universal Heteronomy possible?

The answer to this question lies in the scientific criteria and goals psychology has set for itself. The canons of objectivity, verifiability, replicability, predictiveness, quantifiability, and so on are subscribed to without question throughout most of the psychological community. Consequently, it is not surprising that they are endorsed, albeit with varying emphasis, by virtually all socialization theorists, as well as by psychoanalytic theorists (though perhaps not by so many of their clinical brethren) insofar as psychoanalysts also understand morality as the acquisition and maintenance of social norms. Furthermore, to the extent – often considerable – that developmentalists and personality theorists also subscribe to these canons, their scientific self-image makes it difficult for them to take a consistently internalist metaethical perspective, as we shall see later.

In other words, the externalist metaethical perspective from which most psychologists understand moral motives is part of a more general reductivist stance taken toward the personal. I shall call this stance 'objectivism' because it objectifies human consciousness, treating it as a naturalistic system of causes and effects and ignoring its irreducibly subjective features. This pejorative sense of the term 'objectivism' is not to be confused with the epistemological objectivism of moral realists for whom values are 'out there' independently of subjective desires or beliefs. The latter sort of objectivism is a metaethical perspective that is itself a manifestation (misguided but not basically pernicious) of the impersonal point of view that in the last chapter I called objective thinking about moral issues. However, what I am talking about here is an altogether different and indeed quite pernicious sort of objectivism, namely, the objectivizing conception that contemporary psychology normally has of itself as well as of human functioning in general. This conception is not so much an epistemological thesis as a methodological prescription and, ultimately, a metaphysical postulate. Hence the difference between the two sorts of objectivism can be characterized by saying that the epistemological form of externalism objectifies morality's *subject matter*, whereas psychological externalism objectifies the moral *subjects* themselves. The latter sort of objectivism has been the direct target of sustained critiques by numerous anti-mechanist philosophers of the human sciences, such as Charles Taylor (1971, 1983) and Rom Harré (1980, 1984), whose arguments I shall not repeat here. But as my comments over the next paragraphs plainly show, I share their dissatisfaction with the objective, theory-neutral status assigned by psychology to the environment surrounding the person as subject as well as to the personal responses elicited by that environment.

The self-defeating nature of externalist moral psychology

I take it for granted that in moral psychology as in other sorts of theoretical activity, the theorist is committed in a general way to the metatheoretical goal of reflective equilibrium.[6] As I have tried to show elsewhere (Wren, 1990), the reflective equilibrium at stake in moral psychology is a congruence between two kinds of theoretical attitudes having to do with morality: the psychological theory within which moral behavior is accounted for, and the metaethical theory, implicit or explicit, within which the meanings of moral categories are laid out. Both sorts of theory have pretheoretical foundations, which may never be completely atheoretical but which are sufficiently immediate in our experience to warrant being called 'intuitions.' Insofar as the intuitions of a behavioral scientist are drawn from the same life-world that a moral philosopher inhabits, it is reasonable to expect some congruence between their respective theories, or at least no radical incompatibility. After all, we generally tend to think that reality is one – which explains the attractiveness of the long-range prospect of achieving reflective equilibrium between the deliverances of moral psychology and moral philosophy.

In the present context, which has to do with the psychological status of postulates about human subjectivity, there is an additional attractiveness, perhaps even a certain moral urgency, in the prospect of a moral psychology that would leave intact our metaethical intuitions about freedom and responsibility. In contrast, an unrelentingly objectivist conception of moral motivation with the consequent externalist view of moral motives would preclude genuine self-respect on the theorist's own part, especially where moral values are concerned. This is a severe judgment, but it seems unavoidable: a theorist who takes the Principle of Universal Heteronomy seriously would necessarily regard all moral commitments, including whatever commitments underlie his or her own professional activities of teaching and publishing about morality, as parts of a great social con game. Or at least this would be the case if the theorist ever came to understand his or her own externalist theory completely and without self-deception. It is only thanks to personal inconsistencies on the part of individual thinkers that the history of Western thought includes psychologists and other sorts of theorists who have refused to attribute intrinsic value or motivational import to morality and yet have lived decent lives. We have no record that Thrasymachus was a villain, even though he has been immortalized in Plato's *Republic* for his cynical insistence that justice is the advantage of the stronger. Ben Franklin found Bernard Mandeville to be a charming person as well as an intellectual debunker of the altruistic virtues. B. F. Skinner was much admired and personally respected by those who worked with him. And so on. But whether or not such theorists have ever personally acknowledged any disequilibrium between their own decency and their metaethical cynicism, it is hard to see how they could avoid doing so once they reflected on the matter.

To clarify the point at stake here, let us consider a related point drawn from the linguistics of assertive discourse, where certain factual and epistemic commitments are held in tandem in such a way as to co-implicate each other. The reflective equilibrium between them is so firmly established that it is truistic to observe that a factual assertion, call it X, carries with it a commitment to the higher-order assertion 'I believe X.' The latter assertion, which can be expressed more verbosely as 'I believe that X is true,' is a self-report describing the speaker's own epistemic relation to the fact mentioned in X. However, it also carries with it a commitment to a still higher-order belief about the relationship between these two assertions, such that one who asserts X is also prepared to assert that the psychogenesis of his or her belief in X came about as it did *because X is true*. Since we are talking here about belief, not knowledge, it is not necessary that X really be true: all these first-person assertions could be made, and made with perfect intelligibility, even if X happens to be false. But this last observation is made from outside the believer's own understanding of the situation. The believer cannot combine the belief that X with a belief that X is false, or with a belief that the historical chain of events leading up to this belief does not include those worldly happenings in virtue of which X is true. This is not to say that we can always trace out the psychogenesis of our beliefs, nor is it to say that their history might not really be just a sequence of coincidences, indoctrinations, or otherwise nonrational causal conditions, rather than a chain whose links include events that are, or are triggered by, the truth-making conditions of X. It is only to say that, were a person to think that his or her disposition to believe X is the outcome of epistemically irrelevant conditions (and only these), that person could no longer take the belief seriously, in the sense of feeling even remotely justified in believing that X.

A similar devaluation takes place in the moral order when moral beliefs are regarded as the outcome of fortuitous, morally irrelevant conditions (and only these). Some of these determinants are probably innate biological structures, though sociobiology has yet to clarify their nature. Still others are structural features of the physical or economic environment, constraining individual human beings in much the same impersonal and inexorable way that biological structures do. But the determinants at issue in moral psychology are those socializing influences thought to operate according to one or another version of the Principle of Universal Heteronomy, so as to generate those cognitive states and dispositions we call moral beliefs. Like factual beliefs, moral beliefs carry with them a commitment to certain views about their own psychological origins, views which can be vague in the extreme but which cannot be repudiated without dissipating the belief in question. The Principle of Universal Heteronomy constitutes just such a repudiation, and there are two related ways in which it dissipates moral beliefs. The first operates at the individual level, undermining one's self-respect by dissolving the grounds for the cognitive and moral integrity that are part of one's self-concept. The second operates at the social level, subverting the social order by dissolving the grounds for confidence in (and for the internalization of) the moral teachings and examples provided by society, even for persons who would normally be regarded as socializing agents themselves.

In both cases the psychological theory of morality is so discrepant with the spirit of morality that the term 'disequilibrium' seems too mild to describe the result of their coming together:

the discrepancy between the two does not produce a growthful back-and-forth of corrective feedback but rather mutual destruction. In the first case, the agent's self-respect is undermined for reasons that go much deeper than the embarrassment one feels upon recognizing that one has been duped. Dupes, after all, care about the epistemic status of their beliefs, which is precisely why one who has been duped is discomfited upon learning that sincerely held beliefs were produced in oneself by epistemically irrelevant causes, i.e., circumstances having nothing to do with their truth, rightness, or other sort of assessment-status.[7] Someone who blithely accepted the fact that one's factual and moral beliefs were generated in this nonrational way could not even regard oneself as a dupe but only as a kind of high-grade parrot, more or less faithfully repeating previously acquired beliefs without regard for their assessment-status. For real parrots, this would be accomplishment enough. But for us who are capable of self-concepts it is not, if for no other reason than that part of the infrastructure of our self-concepts is the tacit belief that we are not parrots.

Cognitive self-respect is not the only casualty incurred when a theorist comes to understand his or her own moral belief acquisition entirely in terms of nonrational determinants such as those provided for in the Principle of Universal Heteronomy. Moral self-respect is also sacrificed, owing to the paradoxes involved in being a socializing agent for a moral tradition that emphasizes norms of honesty, trustworthiness, loyalty, etc. Or at least it would be so sacrificed by fully informed and self-reflective theorists, who would necessarily perceive themselves to be accomplices in an elaborate process of social manipulation, a process whose success depends in large part on deception and, in consequence, on the collaboration or at least the silence of socialized persons such as themselves. Since the psychological strain inherent in such a self-concept would be unbearable if it were fully manifest to oneself, we may expect that any theorists who really did reflect in this manner would deploy defense mechanisms very early in their reflective process, and that these defenses would consist largely in strategies of self-deception. However, the very fact that self-deception is here the appropriate strategy returns us to the first of my two main points, which is that there is an intolerable conflict between the theoretical demands of the Principle of Universal Heteronomy and one's own self-respect.

The second main point was that the *social order* is subverted by any psychological theory that regards moral beliefs as externally induced in the manner asserted by the Principle of Universal Heteronomy. To appreciate this point we may consider the distinction between benevolence and beneficence, the former being a matter of good intentions and the latter a matter of good consequences. As the literature makes very clear, moral beliefs are considered by most socialization theorists as devices for constraining certain actions and fostering others, so as to ensure the common good. Although in practice these beliefs are normally promoted by the socializing agent as being important *per se* and not simply *as devices*, for the socialization theorist their ultimate importance is conceived instrumentally, their significance being thought to reside in the anticipated beneficent outcomes rather than in the benevolent intentions usually intertwined with those beliefs. To the believer, however – which is to say, to the socialized agent for whom the moral beliefs have come to be intrinsically important – things are the other way around. Moral beliefs, dispositions, and the rest of one's moral character are not devices for making the world a better place, but rather, as Williams (1985, p. 108) has put it, the believer 'sees the world from that character.' In fact, the believer not only sees the world from that character but *feels* it from there, since sincerely held moral beliefs generate emotional states (gratitude, outrage, loyalty, etc.) as well as actions.

It is hard to imagine a moral psychologist expressly denying either the truth or the importance of these claims, since moral beliefs are usually most effectively beneficent when they are most deeply internalized by moral believers. But just who is it that a socialization program is supposed to transform into moral believers? There seem to be two ways of answering this question, one that begins by looking outward and one that begins by looking inward. The first way is to think of the products of moral socialization as a specific group of *other* people. This was the approach taken by the nineteenth-century British philosopher Henry Sidgwick toward the lower classes, whose social and intellectual circumstances rendered them unfit for the careful theorizing about the nature of morality demanded by his esoteric utilitarian theory.[8] In his day, class barriers were sufficiently great to make it possible for Sidgwick to hope that people would accept and internalize the traditional nonutilitarian moral beliefs that had kept the status quo intact even though (in his view) those beliefs could not be justified philosophically. However, in our century the lowering of those barriers and the higher general level of education make it much more difficult to run a successful con game on a grand scale. For instance, the moral socializers' secret is let out every year when thousands of college freshmen are taught in Psychology 101 that socialization is reducible to processes of external inducement. Presumably the reason our social order has not completely dissolved by now is that most students either fail to appreciate the significance of this claim or are too preoccupied with other matters to have any interest in testing its limits when they leave the classroom.

The second way of answering the question, Who are the socialized moral believers? is to look inward and think of *oneself*, or one phase of oneself, as the prototypical believer. When this answer is subsequently projected outward, as of course it must be if it is to be part of a theory of socialization, the result is reassuringly non-elitist: instead of viewing society as divided into a small inner circle of socializers and a vast outer one of socialized pawns, virtually everyone except psychopaths and very young children is considered a product of moral socialization activities, including the socialization theorists themselves. Like everyone else who has been successfully socialized, the theorists make moral decisions and entertain moral beliefs, though unlike everyone else they sometimes step back from their practical activities in order to explain them. The fact that for this latter, purely theoretical purpose they employ the Principle of Universal Heteronomy is, we are to suppose, of no special consequence for their practical, moral purposes; it is as irrelevant as the fact that they employ computers, research assistants, and foreign languages. But this proposal only replaces one form of deception and dissociation with another, more self-directed one. The theorist is expected to be a moral agent who sees the world from a highly personal point of view made possible by a complex network of beliefs, feelings, and concerns, all of which are to be thought of as constituting his or her own 'self' in some very intimate sense of that term. And yet the theorist is also expected to step back from that self-constituting point of view, to see it from some other point of view that is more scientifically respectable precisely because it is more objective, i.e., more independent of the subject who takes it. But is it desirable or even possible to split off one's theorist-self from the self that has the dispositions under investigation? Such a split seems profoundly unsatisfying, to say the least. Only by means of what Williams has called a 'willed forgetting,' a notion corresponding to the existentialist category of *mauvaise foi* and the psychoanalytic one of defense, could one's theoretical reflections on morality be so alien to one's personal moral sense. But this notion presents in different guise the unwelcome problems associated with the esoteric view of morality, since, as Williams observes, willed forgetting is 'an internal surrogate of those class barriers on which Sidgwick relied, to keep the committed dispositions from being unnerved by instrumental reflection when they are under pressure' (p. 109). Furthermore, such a separation makes for bad theory as well as diminished self-efficacy, for by refusing to treat moral dispositions such as fidelity, fairmindedness, and so on as intrinsically significant and motivational, it flattens out some of the most central data of moral psychology. We are left with the dubious consolation that the data surviving the separation are relatively easy to quantify and analyze.

Conclusion

In the next chapter we shall consider in more detail the externalist nature of those approaches to moral psychology that have dominated the English-speaking world over the last decades. Specifically, we shall consider how Anglo-American psychology, especially in its various theories of socialization, has dealt with morality and morally relevant phenomena in increasingly cognitive terms without becoming any the less externalist in its underlying metaethical perspective. This metaethical externalism is a consequence of the psychological objectivism criticized above for its mechanistic view of human functioning.

Psychological thinking is not as blatantly mechanistic as it used to be, which is not surprising considering the cognitive *Zeitgeist* now in force throughout the behavioral sciences. Since the 1950s, cognitive categories have regained much of the respectability they had enjoyed before Watson's (1919) announcement that thought is but subvocal speech. Since socialization theories in general have become increasingly cognitive, it might seem that the bad old days of mechanism are behind us, at least as concerns moral psychology and its general notion of moral motivation.

Sad to say, this is not the case. The current vogue of invoking lofty cognitive categories to explain social behavior disguises a fundamentally unregenerate commitment to mechanism, an orientation whose roots are lodged in the principles of reinforcement taken for granted by nearly all social psychologists interested in morality and morally relevant subject matters such as helping behavior. This commitment marks a wide range of 'moral psychologies,' many of which have considerable latitude in their notions of reinforcement, especially as regards the relation between classical and instrumental conditioning. As far as what I have called the Principle of Universal Heteronomy is concerned, the *locus classicus* in this tradition is undeniably Thorndike's (1932) formulation of the Law of Effect, upon which social learning theories of moral behavior and their kindred theories of socialization are built. The Law of Effect has had many versions since Thorndike's original formulation, but they all suppose that when a subject learns, he or she always does so reactively, as part of a psychosocial process objectively determined by causal forces and explicable by universal laws. In short, in every case of learning, including those considered as moral development, the crucial motivational dynamic is the fact that one is responding to circumstances that are arbitrary in the sense of being logically extrinsic to one's own response, even though in another sense (that which is the opposite of randomness) they are anything but arbitrary.

Physical punishments and rewards are the most obvious instances of these behavior-shaping circumstances and of course are the ones that dominated the early influential discussions of reinforcement. Skinner called the events constituting these circumstances 'contingencies' in order to emphasize that their occurrence was in some way *causally contingent* (dependent) on the subject's behavior. However, it is important to remember that for all their *de facto* interdependence, the behaviors and the reinforcing contingencies are conceptually distinct from each other, a relationship philosophers call *logical contingency* since the truth of any proposition linking the terms in question depends on the truth of some other, purely empirical proposition. This second sense of 'contingency' is of course precisely the same kind of distinctness we saw to be the defining feature of the externalist metaethical perspective. Thus we are reminded that externalism is a part of an objectivist psychological perspective on human functioning as well as a metaethical perspective on the meaning of moral judgments. It is hardly surprising that these two sorts of externalist perspective are found together, once we recognize their common logical structure. Both assume that propositions about one topic (in psychological externalism, positive and negative reinforcers such as food pellets and electric shocks; in metaethical externalism, sanctions such as hell-fire, withdrawal of affection, or internal states of anxiety) can be asserted without any automatic reference to, or any implicit assertion of, propositions about some other topic (in the first case, operants such as pushing a food bar; in the second, moral acts such as telling the truth). The difference is that in the first case, i.e., the reinforcement-oriented perspective of socialization theorists, the logically independent terms that are paired together psychologically are generally conceived as *overt* occurrences (behaviors and contingencies), whereas they are usually conceived as *covert* ones (moral judgments and motives) in the second case, i.e., the semantically oriented perspective of metaethical externalism. Except for this difference, we may apply the famous maxim of Butler (1726/1983) to both sorts of externalism: in each case an event, be it overt or covert, 'is what it is and not another thing.'

In short, the psychology of socialization has moved away from its behaviorist origins, but the conceptual distinctness between behavior and its reinforcements remains. The empirical connections postulated between behavior and reinforcement have become more intricate and harder to isolate, so much so that one regularly comes across articles written by cognitively oriented psychologists that decry the cruder reinforcement accounts in ways that at first glance seem tantamount to advocating the overthrow of the reinforcement paradigm itself. Ambiguities are further multiplied when the reinforcing process under discussion is the motive-modifying one of *moral socialization*. The metaethical perspective tacitly dominating those discussions no longer has the crudeness characteristic of the brave early days when psychologists were occupied almost exclusively with rat and pigeon learning. Nevertheless, we shall see in the next chapter that, for most psychologists concerned with morality, externalism remains the only game in town.

3

EXTERNALIST MORAL PSYCHOLOGIES: SOCIALIZATION THEORIES

It is now time to get more specific about the concepts of moral motivation and moral motives operating in externalist moral psychologies. In the present chapter we shall consider several theoretical approaches to socialization that, because of their relevance to moral behavior, can also be read as rudimentary theories of moral psychology. They will be familiar to any moderately well-read psychology student, who will have found their many twists and turns described in various social and developmental psychology textbooks and state-of-the-art essays. Although I believe that the significance of the above-noted cognitive turn has been exaggerated, it is nonetheless useful to think of morally relevant theories of socialization as lying along a spectrum of more or less cognitive approaches to moral experience. (See Figure 1.) The present chapter begins at the noncognitive end of the spectrum with a sketch of radical behaviorism, and ends with an examination of a few fairly cognitive – though still thoroughly externalist – theories of socialization. The upshot of this review will be the conclusion that exclusively externalist theories are, for all their complexities, fundamentally inadequate as accounts of the moral experience of mature adults and are at least very questionable as accounts of the moral experience of children and other relatively immature moral agents.

For convenience I shall continue to refer to all these socialization accounts as 'moral psychologies,' deliberately suspending any unsettling philosophical doubts about whether they are really psychologies about morality at all. In view of what was said in the first chapter concerning the mark of the moral, it might seem inappropriate to use the label 'moral' for exclusively behavioral studies of so-called moral conduct, and better instead to devise

40

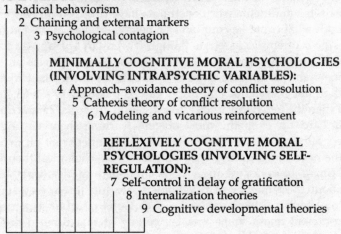

NONCOGNITIVE MORAL PSYCHOLOGIES (INVOLVING NO INTERNAL REPRESENTATIONS):
1 Radical behaviorism
    2 Chaining and external markers
       3 Psychological contagion

MINIMALLY COGNITIVE MORAL PSYCHOLOGIES (INVOLVING INTRAPSYCHIC VARIABLES):
    4 Approach–avoidance theory of conflict resolution
     5 Cathexis theory of conflict resolution
      6 Modeling and vicarious reinforcement

REFLEXIVELY COGNITIVE MORAL PSYCHOLOGIES (INVOLVING SELF-REGULATION):
    7 Self-control in delay of gratification
     8 Internalization theories
      9 Cognitive developmental theories

Figure 1   Spectrum of moral psychologies

some other term for them, such as 'quasi-moral' or even 'proto-moral.' Such a neologism would signify the relatively poor fit of these theories with the semantically deep cognitive categories that are the core features of the moral domain. However, I shall refrain from taking that high linguistic road, not only because neologisms are distracting but also to avoid suggesting that morality is an all-or-nothing sort of referent rather than one that can be conceptualized in different ways and with different degrees of adequacy. Furthermore, I am not convinced that in their actual theorizings behavioristic moral psychologists are really so utterly nonmentalistic and nominalistic. As I suggested in the opening chapter, they tend to assume at least one formal and cognitive principle of moral salience, namely, that moral actions exhibit an *intention* to act in a helpful way. Ideally, theorists making this assumption should acknowledge it and perhaps indicate why they make it. However, even when they do not, it remains true that simply by their choice of subject matter they have tacitly recognized that an utterly noncognitive moral psychology is a paradox or logical impossibility.

I should also note in passing that the following exposition of moral psychologies is not strictly chronological, though there does happen to be a rough temporal order as well as a topical one in our list of morally relevant socialization theories. Suffice it to say that over the last few decades, especially in the 1960s, the extreme antimentalistic constraints have dropped off concerning both what could be counted as a behavior (even moral judgment is now often discussed as though it were an operant) and what could function as reinforcement. This development was probably inevitable: at any rate, even by 1963 Skinner himself had admitted that 'the skin is not that important as a boundary' (1963, p. 84). When the behaviors under investigation are social interactions, it is hard for even the most austere learning theorists to avoid cognitive categories altogether. Hence Skinner went on to admit the need for 'cognitive way stations' in psychological theories of human behavior, though he complained in the same breath about the tendency of psychologists to turn these way stations into 'terminal explanations' – a dubious pun but a perceptive comment about what was happening at that time in the psychology of social learning.

Noncognitive theories: reinforcement without internal representations

Radical behaviorism

The first and least cognitive of the socialization theories to be considered under the rubric 'moral psychology' is that of radical behaviorism. The most important representative of this view is of course Skinner (1953), whose behaviorism, or as he often called it, 'peripheralism,' eschews even the most stripped down centralist or cognitive categories. In its most precise formulations, the peripheralist constraint rules out reference not only to desires, feelings, and self-concepts, but even to *rewards* and *punishments*, since these latter categories are related to the subject's expectations as well as to other experiential features. Hence, Skinner (1971, chs 6–7) has unabashedly philosophized that the Good is whatever is positively reinforcing – either for the individual, others, or society, as the case requires. This metaethical conclusion follows naturally – and naturalistically – from his methodological view, whose call for the systematic exclusion of experience-referring terms is the heart of radical behaviorism. As already noted, in this view such terms are redefined in terms of observable response probabilities rather than feelings, images, or even expectations, all of whose usual definitions suppose some capacity for mental representation. Accordingly, radical behaviorism and the other theories at this end of the spectrum have completely mechanistic and hence non-semantic views of moral motivation.

Even today there is no shortage of theorists willing to work under these stark conceptual constraints. However, their research is seldom very relevant to the philosophically interesting features of moral experience, which have to do with its intentionality. Hence the noncognitive side of the spectrum of moral psychologies is rather sparsely populated, especially in the end zone. More specifically: it is difficult to find in the behaviorist and neobehaviorist literature morally relevant discussions of altogether noncognitively reinforced behaviors. This difficulty is hardly surprising. Except for a few outdated discussions of 'the consciences of dogs' and their 'resistance to temptation' (e.g., Solomon, Turner, and Lessac, 1968), there are no suggestions by psychologists of any school or methodological orientation that morality is not an exclusively human phenomenon. But it now seems to be established within psychology that specifically human conditioning usually, perhaps always, involves an awareness on the subject's part of the reinforcing character of the reinforcement (Brewer, 1974). It remains to be seen just how representational or otherwise cognitive a person's awareness must be for the socializing forms of conditioning to take place, but it seems that not even a standard conditioning paradigm (classical, instrumental, or whatever) can completely avoid looking inside the subject's head when the behavior under investigation is a socially interactive sort of behavior such as morality.

Allowing, then, that even in these psychologies some degree of mentalistic 'taint' is inevitable just because their human subjects cognize reinforcements as rewards or punishments, we can think of the noncognitive section of our spectrum of moral psychologies as comprising a variety of theoretical models (and corresponding intervention strategies) having to do with such morally relevant behavior areas as aggression or helping activities. 'Clockwork Orange' examples of desensitization come to mind here, in which a violent, perverse, or otherwise 'immoral' act (in slightly more cognitive versions, an image or cue representing such acts) is immediately associated with an aversive stimulus and is thereby eliminated from the subject's active repertoire of behaviors. The conditioning involved in such therapies is often conceived under the classical conditioning paradigm, in the sense that the new response or nonresponse is thought to result from a stimulus whose own valence derives from some other, unconditioned stimulus. Here the connection between the two stimuli is altogether noncognitive, since it is a completely arbitrary connection as far as either natural or semantic structures are concerned. For instance, in the celebrated case of Pavlov's dogs there was no intrinsic linkage, organic or conceptual, between the meat powder and the bell that stimulated the dogs, and hence no question of their having any 'reasons for action' in the usual cognitive sense of that term. However, in many social contexts the classical conditioning paradigm overlaps with that of instrumental conditioning, for the simple reason that people *like* stimuli that are associated with rewards (Byrne, 1971; Byrne and Byrne, 1977).

Chaining and external markers

Socialization theorists are now generally nonchalant about the extent to which their own research questions employ and are directed toward cognitive categories. But it was not always so. Some resolutely noncognitive theorists (besides Skinner, 1938, pp. 52ff., 102ff., see Ferster, 1953, and Herrnstein, 1966) were so unwilling to invoke representational constructs – specifically, expectations – that they preferred an alternative now generally regarded as a dead end. They posited that in cases of remote reinforcement, which could be extended to include the learning of moral and other social behaviors, sequential components of behavior become 'chained' together through the reinforcement value that their proprioceptive cues have acquired in the learning process. This sort of explanation has also been applied where external reinforcement is simply absent, an area that includes not only the 'superstitious' (seemingly irrelevant to rewards) behavior of animals but also, we may generalize, the behaviors of moral agents, at least their nonutilitarian behaviors.

The chaining model is, then, radically behavioristic in a way that studies of cognitively reinforced moral behavior are not. It probably is of minimal intrinsic interest, but it gets a brief mention in our list since it illustrates the limits of noncognitivism as far as moral psychology is concerned. The introduction of the idea of chaining not only was a last-ditch effort to explain human action by means of the exclusively noncognitive terms of radical behaviorism, but also relied on the metaphysically incoherent idea of backward yet nonteleological causation. For this reason it was soon discarded, even by theorists otherwise sympathetic to the general idea of conditioned responsiveness. Thus Aronfreed (1968b, p. 73) complained that theories of chaining seem to rest 'on the assumption that a gradient of reinforcement value from the final rewarding outcome would move backward in time across the components.'

A few radical behaviorists (e.g., Bixenstine, 1956; Ferster and Hammer, 1965; Kelleher, 1966) tried to avoid the assumption of backward causation by replacing the notion of intraorganism chaining with the model of 'external markers.' This line of explanation is somewhat more interesting in the present context, since it foreshadows the more robust cognitive accounts of moral socialization in which parents and other socializing agents discuss (and hence verbally represent) an act whose commission or omission has already taken place sometime prior to the verbal dispensation of rewards or punishments. Although the markers were thought of as existing in the environment rather than within the organism (hence inner events do not themselves influence behavior but only transmit external influences), they were presumed to have an affective value as signals, or parts of signals, of the final pleasurable or aversive outcome. Insofar as this compromise account can be thought of as a view of moral socialization, it would have to be located in the noncognitive side of our spectrum of moral psychologies, a point that is underscored by the fact that this model has been applied to the conditioning of animals (Skinner, 1948; Herrnstein, 1966) as well as to that of humans (Strickland and Grote, 1967). However, it ought to be set toward the middle of the spectrum – or better, relatively near the threshold – since it is questionable whether the model of external markers is really as thoroughly noncognitive as its authors suggest. On the contrary, insofar as the markers posited in this model truly 'mark,' we are offered a rudimentary informational, semantically efficacious, freighted-with-meaning sort of model after all. To my knowledge this model has not been applied to any notably moral or immoral sorts of behaviors (Strickland and Grote did study gambling, but not as a morally significant phenomenon); still, it gives us an idea of how theorizings about morality from a predominately noncognitive perspective tend to go beyond the limits set by their own methodologies.

Psychological contagion

A third form of noncognitive moral psychology should be mentioned, which for lack of a better label I shall call 'contagion theory.' Among social psychologists the term 'contagion' is usually used to refer to widespread imitative behavior, such as the 'June-bug epidemic' studied by Kerckhoff and Back (1968), in which over sixty workers in a southern fabric mill reported physical symptoms, initially attributed to a mysterious disease-bearing insect but eventually traced to a pattern of social modeling found among the more popular people in the mill. But my use of the term, which is closer to Wheeler's (1966; Wheeler and Caggiula, 1966) notion of 'behavioral contagion,' refers to noncognitive imitative behavior by a single person, who copies – perhaps altogether unintentionally – another's behavior simply because of some affect-arousing feature of that person or perhaps of the behavior itself. The source of this sort of influence is, by definition, not the reasonableness or any other rational quality of the action in question. In particular, it is not the action's payoff potential as related to a cognized schedule of reinforcements.[1] On the contrary, the influence of such a model is thought to be a function of that person's affective relationship to the subject, an idea that could be expressed either in terms of the needs and affective states of the subject or in terms of certain significance-making features of the model, the most important of which are supposedly the model's power and nurturance.

Obviously, not all instances of psychological contagion take place in specifically moral contexts. Some of the most unambiguous experimental work on this topic are 'vicarious arousal' studies inspired by Berger (1962; cf. Bandura, 1986, pp. 307ff.), in which observers are conditioned to experience emotional arousal (usually painful) from certain stimuli, such as audible tones, simply by exposing them to the sight of other persons being aroused (i.e., grimacing, etc.) by those stimuli. Matters are somewhat different, though, when the result sought is a disposition rather than an occurrent event. Attempts to inculcate empathic response-patterns, altruistic tendencies, and other sorts of moral attitudes by vicarious conditioning have been less successful, or at least less clearly classifiable as instances of purely noncognitive 'contagion.' Compared to empathy, aggressive feelings and dispositions are a little easier to inculcate by noncognitive modeling, an empirical finding that has an inverse significance for moral psychology. It seems to suggest that the motives for paradigmatically moral actions, such as helping an injured person, are typically mediated by inherently cognitive and cross-situational meaning-structures, such as justificatory principles and values, whereas nonmoral motives, which can prompt bad actions as well as neutral ones, can easily operate without any such mediation – in particular, without any regard for justificatory reasons or excuses.

But this way of contrasting moral and nonmoral motives is deceptively simple. Here as elsewhere in the literature on vicarious arousal there is more controversy than one might expect from laboratory-produced studies. The results of experiments such as those of Berkowitz and Geen (1966), Wheeler and Caggiula (1966), Geen (1978), and others are conflicting. However, a consensus has emerged (see Aronfreed, 1968b, p. 122; Bandura, 1986, p. 311) on at least two points: that the simple observation of another person's aggressive behavior can have a motivational effect on the observer, and that such observation always involves some interpretation placed on the arousing event by the observer – which means that the medical metaphor of 'contagion' is much more limited than is suggested by early literature of modeling as well as by such everyday expressions as 'infectious laughter' or 'the contagion of fear.' Clearly, for the motivational effects of vicarious arousal to be transformed into the sort of social action or interaction of interest to moral psychologists, more than simple observation is necessary – a conclusion also drawn in the more recent literature on modeling. For instance, for one's anger to be aroused by exposure to an angry model, it is also necessary that one be sensitive to social cues providing information about how and when one's own anger is to be acted out. It also seems necessary that one have a certain 'readiness' to become angry, a predisposition that probably has its own highly cognitive structure. And so on. It is, of course, no news to moralists that learning by example is a much more complex sort of personal change than, say, catching the flu. Hence when we study moral socialization, the theories of modeling proposed by recent cognitive social learning theorists are much more interesting, as we shall see when we move into the cognitive sector of the spectrum of moral psychologies.

Many other basically noncognitive approaches to the moral side of social experience could be mentioned here. Some seem more cognitive than they really are because they involve experimental procedures that willy-nilly introduce elementary cognitive constructs. For instance, Aronfreed and Paskal (1965) studied the development of empathy as a (nonvicariously) conditioned response to conditioned and reward-producing stimuli. Since they proposed empathy as a motivational base for altruistic behavior and since the central explanatory role in these accounts is played by mere *contiguities* of the stimuli, it seems reasonable to represent their work and other research inspired by it (e.g., Hoffman, 1976) as located on the noncognitive side of our spectrum of moral psychologies. Another, slightly more cognitive (perhaps because it is more adult-oriented) approach to altruism was taken by Moss and Page (1972), who studied whether the act of giving directions to a stranger on the street (itself a richly cognitive performance as well as an altruistic one) could be noncognitively reinforced by the affective tone of the stranger's reaction. Their expectation was that the subject would be more likely to refrain from helping a second stranger in need if the first one reacted to the help rudely, and more likely to help a second one if the first stranger was grateful – polite, smiling, and so on. (They found evidence for the first hypothesis, by the way, but not for the second.) But in spite of their cognitive tinge, at bottom these approaches are as resolutely noncognitive as those discussed in more detail above. Statements about intentions and inner representations might slip in from time to time; but when they do, their reference is only to the enabling conditions or causes of the behaviors under investigation – never to the subject's *reasons* for action.

The list of noncognitive studies of morally relevant behavior is long and not always easy to catalog. However, it seems safe to predict from the studies considered so far, which are representative of the literature, that no utterly and absolutely noncognitive account of moral motives will accommodate our prescientific conception of morality as an action-determining process that is both motivational and reason-sensitive. In the opening chapter I urged that the moral domain should not be narrowly construed, which suggests in turn that 'moral psychology' is itself a fairly broad and open-textured concept. But however broadly moral psychology is understood, it cannot be purely 'noncognitive' in the radically nonsemantic sense employed in the preceding pages, even though a theory need not be intellectualist or rationalist to count as a moral psychology.

Theories of conflict resolution

Once we leave the noncognitive fringe of the spectrum we can find other, more plausible sorts of moral psychologies that while still relatively noncognitive use at least a few intrapsychic categories in their approach to moral socialization. Since these categories refer to the subject's own actions, they render the theories that invoke them distinctly more cognitive than those considered so far. For our purposes, they can be divided into approach–avoidance and cathexis theories. Both types deal with motivational conflict, envisioned either from the field of interpersonal conflict, as with approach-avoidance theory, or from the subpersonal field of clashing energies, as with cathexis theory. In either case, the underlying assumption is the essentially cognitive one that intrapsychic conflict can occur only to the extent that the subject can represent to him or herself a plurality of possible outcomes. If we take this assumption seriously, as I think we must, it seems unlikely that the radically noncognitive theories described in the last section can be applied profitably to the experience of moral conflict – which provides us with still another reason not to consider them full-flown moral psychologies. Moralists and moral philosophers differ greatly in the significance they assign to motivational conflict, but some form of the 'war of the passions' has always been thought to constitute at least part of the object of morality. Even Aristotle, who in the *Nicomachean Ethics* distinguished what he called *continence* (doing the good thing regretfully, i.e., while also wishing to do the opposite) from moral *virtue* (doing the good thing with relish), included on his list of virtues the habits of temperance and courage, both of which are self-monitoring dispositions that presuppose the possibility of countervailing motives.

However, most of the empirical literature on motivational conflict is still a long way from anything that could reasonably be considered a worked-out psychology of *moral motives*, assuming these motives are of a conceptually different order than purely 'wanton' impulses and affects (no matter how benign or prosocial the latter might be). As Alston (1977, p. 91) has pointed out, the standard intrapsychic picture drawn by psychologists is that of a motivational field in which various tendencies – moral, nonmoral, and immoral – engage in a single interaction for the control of behavior. Or to use Gilbert Ryle's (1949) categories, which tie us back into Butler's view and my own remarks above and elsewhere (see Wren, 1982) about mechanistic models of human processes, the prevailing idea is that the resolution of conflict is *paramechanical* rather than *parapolitical*. This idea holds even for specifically moral conflicts of temptations and ethical dilemmas, where the forces involved include charity, respect for life, and other action tendencies considered *moral* motives because they are usually defined in reference to moral values. Supposedly, when such motives determine the direction of an agent's behavior, they do so not by any privileged status or authority (as in a political system) but only by their greater strength or power (as in a mechanical system).

Approach–avoidance theory

We need not carry this last point beyond the perimeters of ordinary language. Since morality deals with conflict, especially that inner psychic conflict often referred to simply as 'the moral struggle,' conflict resolution theory in general can be regarded as a rudimentary moral psychology, using the latter term in the loose sense adopted at the beginning of this chapter. However, we must not let ourselves be misled by this usage, or by the reference to intrapsychic variables made in conflict resolution theories, into thinking that these theories are more cognitive than they really are. They depict the subject as caught in an inherently nonrational force-field of desires, simultaneously inclined toward and away from some global state – similar to a rat for whom getting food also involves getting a shock. Philosophers will recognize this as Thomas Hobbes's picture of the human condition, as well as that of the ancient atomists. Its most famous moral instance is probably that of the person struggling against unruly sexual desires, as represented in Plato's *Symposium* or Paul's *Letter to the Romans*. The most important recent philosophical statement of this view is probably Richard Brandt's Locke Lectures (1979). In modern psychology its most influential version is the approach–avoidance picture of conflict, developed by Kurt Lewin (1938) and a decade later by Neal Miller (1948a). In this picture, as well as in the related ones of approach–approach (the subject is pulled by two competing goods), avoidance–avoidance (involving two evils), and double approach–avoidance (involving two good–evil pairs), conflict is envisioned as a competition of desires, some of which function as moral motives. In each case the respective pro and con desires vary with regard to a variety of factors such as the distance from the goal, the strength of the underlying drive, and (since cognitive categories are not completely excluded) the probabilities with which the goal or threat is perceived and expected. Ideally, all these factors could be represented in machine table form, which as Ashby (1968) has explained represents the complete sequence of states and outputs a machine or any mechanistically conceived organism will run through under a given set of input conditions. In reality, of course, no one seriously expects the pulls and pushes of conflicting human desires to be represented by a machine table, since desires are so varied and their interaction is so complex. But for all their complexities, all conflicts are understood in the approach–avoidance account as being ultimately resolved in favor of the strongest current desire. In fact, even this formulation is misleading: the resolution of a desire conflict is not a victory or something awarded by the agent to the strongest desire the way a prize is awarded by a judge to the fastest runner, but rather simply is the fact of one desire having overpowered the others. Here there is no question of a desire's entitlement or its being 'declared' the winner – hierarchical notions that suppose a judge and a set of rules under which a contender's efforts are evaluated from a higher level – but only of whether or not it has prevailed.

In the early psychological literature the original approach–avoidance picture was drawn in language appropriate to drive- or tension-reduction theories rather than in terms of expectancies, but that fact is not important here. Like the Law of Effect on which it is based, the approach–avoidance account is compatible with either of those two conceptions of the general conative notion whose nontechnical name is simply 'desire.' After all, any expectancy theory of motivation owes its intelligibility to the assumption – often tacit – that we have certain pre-established conations whereby most if not all of our affective states are motivational. From a strictly logical standpoint, there is no necessary connection between any given affective state (or the prospect thereof) and its corresponding desire, though from an evolutionary point of view there is necessarily a highly probable connection between them. (Organisms not aversive to pain states would have dim chances of survival or of reproductive success.) It is, then, not surprising that as the psychology of motivation developed, theories stressing the cognitive element of expectation emerged in the wake of drive theories of motivation, in a manner reminiscent of the dialectical notion of *Aufhebung*, i.e., simultaneously denying and incorporating the earlier position. Hence it is not important for our purposes to disentangle the 'push' theories from the 'pull' theories of motivation. Whether one begins with a notion of drive, energy, tension, etc., or with that of incentive, valence, cue, etc., the picture of moral motives presented in this theory remains that of a non-hierarchical power struggle, which is quite different from the standard philosophical conceptions of moral motives as reasons that dominate a hierarchical process of self-regulation.

Obviously, the approach–avoidance conception of the conflict problematic presupposes that it is possible at least in principle for an onlooking theorist (though not necessarily the agent him or herself) to quantify that agent's desires or at least to rank them as being more or less strong. In general, there are two circumstances in which we speak of a desire as 'strong': when one wants something very much, and when one wants very much of something. These two ways of conceiving a desire's strength correspond to the two general ways already mentioned of conceiving the nature of desire, i.e., as tendency and as expectancy, and are similarly reciprocal in their broad outlines.[2]

Regardless of which way was used, the early experimental work on conflict situations studied conflicts of a rather elemental nature, usually with nonhuman subjects or nonmoral problems. But we see the same logic at work in contemporary psychological analyses of higher sorts of conflicts, in which conscience or its equivalent is conceived in the same way (i.e., as mechanical rather than parapolitical) that hunger and fear of electrical shock were conceived in Miller's approach–avoidance model. What is different about moral motives is the way they are thought to be acquired in the first place, not the way they engage with nonmoral motives or with each other. Nor are moral motives thought of as all acquired in the same way. For instance, Hoffman (1976) explains the genesis of directly benevolent desires as a combination of nature and nurture, involving early experiences of empathic distress in situations where self and other are not well-differentiated. Other moral motives that are only indirectly benevolent, such as an aversion to lying or a desire to tell the truth, are acquired 'inductively,' a term Hoffman uses to describe methods of education that develop desires and aversions by explaining or otherwise demonstrating consequences of certain actions. Still other morally toned desires and aversions are acquired as a result of punishment, and so on. But – and this is the main point of the present discussion – when a moral motive such as benevolence or the desire to keep a promise prevails over other, nonmoral or 'wicked' desires, it does so not because of some independently established worthiness or reasonableness ascribed to it by the agent, but only because it has combined with one's other desires to form the strongest action-tendency. As Atkinson and Reitman put it, 'The resultant motivation is the algebraic summation of approach and avoidance' (1958, p. 279; see also Littig and Petty, 1971; Raynor, 1974; Brandt, 1979, ch. 3).

Cathexis theory

The approach–avoidance account of intrapsychic conflict has a psychoanalytic analogue in Freud's early theory of repression, whose central concept is that of *cathexis*, i.e., the notion of psychic energy or drive channeled to an object. Like the former account, this theory forms a rudimentary moral psychology when it is applied to the socialization of one's appetites, especially sexual passion, and – also like the former account – it is a modestly cognitive moral psychology in that it presupposes some internal representations on the part of the subject. Thus Freud's essay 'Repression' (1915/1957) suggests that repressing lustful desires is a strategy for resolving the conflict between one's sexual desires and other wants, for instance the desire not to betray a friend whose spouse is the object of one's lust. The technique consists in first separating the thought of the desired object from the feeling animating the desire, and then displacing that feeling onto another object – or, more exactly, onto another idea or representation of that object.

This picture of repression and cathexis was originally outlined in his 'Project for a Scientific Psychology' (1895/1950), which he did not publish in his lifetime even though 'it haunts the whole series of Freud's writings' (editorial note in ibid, p. 290; see also Amacher, 1965, and R. R. Holt, 1965). It was redrawn by him over the next two-and-a-half decades, but once he moved from the drive paradigm to that of ego and superego, the picture faded so rapidly that today few books and articles about Freudian theory contain more than a passing reference to his notion of cathexis, and rightly so.[3] Like the models of chaining and external markers discussed above, Freud's early theory of repression is significant for our study primarily because it illuminates another, longer-lived and better-known model of moral psychology.

As I have just said, his picture of cathexis is analogous to that of the approach–avoidance picture of conflict resolution at the personal level, even though Freud's motivational construct was that of a drive rather than an expectancy. Thus Miller (1948b), himself no Freudian but at the time something of a 'push' theorist and so not unfriendly to the cathectic (drive-attaching) paradigm of repression, noted the similarity between Freud's notion of 'displacement' and that of what experimentalists like himself called 'stimulus-response generalization.' The one approach originates in the clinic and the other in the laboratory, but both hypothesize that motivational tendencies can be redirected – Freud would have said cathected – when for some reason or other their original objects are not available. Repression, which Freud always considered the standard modality of moral experience, is the unconscious version of this process. It is in effect a form of conflict resolution, in that repression takes place when (to return now to the jargon of experimental psychology) the direct response to the original stimulus is prevented by conflict and so is displaced in the direction of stimuli more or less similar to that which originally elicited the response or response-tendency (see Miller, 1948b, p. 177). It followed for Freud that the forge of moral motives, i.e., socialization, could be understood as the set of culturally induced processes by which the direction and distance of displacements are determined, though he did not claim that all displacements must be socialized ones any more than he claimed that all repressions must function as moral censorship.

Of course Freud's later theory, especially his construct of the superego in *The Ego and the Id* (1923/1961) and *Civilization and Its Discontents* (1930/1961), develops the idea of moral constraint with considerably more sophistication concerning the executive dimension of self-regulation than is contained in the non-hierarchical, force-field pictures of either the approach–avoidance account or cathexis theory. (Hence even Rapaport (1951, p. 65), for all his enthusiasm for the concept of cathexis, could plausibly reject, in the name of psychoanalysis, the idea that human behavior is produced in a motivational Battle of the Titans.) We shall look at the superego in the next chapter. But it is interesting to note here that, well before *The Ego and the Id*, Freud had conceived of morality as a cross-situational anchor whose stability was explained not as cognitive self-regulation but only as a noncognitive set of psychic energies already at play within the organism, constant in quantity and only requiring realignment or counter-cathexis in order to be able to assume what Freud regarded as the typically repressive role of morality. Although this is not the place to trace the intricacy of Freud's notions of cathexis, counter-cathexis, bound cathexis, hyper-cathexis, etc., it is worth observing that this path would eventually lead us to Freud's idea of anxiety, which changed from the notion of a toxic reaction to undischarged sexual tensions and finally to the notion of a vehicle for discharging the affects of repressed ideas. In its later formulations (see Freud, 1926/1959), anxiety was an affective construct functioning both as an alarm signal and, in the cases of neurotic and moral anxiety where the danger is not objective (except indirectly, e.g., through punishment), as the aversive stimulus to be avoided for its own sake. This second function corresponds to the expectancy view central to learning theories of socialization, since in both cases the agent is motivated not by the intrinsic meaning of his or her behavior but rather by logically extrinsic outcomes of that behavior. Hence it was no coincidence that tough-minded empirical psychologists like MacCorquodale and Meehl (1953; cf. Tolman, 1945) used Freud's term 'cathexis' to refer to the incentive value of a stimulus anticipated by the agent as the consequence of a response that he or she is in a position to make to some other, already impinging stimulus.

It may be wrong to read Freud as saying, at any stage of his career, that human motivation is just a network of blind forces, since the importance of his work consists largely in its recognition of unconscious purposiveness (see Peters, 1958). But it is undeniable that he continued to advocate as a scientific ideal an 'economic point of view' that would do away with qualitative, teleological accounts of motivation in favor of quantitative ones that could be manipulated algebraically, even though Freud eventually came to regard the coercive power of libidinal or psychic energies as that of a force – a vector quantity – rather than that of raw energy – a directionless scalar quantity.[4] In his later work Freud held a teleological view of the vectors that constitute moral self-direction, in which they seemed to him eligible for such qualitative predications as 'better' and 'morally right' as well as 'stronger' and 'greater.' However, the extent to which this view replaces his earlier, more mechanistic view of human motivation is an in-house issue that we can leave to Freud scholars to sort out (see Solomon, 1974).

Two qualifications

In the last two sections I have gathered experimental and early Freudian accounts of intrapsychic conflict together under the general rubric 'moral psychology.' Since moral issues, especially sexual ones, are often thought of as a struggle between competing motives or clusters of motives such as what Paul called urgings of 'the flesh and the spirit,' it seems reasonable to reserve a place for these accounts in our spectrum of moral socialization theories. But this decision needs two qualifications. The first and less problematic one is the reminder that these conflict theories are 'moral' in a real but quite limited sense, since inner conflict resolution is only one part of morality and much moral behavior is carried out with little or no struggle. The second qualification is more problematic, because it involves the recurring question of how far moral psychology must go beyond purely behavioral categories in order to do justice to its subject matter. To parallel my first qualification, the second one can be formulated as the observation that the conflict models discussed here are 'cognitive' in the weakest possible sense of that term. As we have just seen, they presuppose some minimal representations or semantic activities on the part of the subject whereby objects and alternative courses of action are envisioned and valenced, but not any evaluative cognitions in terms of which these conceptualizations might take on new, specifically moral meanings. Since the conceptual schemes used to represent intrapsychic conflict involve *representations* of reality as well as behavioral *responses* to it, we may think of these theories as standing on the threshold between the cognitive and the noncognitive portions of our spectrum, perhaps adding that the moral psychologists who use these schemes have sometimes quietly slid over that threshold when the behavior under investigation included a good deal of verbal behavior. However, the threshold has been crossed openly and decisively by the moral psychologists to whom we now turn: those socialization theorists whose interest in the dynamics of teaching by example (modeling) has led them to explain moral motivation in terms of the idea of vicarious reinforcement.

Modeling and vicarious reinforcement

A full review of modeling theories would call up its own subordinate spectrum of noncognitive and cognitive accounts of the power of personal example, which we cannot systematically traverse here (but see Bandura, 1971a, 1986, esp. pp. 47–9). The best-known approach to the general topic is that of Albert Bandura and his associates (Bandura and Walters, 1963; Bandura, 1965, 1971b, 1977, 1986; Rosenhan, 1972), which since the 1960s has dominated the literature on observational learning. In their various discussions of observational learning they argue that *any* behavior, moral as well as nonmoral, can be acquired through modeling. As we have already seen, the early, relatively noncognitive accounts of imitative behavior treated modeling as a form of psychological contagion: under certain circumstances, the simple act of observing another person was considered a sufficient condition for the occurrence of imitative behavior, with no provision made for any distinction between mimicry and more sophisticated forms of imitation. But the social learning theorists just mentioned (Bandura himself now prefers the name 'social cognitive theorists') have transformed the conceptually lean idea of simply 'observing a model' into a semantically richer idea, and hence a much more cognitive one. For them, modeling involves the vicarious experiences of observing not only the model's overt behavior but also its consequent reinforcements; it also involves the internal use of verbal and nonverbal images whereby imitation goes beyond mere mimicry of specific acts to more generalized sorts of matching behavior.

Accordingly, a calculative requirement was added to the three other necessary conditions generally recognized as having to be met if one is to learn from a model (Bandura, 1971a). The subject not only must (1) observe the model's behavior, (2) retain what has been observed, and (3) have the skills needed to reproduce the model's behavior, but must also (4) perceive the consequences of the model's actions as desirable or reinforcing. The cognitive dimensions of this now standard explanatory scheme should be obvious. For instance, the first of these requirements is that the subject *notice* and *attend* to what the model does, operations that are not themselves overt activities. The cognitive dimension of the second requirement is especially intricate, since, as just mentioned, the subject is thought to *retain* what he or she observes by encoding it in some semantic vehicle, either a nonverbal 'image' or its verbal equivalent, such as a label, propositional value judgment, or rule. This semanticity recurs in the third and fourth requirements. The 'skills' needed to *reproduce* the model's behavior include not only motor skills but also cognitive skills of applying and manipulating images, labels, criteria, values, and other rule-like units of meaning. Similarly, these or comparable skills are needed for the *hypothetical thinking* described in the fourth requirement, which involves not only calculating the affective benefits of a vicariously experienced state of affairs but also doing so from another perspective (i.e., the model's).

One result of the 'cognitivization' of modeling theory over the last two-and-a-half decades is that its analysis of observational learning tends to toggle back and forth between what is learned (contents) and the subject's cognitive competence (skills) for learning it, a development that is especially evident in the analysis of moral learning. Social cognitive theorists often say that what is learned just *is* the image, rule, etc., that organizes the behavior and makes it possible for a subject to imitate the general outlines of another's behavior but not its irrelevant or inappropriate details. Thus Bandura (1986, pp. 19, 47) writes:

The capacity to learn by observation enables people to acquire rules for generating and regulating behavioral patterns without having to form them gradually by tedious trial and error....By observing others, one forms rules of behavior, and on future occasions this coded information serves as a guide for action....Throughout the years, modeling has always been acknowledged to be one of the most powerful means of transmitting values, attitudes, and patterns of thought and behavior.

Another development in modeling theory that has special relevance to moral learning is the emphasis by social cognitive theorists on certain inner states or feeling tones, which the model experiences directly and which serve as vicarious reinforcements for the subject. These feeling tones include the anxiety or 'guilt-feeling' associated with misconduct and the warm glow or 'good feeling' one has as a consequence of having engaged in altruistic behavior. (Presumably the model's own experience of these feelings is the product of other conditioning processes, e.g., physical punishment.) In these cases, it is usually necessary that the model engage in some self-expressive activity in order to inform the subject that an apparently unrewarding act really has positive consequences for the agent or vice versa. For instance, Bryan (1971) described the production of 'imitative generosity' in children who heard a model report 'This is fun' and 'I feel wonderful' (positive affects that provide reinforcements) immediately after he was observed acting generously. But there are also many cases whose explanation requires no appeal to inner states. These are the garden-variety cases in which the reinforcing consequences of the model's actions are immediately obvious to the subject, as when a child sees or hears an older sibling receive parent-administered rewards or punishments. Either way, the act and its reinforcing outcome are correlated with each other in the same externalist fashion we have seen operating in all the other moral psychologies reviewed so far. Although the possibility remains open that the modeled behavior might eventually be engaged in for its own sake by the subject, the whole idea of acquiring patterns of behavior or their underlying rules by vicarious reinforcement prescinds from any intrinsic motivational factors that might exist then or later.

Thus Bandura and his associates supplemented the familiar stimulus-response accounts drawn according to the Law of Effect with another postulate that soon became fully orthodox and formed the heart of social learning theory: that the association of affective stimuli and actions can be wrought vicariously as well as by instrumental and classical conditioning. In doing so they made the important point that reinforcement by vicarious association works in virtue of the cognitive character of the mediation between observing the model and acting accordingly. But this is still a relatively limited sense of 'cognitive,' for two reasons that are especially relevant to moral theory. One is that, within the standard social learning theory accounts of imitative behavior, the proclaimed 'cognitive mediation' has no intrinsically *motivational* dimension; the other is that it has no *epistemological* dimension.

The first of these two missing dimensions may not seem all that important to psychologists already committed to studying morality from a thoroughly externalist metaethical perspective. For them, views about observational learning do full justice to the cognitive dimension of socialization, including moral socialization, simply by positing some general internal standards for conduct: no need is felt to construe these standards as being affect-laden or motivating in themselves. The internal image or semantic vehicle acquired by a subject in observational learning represents not only the model and the model's behavior, but also – because it recapitulates the model's own reinforcement schedule – social information about standards of appropriate behavior. Thus Bandura's remark, cited above, referred to rules as *guides* but not as motives ('By observing others, one forms rules of behavior, and on future occasions this coded information serves as a guide for action'). Even in this relatively cognitive version, modeling theory offers no suggestion that rewards and punishments have any intrinsic connection with the behavior that fetches them, as would be the case in a theory tracing imitative behavior back to some intrinsic motivation such as curiosity. As we shall see below, in the latter sort of theory the same features that make an observed action interesting enough to engage the subject's attention in the first place also supply the motives to imitate that action (see Kohlberg, 1969/1984). But in standard modeling theory the sanctions that provide the subject with motives for imitating the model are regarded as completely arbitrary, emanating from the ungrounded volitions, habits, and preferences of the socializing agents lurking in the background. Or (to cast the same point in the metaethical terms used in this study), within vicarious reinforcement accounts of modeling there are no logical, semantic, or conceptual ligatures between statements about one's moral images (ideas) acquired by observational learning and statements about one's moral motives to act on those images. Metaethical externalism, which postulates a conceptual gap between cognitions and motives, remains the order of the day regarding both the transition from image to action and the general dynamics of acquiring and (especially) continuing to cherish such images.

At first sight, there seems to be a glaring discrepancy between the externalist character of learning by vicarious reinforcement and the eminent standing enjoyed by moral exemplars, who seem to be admired and followed for their own sakes without regard to bribes or threats. However, the necessity ascribed to external sanctions is really a logical corollary of one of the most basic propositions in social learning theory, namely, Tolman's (1949) axiom that the acquisition of any given repertoire of behavior does not guarantee its performance. Socialization theorists who stress the importance of imitative behavior take Tolman's axiom for granted and apply it across the board of moral learning. Unfortunately, by doing so they forestall consideration of serious motivational issues that are, or at least should be, crucial in the application of modeling theory as a theory of conscience. For instance, why in the course of moral learning does a subject acquire one rather than another, perhaps less 'worthy' image or ideal that might have been drawn from the model's total display of behaviors, strategies, etc.? Still more pointedly: why does the subject continue to maintain a certain image as a standard of conduct even when it leads him or her to strenuous or even painful courses of action? Learning theoretic discussions of modeling offer no answers to such general questions. They do, of course, frequently refer to certain relatively noncognitive factors such as the nurturance, power, attractiveness, or status of a model. However, such references are better suited to contagion theories of modeling than to vicarious reinforcement theories, where they tend to be quite vague if not circular when analyzed closely (e.g., Kelman, 1958; Weissbrod, 1975). That this is so should not surprise us, once we recall the point made at the beginning of the previous chapter about how the distinction between moral motives and moral motivation operates within externalist moral psychologies. Although these theories vary in their accounts of how people are motivated to carry out moral actions, they all rest on the same deep-level concept of moral motivation, namely, that what brings people into morality in the first place is the likelihood of rewards or punishments.

The second of the two missing dimensions, which I have called 'epistemological' to emphasize its reference to truth- or rightness-making conditions, is at least as important here as the first dimension. Admittedly, from a cognitive point of view the recent work on vicarious reinforcement must be counted as an immense improvement over previous, purely peripheralist accounts of imitative behavior, where conscience was not even allowed the status of an informational guide. It is no longer correct to complain that in the literature of social learning theory, no inferential or computational processes are posited beyond the general, undifferentiated ones of imaginative representation and hedonic calculation. But it remains the case that in this literature no *truth-making*[5] values are ascribed to the representations posited in cognitive modeling theory. To be fair, we should recognize the increasingly reflexive character of Bandura's recent work, especially regarding the general categories of the self and self-regulation (Bandura, 1977, 1986). Nevertheless, he has continued to minimize the referential or epistemological import of evaluative symbols that are acquired in modeling and used in self-regulation. For instance, although an internalist moral philosopher would applaud his statement, 'Values can be invested in activities themselves as well as in extrinsic incentives' (Bandura, 1977, pp. 139–40), his very next sentence makes it clear that these values are not truth-bearing meanings but only portents of contingent, affective experiences: 'As we have seen, the value does not inhere in the behavior itself but rather in the positive and negative self-reactions it generates.'

In other words, in contemporary modeling theory the general view of moral motives is that the subject does not imitate a moral action or a moral model because it seems right (good, appropriate, etc.) to do so, but rather an action is right for the subject precisely because it has been successfully modeled. Bandura admits that the observer's attention to the model is selective as far as the intentions of both parties – the model and the observer – are concerned. However, he gives no account of what we might call the truth-developmental side of observational learning, i.e., the process whereby criteria for selecting one's models are generated and revised. For such an account we must go beyond the reinforcement paradigm altogether, to the work of cognitive developmentalists such as Piaget (1951) and Kohlberg (1969/1984). We shall consider those theorists in their own right later; suffice for now to note that their disagreement with the view of modeling now under discussion is based on their claim that imitation presupposes epistemic structures that are themselves capable of being differentiated and ranked in terms of their cognitive adequacy. Bandura (1986, p. 83) has explicitly criticized Piaget's theory of cognitive structures for having failed to provide reliable means of certifying what cognitive schemes children or other imitators possess, which is an issue that I shall not take up here. But whatever be the merits of this and other critiques of cognitive structures, the partisans of vicarious reinforcement have not done much better. They pay their cognitive dues, but just barely. With much fanfare they reassert the undeniable fact that people are able to learn sophisticated, rule-governed sorts of behavior by observation as well as by trial and error. However, no account is offered wherein the subject generalizes from a set of particular observed behaviors to an abstract form or structure capable not only of affecting any number of his or her own potential behaviors but also of representing something – be it the social environment or the subject him or herself – more or less 'rightly,' however that elusive normative term might be defined.

The absence of any such account within social cognitive theories of modeling is all the more striking when one reflects on their common view that some of the most powerful reinforcers are words of praise and blame, as well as nonverbal signs of approval and disapproval. One may well ask just why it is that approval and disapproval are such powerful levers on imitative behavior. As I intimated a few paragraphs back, other, more cognitive alternatives to the social learning theorists' account of imitative behavior are available. These turn upon the idea that people have a generalized desire for competence or success in whatever tasks they undertake, a desire that has been discussed under various titles, such as 'assimilation' (Piaget, 1952), 'effectance motivation' (White, 1959), and 'mastery motivation' (Yarrow *et al.*, 1983). However it is labeled, the desire for competence is regarded by these authors as an intrinsic motivational tendency whose specific shapes come from the definitions of success provided by socially defined norms and ratified by socially administered rewards for following those norms. When construed in this cognitive way, social reinforcements have the same norm-based leverage on behavior regardless of whether they are experienced directly or vicariously. Directly experienced reinforcements are norm-based in that rewards are cognitively apprehended signs one has acted successfully; vicarious reinforcements are even more cognitive, in that they are mediated by a model who provides norms (criteria of success) precisely because one perceives the model as being more competent than oneself.

For adults, the cognitive relationship between social reward and competence is a matter of simple common sense: I value approval from other people or groups because I respect them, but if they are exposed as frauds their praise or endorsement means nothing.[6] The same common sense leads me to admire and take as models persons who seem to enjoy the approval of those I respect, but not Nazi officers, terrorists, and others who are approved or otherwise rewarded by those I regard as wicked, foolish, or generally incompetent dispensers of praise, etc. However, for children the standards of success and failure are more elusive, even when considered from common sense. Not only is the line between success and failure, right and wrong, good and bad, hard to discern when one has had only a little social experience, but the very notions of correctness and of being rewarded are barely conceptualized and hence not well-differentiated in the mind of the young child, who tends to assume there must be a rule according to which rewards are given. Thus, studies show that 4- to 6-year-olds not only say 'Good guys win' but believe one can know who the good guys on television are *because* they win (reported in Kohlberg, 1965). This finding does not mean young children are not also interested in success or correctness for its own sake, but it does explain why they appear to be governed solely by the prospect of rewards and punishments, including those cognized in observational learning. Bandura's own view is quite different, as one may expect: he accounts for the children's identification of winners as 'good guys' by saying it is their rationalization for the imitative behavior they want to carry out for vicarious rewards (Bandura, 1969). In contrast, the alternative accounts I have alluded to postulate that the children's naïve cognitive identification of winners with good guys is causative, and that this vicarious reinforcement effect would not occur with older children because they are able to differentiate goodness from the success, or pseudo-success, of being given arbitrary rewards. (Kohlberg (1969/1984, p. 129) expanded this postulate into a structuralist claim that 'long-range maintenance of [socially approved] behavior depends on the cognitive stability of the children's definition of the behavior as "good," or "right".')

It has been said that the modeling theory of cognitive social learning theorists and the structuralist theory of cognitive developmentalists tend to converge in their treatments of the socializing process producing moral judgments (Casey and Burton, 1986). But the modeling theorists' heavy use of cognitive nomenclature such as 'symbolic manipulation' or 'rules for organization of behavior' should not be interpreted as signaling an internalist metaethical perspective in which moral motives are considered inherently rational and moral judgments inherently motivating. Modeling theory remains externalist as long as it continues to be based on the reinforcement paradigm of learning. As we have just noted, in this view the affect attached to a cognitive process is not primarily a function of the meaning of the image, as cognitive developmentalists would hold, but only of the logically contingent associations enjoyed by that image in the learning history of the agent. Here as in the more starkly noncognitive forms of socialization theory discussed at the beginning of this chapter, the implication for our inquiry into the nature of conscience is unsatisfyingly negative: according to modeling theory, whatever motivational power moral ideals and principles might possess, they have that power independently of any cognitively privileged status they might enjoy in virtue of being rational, impartial, or otherwise 'good' reasons for acting in this or that way. Their existence and power are also independent of one's self-concept or any other self-referential cognitions one might have, a point that will become more obvious in the next section. The image of the model that the agent cognizes is thought to be effective thanks solely to the vicarious, but fundamentally alogical and externalist, conditioning of affect (typically but not necessarily negative affect) to certain behavioral responses and outcomes. Inner representations determine behavior in the same general way as do the early expectancy constructs applied to animal learning, namely, by way of portending those stimuli – noxious or pleasant, depending on whether the behavior determination is envisioned as repressing or inciting – that somehow have come to be associated with the acts in question. No evaluation is made by the subject, from a structurally higher perspective, of the *quality* of the motivations and behaviors that are inhibited, or at least no such evaluation is considered by the modeling theorist to be part of the subject's inhibiting or self-regulating process *per se*. And no evaluation is made of their adequacy as expressions of one's deepest sense of self.

Self-control in delay of gratification

We turn now to another psychological account of moral socialization that, because of its unqualified reliance on the Law of
Effect, has an externalist perspective on the nature of moral
motives and moral motivation. It embodies a conception of
human action far more cognitive than those considered so far in
this chapter, though it overlaps in important ways with the
conceptions of vicarious reinforcement just discussed. It is the
account given by recent social learning theorists in which all
socialized, norm-governed behavior – including that associated
with specifically moral norms – is portrayed as a certain kind of
self-regulatory process, namely, as the deliberate postponement of
the gratification of one's own desires.

It should go without saying that self-regulation is a very
general concept.[7] It can be found, in various conceptual garbs, at
the center of many psychological systems and theories, not just
those socialization theories explicitly identified with or founded
on learning theory. Indeed, its central position in contemporary
social learning theory is a bit incongruous, considering the
latter's origins in radical behaviorism. In spite of the great diversity
of its theory-specific conceptualizations, self-regulation is by its
very nature a covert activity rather than a piece of overt, observable
behavior, though of course it has many observable indications.
Its intentional object is a state of the self, one whose behavioral
issue is actually a nonbehavior, i.e., a negative action or forbearance. Theories of self-regulation are, therefore, cognitive in a
very special way. They lie somewhat nearer the cognitive end of
our spectrum of moral psychologies, not only because the representations they employ tend to be abstract, complex, and verbal
– in short, propositional – but also and more basically because
they operate under the assumption that holistic and reflexive
categories such as the 'self' are fundamentally intelligible.

In what follows, I shall use the term *self-control* to refer to the
form of self-regulation usually studied by social learning theorists
interested in the general topic of socialization and, more specifically, in the acquisition of those standards of conduct regarded by
one's society as moral. As W. Mischel, F. H. Kanfer, and others
have emphasized, a major part of being socialized is learning to
control one's own behavior from within (see Mischel, 1968, 1974;
Mischel and Mischel, 1976; Kanfer, 1970, 1971; Kanfer and Karoly,

1972). Socialization is represented as a generic process in which what is learned is not a first-order, behavior-determining tendency, such as the tendency to look for cars before crossing a street or (for monks and maidens) to drop one's eyes when talking to someone of the opposite sex, but rather a second-order, tendency-determining tendency, namely, the disposition to inhibit present inclinations for the sake of later rewards. The postulate of self-induced inhibition is analogous to Freud's construct of a conflict-free zone as well as to Ben Franklin's conception of prudence and Aristotle's notion of the *enkrates* ('continent' man). As the empirical research of both Bandura and Mischel illustrates, the formation of such tendencies involves much more than the psychological contagion of cognitively undifferentiated affectivity associated with an attractive or powerful model's example. It also involves more than observing someone else being rewarded or punished for engaging in certain overt behaviors, although in this explanatory scheme observation functions as a condition for the development of self-control when what is modeled is restraint and what is observed are the payoffs gained by such restraint.

It is seldom necessary to choose one of these explanatory conditions to the exclusion of the others, since the workings of *moral* example are often best explained by accounts invoking multiple causes. As Bandura (1986, p. 340) observes, the judgmental function of how well one is doing includes several subsidiary processes. Subjects exposed to models adhering to a stringent performance standard are more likely to adopt that standard when the behavior that embodies it is 'contagious' in ways already mentioned, e.g., by being associated with powerful, nuturant, or otherwise appealing models (Akamatsu and Farudi, 1978). For instance, multiple-cause accounts seem well-suited for cases in which a child learns self-control through the inspiring but also well-rewarded examples provided by an older sibling, stories of saints and heroes, or the personalities of athletes and television stars. However, although social learning theorists are willing to count contagion among the causal factors for the acquisition of self-control, they assign it a subordinate role to the reinforcements that are apprehended first vicariously, by observing the model's consequent gratification, and then personally, when the subject reaps the fruits of his or her own self-control.

Socialization theorists have further subdivided the concept of self-control into three research areas, which they usually treat under the rubrics of *delay of gratification, resistance to temptation,* and *tolerance of pain.* Only the first of these is directly relevant to *moral* socialization, since the second is a misnomer and the third does not refer to a form of socialization at all. By now it should be obvious that the first rubric refers only to self-imposed delays and not to the many delays of gratification caused by external circumstances ranging from bad weather to incarceration.[8] The only thing to note about the second rubric (about the third, nothing at all needs to be said here) is that in spite of the moralistic ring of the label 'resistance to temptation,' it does not refer to what is ordinarily conceived as moral struggle. The phenomena studied under this heading are virtually any instances of behavioral maintenance under aversive circumstances in which the aversiveness in question 'is produced by the presence of rewards that must be foregone' (Karniol and Miller, 1981, p. 32). Resistance takes place not because the actions in question are qualitatively wrong but only because their pleasurable consequences are perceived to be offset by other outcomes, remote but nonetheless unwelcome. Accordingly, there are no dimensions of any special moral interest to be found in a program like Cautela's (1971), which was developed as a technique of 'covert conditioning' for clinical populations of obese and alcoholic subjects wherein the therapist provides images of the consequences of the client's resisting or not resisting temptation, such as becoming slim or getting sick. By this means as well as by other thought processes, such as learning to verbalize and otherwise generate plans for resisting temptation, people are taught to make changes in their own evaluations of potential outcomes and thereby 'resist.' Of course this conception of self-control is not completely disconnected from the moral order, but it is related only in the same broad sense that this or any other technique for efficient living can be said to promote a person's moral life.

Returning to the first of the research areas just mentioned, we may note that there is some historical overlap between the research done on the delay of gratification and the more cognitive studies of modeling. (For instance, Walter Mischel is a major contributor to both sets of literature.) But those working in the former area have focused more on the active, self-interventional aspects of norm-governed behavior than on the element of conformity that tends to be emphasized in discussions of the impact of a model's example. True, socialization in its broad sense includes both of these features (see Bandura and Mischel, 1965), but because it is a mode of self-regulation, socialization theorists' discussions of self-control tap into something that is associated much more closely with morality than imitative behavior is.

In the earlier stages of research on delayed gratification there was relatively little stress on the cognitive reflexivity of self-regulation, whereby one represents oneself to oneself. Discussions such as Mischel (1966) were so closely tied to the standard social learning theory emphasis on expectancy-value that, although they certainly had a self-referential dimension, their specific conceptualizations were unequivocally outcome-oriented. In other words, it was assumed that when a subject decided to delay gratification his or her decision was primarily if not solely a function of (1) the relatively greater value of the long-term reward as compared to the short-term reward, as well as of (2) the expectancy or subjective probability with which the long-term reward[9] was anticipated. Consequently, the research done from this perspective focused on situational variables that strengthened or undermined the subject's confidence in the environment's capacity to deliver on schedule whatever birds in the bush happened to be the object of his or her anticipations.

As the research focus broadened to include variables having to do with the maintenance of prior decisions to delay gratification, theorizing grew still more cognitive in that it posited more cognitions of a self-referential nature. Subjects were thought of not only as representing distal rewards to themselves but also as acting upon those very representations by self-manipulative procedures, such as verbalization to oneself or others, redirecting one's attention, and so on. True, it was assumed that the acquisition and exercise of self-regulating skills – or as philosophers are wont to call them, executive dispositions – proceed in the same way as that of any social behavior pattern, which as we have seen includes various sorts of modeling and related sorts of observational learning, conditioning, direct and vicarious reinforcement, generalization, and discrimination. As Mischel (1968, p. 188) pointed out, these processes can be the antecedents of extreme dependency, aggression, and other maladaptive or antisocial patterns, as well as of prosocial patterns of self-control. What was deemed special about self-control was that in it some of the reinforcing consequences of behavior are mediated by the individual's dispositions and decisions rather than dispensed directly by the external physical or social environment. More recent research, which focuses on the decision to terminate the delay, continues this emphasis on self-referential cognition (Kanfer, 1977; Karniol and Miller, 1981; Meichenbaum and Cameron, 1982) in that it is concerned with changes that occur in the subject's own perception of the waiting situation.

The acknowledgment of self-referential cognition constituted a quantum leap in cognitive sophistication for the learning theory approach to socialization. Nevertheless, what Karniol and Miller said in 1981 of their own work remains true of the results of the delay of gratification paradigm in general:

> Overall, our research, as well as the related data, suggests that self-control processes depend on how one evaluates the *outcomes of action*....Self-control appears to depend on one's ability to cognitively manipulate the values of these outcomes in such a manner as to make them either less desirable or more desirable.   (1981, p. 50, italics added)

This citation recapitulates the externalism inherent in the delay of gratification paradigm, whose heart is the postulate that, *ceteris paribus*, the self-control responsible for the delay will fetch an externally produced payoff in the form of tangible rewards or intangible ones such as social approval. This postulate does not deny that agents are actively engaged in their own self-regulation; after all, they initially achieve self-regulation by fixing their attention on the more remote consequences and then maintain it by means of a variety of other covert and overt self-manipulative strategies (e.g., muttering to oneself). But for all this internal activity and cognitive functioning, the principles of reinforcement remain fully in place as the theorist's explanatory substructure and, supposedly, as the organism's machine table.

A striking illustration of the externalist and mechanistic character of social learning theory explanations of self-control is provided by the so-called 'closed loop learning model' developed by Kanfer and his associates (Kanfer and Karoly, 1972). In this conception of self-control, the individual is regarded as his or her own behavior-modifier, the goal being to influence the probability of a given response at the end of some behavioral chain. It should be obvious that there is no special moral significance attached to this sort of self-regulation. Its cognitive operations are purely economic, namely, the selection of effective means. As in any therapy game, the only important procedural rule is that the therapy must succeed: at the end of the learning process the subject must be able to function in the absence of immediate external supports. The individual can be weaned away from these supports by whatever manipulative strategies the wit of the behavior-modifier can devise. But in Kanfer's closed loop strategies of self-regulation one substrategy that is always employed is that of setting up 'ad hoc performance standards' in terms of which the behavior is reinforced. Kanfer calls this central element a performance promise or contract, though it need not be an overt act in its own right.[10] Once this intrinsically arbitrary standard has been set, its discrepancies with the person's actual performances can be discerned and reduced by diverse reinforcements. A typical example of the closed loop model in action is that of smokers who give themselves little prizes for smoking only a given number of cigarettes. In the Hullian jargon of Kanfer and Karoly: the person's self-monitoring and self-evaluation produces a judgment, which then serves as an S_D (drive stimulus) 'either for positive self-reinforcement (SR+), if the outcome of the comparison is favorable, or for self-presented aversive stimulation (SR−), if the comparison is unfavorable' (Kanfer and Karoly, 1972, p. 406).

We can see from this and other instances of the delay of gratification paradigm that self-control is not construed in that paradigm as a separate motivational system. Even though the self-controlling subject makes use of self-addressed commands, reminders, and promises, 'the internal monologue may not be *causing* the action so much as reflecting the changing strengths of alternative actions' (Brown and Herrnstein, 1975, p. 194). In other words, the delay of gratification paradigm involves no hierarchy of motivational functions, since local control is retained by the agent's diverse subsystems of wants, needs, hopes, etc. The motivational components (though not the attention-selecting ones) of the agent's self-regulative dispositions are thought to work on the same level as the other desires and tendencies they are supposed to direct.

Consequently, the extensive psychological research into delayed gratification has yielded no new ways of understanding the motivational structure of morality, notwithstanding its greater

71

cognitive complexity compared to the other moral psychologies of socialization we have considered so far. We may conclude, then, that the delay of gratification paradigm is but a particular application of the Principle of Universal Heteronomy. This conclusion is also drawn in Brown and Herrnstein's influential introductory textbook for psychology, which continually reaffirms the Law of Effect. For instance, a few lines after the passage just cited, they redescribe the agent's internal feeling of autonomy in having made a self-regulating decision to, say, stop smoking:

> The internal feeling is just a link in the chain of causation from environment to behavior. Our position here is that the *real* reason for human self-control is again the law of relative effect, and that the subjective stream of thought reflects the moment-to-moment strengths of various actions.

The semantic medium of self-control, viz., language, is regarded as simply 'a medium of reward and punishment,' albeit a 'peerless' one in that language enables humans to keep in view an extraordinarily large set of influences, drawn from the past, present, and future. From this the authors conclude that, although self-control can be ascribed to animals as well as to humans, the difference between the two sorts of self-control is found 'not in the mechanism of action – which is the law of relative effect in all cases – but in the complexity of the associations that form the channels between reward or punishment and action' (p. 194).

To their conclusion I would add that the delay of gratification paradigm is but a simulacrum of moral conscience, involving no special, parapolitical relationship to the other motivations that constitute the agent's personality. As Alston (1977, pp. 95–6) has complained in a similar context, what is crucial in this account of self-control is affective anticipations that are logically independent of the nature of the activity in question. In contrast, the core idea of *moral* motives – as opposed to the fortuitous affections of a happy wanton or, to use a more lifelike example, such isolated prosocial affections as an otherwise ruthless gangster's fondness for children (Kant's 'pathological love' (1785/1959, pp. 16–17)) – is that an agent acts, or abstains from acting, in accordance with some norm that is *independently cherished* and hence motivationally antecedent ('pre-scribed') to the specific, first-order desires and action tendencies embodied by specific moral behaviors. This kind of self-regulation may be considerably more rare than moralists like to think, but that is not the point here. The point is that in spite of its emphasis on the cognitions in self-control, all we are given in the delay of gratification paradigm is (to adapt Aronfreed's (1968b, p. 278) phrase) a transsituational 'cognitive schema for the economical coding of information' about motivation-producing features of actual and possible worlds. In this formulation, the psychology of self-regulation is just as mechanistic as we saw the less cognitive members of our spectrum to be.

Conclusion

I shall conclude this chapter by noting that once again we find ourselves with a theory of moral socialization that offers a picture of moral motives but has nothing to say about moral motivation that is not already contained in the Principle of Universal Heteronomy. In the motivational picture latent in these self-regulation theories, the passage from thought to moral action is under the agent's own control in the sense that the reinforcement schedule is presented by the agent to him or herself. But *how* reinforcements are 'self-presented' is not under the agent's control. In this picture it only varies according to the nature of the eventual reward or punishment, since the literature on delay of gratification views the incentives for self-control from the externalist perspective taken in less cognitive moral psychologies. What is externalist is, of course, the metaethical point of view from which the delay of gratification paradigm is constructed, not the locus of the reinforcements themselves, which can lie either inside or outside the subject. Kanfer regularly discusses the presentation of external tokens (i.e., tangible prizes, such as an extra helping of dessert) one bestows upon oneself. But Mischel (1968, p. 166) recognized quite early that in the course of controlling themselves, people also have other, more internal resources with which to reward or punish themselves, namely, self-praise and self-blame or (somewhat more generally) self-reproach. Others have described such incentives for self-control in terms of 'self-esteem costs' (see Bandura, 1977, p. 143).

It should be noted that when the notion of self-esteem is linked to those of self-reproach and self-praise, a bridge is built, one that can take us from the cognitive but still relatively simple delay of gratification model to the more cognitive, internalist forms of self-regulation to be discussed in the next chapters. We need to take this bridge because the notion of self-control involved in delayed gratification fails to do justice to that core feature of the moral domain that I have called its 'executive function,' without which a moral psychology is self-defeating in the manner described in the previous chapter. The motivational account of self-imposed gratification delay is basically the same as that of the other moral socialization theories discussed in the present chapter, in that all sanctions and their dispensations are conceived as morally neutral. Insofar as these sanctions work as mental representations they are internal in the sense of being 'within' the subject (the so-called organism), but they are external to the subject matter (the behavior in question) in the important logical sense of remaining conceptually independent of the activities they reinforce. This is true whether they are intangible sanctions such as social approval or tangible ones such as the external tokens in Kanfer's model: there is nothing in their semantic content that is incompatible, in principle, with their being used as reinforcements for the most immoral sorts of behavior. In the delay of gratification paradigm, no supervening principles or 'good reasons' are involved, no prescriptive moral ideals are imaged, whereby our inclination to wait for the birds in the bush can get an edge over the inclination to take the bird at hand. Thanks to the expected schedule of payoffs, the former inclination just *is* stronger, and regularly so. The machine table works away.

4

INTERNALIST MORAL PSYCHOLOGIES: INTERNALIZATION THEORIES

As we worked our way across the first part of the noncognitive–cognitive spectrum of moral psychologies, virtually nothing was said about moral motivation or, for that matter, about the moral motives/motivation distinction itself. This omission was not accidental. Moral motivation is the tendency to invest one's experience with moral *meanings*, and so implies a cognitive competence for which there are no categories in the noncognitive moral psychologies reviewed in the last chapter. As I argued earlier, their systematic neglect of the semantic dimension of human (including moral) experience is a result of the grip the Principle of Universal Heteronomy has on the methodological infrastructure and metaethical perspective shared by those theories. Within noncognitive moral psychologies the backdrop for specific moral motives is not a more general concept of conscientiousness or moral motivation but rather the Law of Effect itself – with the result that moral motives are divested of any semantic significance they might have as 'reasons for action.'

However, for all its dominance in the social and behavioral sciences, the Principle of Universal Heteronomy is not itself universal. Some theories of socialization have tried, bravely if not always successfully, to build a semantic dimension into moral motives and, by implication, to create room for some construct or other corresponding to my notion of moral motivation. These theories of internalization are the subject of the present chapter. In them the semantic dimension is linked with the conative dimension along the lines of what I have called metaethical internalism, which is to say that within these theories moral motives do indeed function as reasons for actions (albeit not necessarily as moral principles) and vice versa. All this can

75

be summarized by saying that theories of socialization have been developed which are both relatively cognitive in their psychological perspective and at least minimally internalist in their metaethical perspective, and that within these theories one can indeed distinguish between moral motives and moral motivation in the manner described in the first chapter. As I pointed out then, the two terms of this distinction take on new tones in the cognitive portion of the spectrum: moral motives are understood from an internalist rather than externalist metaethical perspective, and moral motivation is understood top-down, as a constitutive rather than merely summary sort of conception. So construed, the moral motives/motivation distinction amounts to the proposal that moral motives are a necessary condition for the passage from moral judgment to moral action, whereas moral motivation makes possible the thinking or reasoning from which the moral judgment emerges. In what follows I shall try to tease out of these theories their metaethical assumptions about motivation, by reconstructing their main ideas in terms of this distinction. There is reason to expect that they can be so reconstructed without undue distortion. They are relatively cognitive theories, in which the category of self-regulation introduced at the end of the last chapter is ratcheted up several notches to include self-representation and self-evaluation, and the criteria along which the self-evaluation proceeds are viewed in these theories not as external constraints but rather as *internalized* moral norms and ideals.

As we shall presently see, the general idea of internalizing other people's evaluative criteria can be found at the heart of certain relatively sophisticated reinforcement and affect-conditioning theories of moral behavior. In the first of these, internalization is based on reinforcements that are dispensed from within, which for all its cognitive-semantic thinness is a richer notion than the crudely externalist one of externally administered rewards. The second case we shall consider is even richer: Aronfreed's account of internalization, in which he tests the limits of the Law of Effect by positing 'evaluative cognitions' that are distinctly semantic and affectively loaded in themselves. However, a much more rich, though quite different idea of internalization is found in Freud's later work on the superego and identification, with its distinctive psychoanalytic notions of introjection and other sorts of internal representation. To these one could add other, somewhat less influential theories not discussed here, such as the moral traits accounts developed in various ways by Peck and Havighurst (1960), Hogan (1973), and others, or cognitive dissonance and attribution theories launched in the 1950s by Festinger (1957; Festinger and Freedman, 1964) and Heider (1958). My own view is that so far the most important (albeit still incomplete) psychological conception of moral internalization is that introduced by Piaget and thoroughly over-hauled by Kohlberg; however, discussion of that conception must be postponed until the next chapter, when we turn to the so-called cognitive developmental accounts of moral socialization lying at what for now is the very end of the spectrum.

Self-regulation, moral cognition, and internalization

The approaches to internalization to be discussed in the present chapter are quite different, but they share the assumption that moral cognitions are major determinants of moral action: that well-formed moral judgments have semantical content whereby they have justificatory, explanatory, and even causal significance within a subject's motivational system. In short, these approaches all make use of some sort of cognitive construct that plays the role of 'moral motive.' However, they vary considerably in the extent to which they assume, or at least are compatible with, the category of 'moral motivation.'

I shall develop these ideas in due course, attending to their philosophical base as well as to their psychological applications. But it is important that we be clear at the outset about the difference in ethical relevance between moral motives and the self-regulative dispositions and cognitions appropriate to delayed gratification, which was described at the end of the previous chapter as the prototypical form of self-regulation. In a world where one cannot have one's cake and eat it too, the ability to delay gratification or otherwise control the course of one's desires is clearly of vital importance. But is this general ability to control oneself inherently *moral*? Presumably not, since although self-regulation sometimes operates in the service of moral principles, it also implements many useful but essentially nonmoral regulatory principles ranging from the rules of etiquette to the martial arts.

There is an interesting conceptual tension here. On the one hand, if we take 'self-regulation' in the broad sense to include all forms of self-control including those specifically keyed to delayed gratification, then self-regulation has no special moral significance in itself. After all, one might argue, if the domain of morality were coextensive with that of self-regulation then nearly everything an adult did would have to count as moral: even Jack the Ripper exercised self-regulation when he monitored his actions to avoid detection. On the other hand, although it would be linguistically eccentric to regard self-regulation as the *logical genus* of adult morality (the executive function is only *one* of the core features of the moral domain), it seems reasonable to view it as a major part of morality's *psychological genesis*. Since self-regulative dispositions, including the simple ability to delay gratification, are valuable qualities in a universe characterized by scarcity and struggle, it is hardly surprising that they are generally esteemed as virtues even though it seems equally clear that they are not the only virtues one can have. That is, a person (Jack the Ripper, perhaps) possessing only the executive virtues associated with self-control is not by that fact alone considered a morally good person. Perhaps they are not even the virtues most worth having, though moral traditions have often singled them out for special praise. Thus Aristotle regarded temperance as one of the four cardinal virtues, the Stoics defined the good life as ataraxia, and Ben Franklin exhorted his readers to develop habits of thrift and punctuality. Even though there are other moralities less preoccupied with the virtues of self-control ('Love God and do what you will,' said Augustine), it is inconceivable that a morality would discount them altogether, since to be any sort of moral agent one needs the general capacities of self-control that make it possible to formulate and abide by one's moral judgments, as well as to acquire and exercise the other moral virtues such as justice and loyalty. An empirical study like Maller's (1934) factor analysis, which found evidence of a common factor of self-control across the tests of honesty, cooperation, and persistence used in Hartshorne and May's (1928–30) famous studies of character, only belabors the obvious.

Research on self-regulation has grown increasingly cognitive in its suppositions about the internal determination of behavior, so that the moral psychologies we shall now examine can be thought of as making up the more cognitive portion of the spectrum of moral socialization theories. However, they do more than just elaborate on the theme of self-cognition introduced at the end of the last chapter, since in at least one major respect they are qualitatively different from the delayed gratification paradigm. Even though that paradigm is a cognitive one in that it involves mental representations, it assumes that the ultimate point of all self-regulation is the achievement of some outcome whose significance consists, wholly and without residue, in the fact that it is contingently associated with a positive affective state. Under this assumption, for any human behavior the product motivates its process, justifies it, and supposedly renders the behavior intelligible both for the subject and for those with whom the subject interacts. But such an assumption, which reflects the externalist metaethical perspective implicit in the Principle of Universal Heteronomy, is incompatible with the view of (adult) moral agency as autonomous, intrinsically motivated, and free to embrace even the most heroic sacrifices. That view is an idealization in the sense that few of us operate in this manner on a regular basis. However, as I argued in the second chapter, to write it off as an utter illusion would abolish the whole enterprise of moral philosophy as well as dissolve some of our most cherished self-perceptions. For moral psychology to avoid such consequences, one or more alternate constructs of self-regulation must be developed, in which affective outcome gives way to moral worth as the principal criterion of successful action.

Such constructs are already in play in the psychological literature, but they have not been the theme of any extended theoretical discussion there. However, another more or less equivalent construct has been developed over the last several years in the philosophical literature, thanks largely to a seminal essay by Harry Frankfurt (1988a, originally published in 1971). In that essay and subsequent writings (e.g., 1988b), Frankfurt proposed a hierarchical model of motivation, centered on the idea of what he called 'second-order desires.' He introduced his model as follows:

Human beings are not alone in having desires and motives, or in making choices. They share these things with members of certain other species, some of which even appear to engage in deliberation and to make decisions based on prior thought. It seems to be peculiarly characteristic of humans, however, that they are able to form what I shall call 'second-order desires' or 'desires of the second order.'

(1988a, p. 12)

Frankfurt's own point was that the ability to endorse our own desires is what distinguishes us as humans. When his point is considered in the light of the internalist perspective on motives, it has an especially intimate connection with the moral dimension of being human.

However, before we take up that or any other metaethical idea, we should get straight on what is involved in the 'meta' level currently under discussion. Among philosophers it is generally agreed that without the logical possibility of acting on a desire, it is meaningless to speak of having the desire.[1] (Thus Anscombe (1963) asked what it could mean for someone to desire the moon.) Two kinds of second-order action come to mind at this point. The first is that of *self-manipulation*, a category which as we saw in the last chapter includes not only strategies of bribes and rewards promised and dispensed by the subject in a self-administered program of desire-modification[2] but also attention-selection strategies, which are sometimes intertwined with bribes or rewards and sometimes distinct from them. The other kind of second-order action is that of *reason-giving*, a category which, to put it mildly, has not been passionately embraced as a research topic by most socialization theorists. For instance, Brown and Herrnstein (1975, p. 289) have advocated a 'two road theory,' according to which people talk about moral issues on one road and act on another road: we are told by these highly influential learning theorists that it is 'naïve...to think that what a person says has anything to do with how he behaves.' But they are not representative of all moral psychologists. Many, including not only cognitive developmentalists but also socialization theorists working outside that tradition, have not hesitated to understand a subject's behavior as caused in large part by the reasons he or she reports as being decisive considerations.

These considerations need not have the form of abstract principles to count as moral reasons. It is enough that they be what Aronfreed has called 'evaluative cognitions,' that is, standards or rules forming the criteria in terms of which moral self-evaluation is carried out at the second level. What makes a criterion count as a specifically *moral* norm or reason is a much-disputed metaethical issue, which we need not go into now. We may instead simply embellish the hierarchical model of motivation with still another distinction, between two sorts of evaluative stances that one can take toward one's first-order desires. The first of these, which I shall call *economic evaluation*, is the self-regulatory cognition characteristic of the delay of gratification paradigm: using strictly means–end considerations it seeks to optimize the workings of one's first-order system – suppressing certain desires, fanning some, postponing others, and so on, all without passing judgment on their intrinsic worth. In contrast, what I shall call *ethical evaluation* is only incidentally concerned with whatever outcomes might be intended in one's first-order desires. Instead, attention shifts from the outcomes to the worth of one's desires, with the details of this shift depending on one's conception of human nature.[3] In what follows, I shall concentrate on this second, more qualitative notion of evaluation and self-regulation, although as we shall see it is not always clear just how important the distinction between economic and ethical evaluation really is for the theorists under discussion.

Even so, the multileveled model of self-regulation provides us with a framework within which our distinction between moral motives and moral motivation now can be spelled out more carefully. As we saw above, the idea underlying that distinction is that moral motives are a necessary condition for any passage from moral judgment to moral action, whereas moral motivation makes possible the evaluative cognition from which moral judgments emerge.

The following scheme portrays this double mediation between the self and the completed action, in a way that recalls the formula introduced at the beginning of this chapter:

$$\text{SELF} > \frac{Moral}{Motivation} > \text{MORAL THINKING} > \frac{Moral}{Motive} > \text{ACTION}$$

The psychological theories we shall now examine construe moral motives in ways that are more or less suggestive of some underlying view of moral motivation. There are two closely related ways in which these theories stand in contrast with those reviewed in the last chapter. The first is that they lie solidly within the cognitive sector of the noncognitive–cognitive spectrum of moral psychologies. The second is that metaethically their cognitivism lies closer to the internalist side of the internalist–externalist debate since they tend to ascribe motivational efficacy to moral cognition. With this in mind, let us return to the spectrum of moral psychologies, picking up where we left off in the last chapter's discussion of the delay of gratification paradigm and moving on to the special class of socialization theories that are often called 'internalization theories.'

As we saw at the end of the last chapter, the standard learning theoretic accounts of self-regulation used the paradigm of delayed gratification to portray an essentially passive subject, one whose so-called self-control is autonomous only in the limited and negative sense that he or she somehow manages to withdraw from the immediate situation in order to progress toward distant but greater satisfactions. The incentives for taking the long view were not portrayed as being under one's immediate control or reflective evaluation, nor were the rewards or punishments that are envisioned by the subject who takes that long view. As far as the dispensation of benefits was concerned, the familiar applications of the delay of gratification paradigm remained faithful to the Principle of Universal Heteronomy. However, all this begins to change once the account of self-regulation is expanded to include the twin concepts of self-praise and self-reproach, as well as the moral motives corresponding to these two concepts. With this shift, the delay of gratification paradigm is transformed into a type of internalization theory, with the result that socialization theory becomes much more recognizable as a moral psychology. True, in the social learning theories of socialization we shall consider, the underlying motivational construct in the revised conception of self-regulation remains that of affective expectancy; however, in this version the expected payoffs not only are intangible but have the self as paymaster.

Nor is this the only relevant version. In what follows we shall move from the learning theoretic picture of self-praise and self-reproach to the pictures of internalization drawn in terms of affect conditioning (Aronfreed) and aggressive anxiety (Freud). For all their differences in vocabulary and historical contexts, these pictures have much in common: they all assume that evaluative cognition is a necessary determinant of moral action and that this determinant is not only cognitive but also affect-laden. In other words, internalized norms function as moral motives.

The reinforcement picture of internalization

As I have just indicated, among socialization theorists working within the reinforcement paradigm, the logical as well as historical transition from the early neobehaviorist accounts of self-control to the later, more autonomous and internalized social cognitive versions has been provided by the concepts of social approval and, negatively, social disapproval and rejection. By their very definitions it is clear that those benefits and disbenefits are dispensed by *other* persons and hence differ importantly from self-dispensed reinforcements, be these the extra helping of dessert discussed above or the self-praise to be discussed below. But the reactions of others can enter into the structure of *self*-control in two ways, which reflect the difference between extrinsic and intrinsic conceptions of motivation. First of all, the reactions of others often provide additional incentives for self-regulation because of their informational value about certain extrinsic rewards and punishments (including intangible ones of praise and rebuke), especially those they are in a position to dispense: the boss's harsh words toward me bode ill for my chances of getting a raise, etc. Secondly and of somewhat greater relevance here, the reactions of others often have intrinsic value, especially when what is sought is the approval of significant others. Furthermore, these two sorts of self-control motivation often come together in real life: being rebuked by my boss can be distressing not only because rebukes portend still other trouble from her office but also because such experiences are usually distressing in themselves.

The internalized counterparts of such familiar experiences are, of course, the processes of self-praise and self-reproach. Among social learning theorists the idea of subjects administering their own rewards and punishments was originally developed as a corollary of the more general ideas of self-control and modeling. In both cases, the idea of self-administered rewards is an important enhancement, one that renders the general theory considerably more cognitive as well as more recognizable as a moral psychology. For instance, in the early studies on self-control done in the 1960s by Bandura and Walters (1963), Aronfreed (1964), and Mischel (1966), several motives were thought to operate simultaneously in the child who passes up immediate gratification for the sake of a larger but later reward. The most obvious motive was, as we saw in the last chapter, the reinforcement value of the later reward. This motive also produced self-criticism when failures in self-control led to regrets for being impulsive. But since the child is surrounded by parents and other socializing agents who *evaluate* his or her efforts at self-control, the child's tendency to self-reproach was produced not only by regret for lost opportunities but also by the hope of thereby forestalling parental condemnation (and its attendant punishments) or securing restatements of their approval (and its attendant pleasures; see Bandura and Walters, 1963, p. 186–7). A somewhat different but compatible motive was proposed by Aronfreed in an article entitled 'The Origins of Self-Criticism' (1964), saying that children are moved to engage in self-criticism because it resembles the point in parental punishment at which the anxiety built up after a transgression is dissipated: the 'air is cleared' by a spanking, and by association, by self-rebukes. Still another, more general motive for self-administration of rewards, including the negative one of self-criticism, was proposed by Mischel (1966) in conjunction with modeling theory: the child learns early on that emulating those who control valuable resources 'is likely to lead to positive consequences for the imitator' – and one of the things that a child can very profitably imitate is the tendency of those powerful persons to criticize (and praise) children, in particular, the imitative subject him or herself (p. 118). These accounts are singled out by Alston (1977, pp. 96–7) as examples of identification-oriented explanations of the origins of evaluative cognitions. And so they are – if we use the term 'identification' in the wide sense of referring to any account of internalization, Freudian or otherwise, in which principles of conduct are taken over from significant others rather than acquired because of the affect attached to the object or contents of those principles. As he puts it,

> These explanations, like the Freudian ones, are independent of any assumption that the contents of the principles involved have any attractiveness or aversiveness to the child *prior to* and as a condition of, his acquisition of the [evaluative stance] in question.
>
> (Alston, 1977, p. 97)

Since the time of the studies cited by Alston, other research has been carried out in which a child apparently imitated not overt actions but rather the inner, judgmental behavior of an adult whom it had observed reinforcing – verbally as well as materially – the child's own overt behaviors (see Bandura, 1986, pp. 349ff.). Presumably what he said of the earlier studies would apply to these as well, for they also purport to explain the origins of internalized evaluative cognition. They roll the relatively specific claims of the earlier studies into a general view of self-administered rewards, which can be summed up as follows: children will proceed to heap praise or blame upon themselves if no one else does it for them. The connection between this view of self-reinforcement and modeling is perhaps best seen in Rosenhan's (1972) discussion of the paradox altruism presents for learning theory. (The paradox he has in mind is that altruism is rewarding yet presumably is engaged in without thought of rewards.) Rosenhan's proposal, which he points out is fully in line with Bandura's view, is that being charitable ('contributing') can contain within itself a special kind of self-reinforcement, described as follows:

> In the context of imitating a model who has just been charitable, this view would hold that children tell themselves that they are 'good' because they have contributed, which allegedly is nearly as good as having someone tell them that they are good, or even giving them money for having been good.
>
> (Rosenhan, 1972, p. 158)

But this account leaves a good deal to be desired, for at least two reasons. The first reason is that it is self-effacing in the same general way that I claimed in Chapter 2 the other reinforcement-based pictures of moral motives are, only more obviously so. Were someone to accept the foregoing account as an accurate description of his or her own motives for engaging in contributing behavior, then that behavior would either lose its significance as 'charitable' or cease altogether. This sort of self-reinforcement can work only to the extent that it is not transparent to the agent, a requirement which when generalized to other moral behaviors would not only turn morality into a form of self-deceit but also make it very difficult to explain how ordinarily intelligent and reflective persons, children as well as adults, could praise and blame themselves for acting in ways considered moral or immoral.

It might be objected that this self-effacing feature is characteristic of many other theories of moral socialization, not just the self-reinforcement theory exemplified in Rosenhan's account of charitable or contributory behavior. And this would be correct, for reasons I presented in Chapter 2 where the Principle of Universal Heteronomy was criticized independently of its specific theoretical incarnations. The self-effacement criticism is fully applicable to the externalist socialization theories reviewed in the last chapter, since one of the basic problems with the externalist perspective is its corrosive effect on the externalist's own capacity for moral commitment. But it is especially pertinent here in view of the internalism, or apparent internalism, that I have ascribed to the reinforcement model of self-praise/blame.

This brings us to the second reason for considering the model inadequate. One might set aside the objection that it is self-effacing, on the grounds that it is built out of data collected from children, who should not be expected to have a very clear understanding of their own motivational processes. But regardless of what one thinks of the model's adequacy concerning altruism in children, it holds little or no promise as an account of how adult benevolence develops. It is not surprising that reinforcement theorists who explain the acquisition of altruistic motives in this manner do not go on to explain how children graduate from the childish pleasure of telling themselves that they are good to more adult forms of altruism: from their theoretical perspective such a graduation is probably not even conceivable. That is, they seem to have no way to resolve a still deeper paradox generated by their construal of altruism as a means for self-praise, namely, the odd consequence that as one grows out of egocentric modes of thinking one would lose the incentive to act altruistically. The ability to put oneself and one's desires into a larger, more objective and long-ranging perspective is a cognitively advanced form of self-regulation associated with adult human functioning and not expected of children. But it seems inevitable that this ability would also dispose the adult subject to question and eventually reject what is supposedly the central assumption tacitly involved in childish self-reinforcement, namely, the assumption that telling oneself that one is good 'is nearly as good' as hearing such praise from another. We have already seen that part of the logic of approval discourse is that if praise is to be normative it must be dispensed by someone whose approval *matters*, someone who enjoys a privileged place in the web of social relations (see Foot, 1978, pp. 189–207). That an adult subject might coherently be said to approve of his or her *own* actions is not the issue here, since the relation of a person to himself or herself is probably always a recapitulation in one form or another of the surrounding interpersonal world. What is at issue, though, is whether our understanding of the moral self-relation is advanced by the claim that self-praise 'is just as good as' (i.e., just as motivationally relevant as) approval from significant others. *Why* is it just as good? is the real question.

We may expect the answer to this question to be different for children than for adults, in view of children's inability to make certain cognitive differentiations between self and other. We may also expect some adults to find self-praise just as good as approval from others for the same reason, which means that in certain behavior domains, such as morality, they do not function as adults. In such cases – which may be far more common than a review of moral philosophy textbooks would suggest – the observance of moral norms is really a regression to infantile forms of self-cognition and motivation. Nonetheless, it would be wrong to say that the reinforcement picture of internalization leaves no room for nonregressive moral behavior. The account it gives of the origins of self-praise/blame is keyed to childhood socialization and is noncommittal on the workings of self-esteem at the adult level. Hence we must go beyond this picture if we want to find an account of the affectivity of self-praise and blame that is compatible with the fact that in adult cognition self and other are differentiated fairly sharply.

The affect-conditioning picture of internalization

One such account is Aronfreed's (1968b) classic study of conscience and socialization. This study, as well as many of those influenced by it (e.g., Aronfreed, 1971, 1976; Hoffman, 1970a, 1976; DePalma, 1975), is more eclectic in its attempt at 'illuminating the contribution that moral judgment makes to conscience' (Aronfreed, 1976, p. 55) than are the learning theoretic studies of Bandura, Mischel, and others cited so far in our discussion of self-control, but its recurring theme is the affective conditioning of evaluative cognitions. To account for the self-regulative activity of conscience, it draws on the classical conditioning paradigm introduced by Pavlov as well as on reinforcement theory, and has important parallels with psychoanalytic concepts introduced by Freud.

As he points out at the beginning of his book, Aronfreed's notion of conscience is restricted 'to those areas of conduct where social experience has attached substantial affective value to the child's cognitive representation and evaluation of its own behavior' (1968b, p. 6; see also Aronfreed, 1968a). The paradigm case of this sort of evaluative cognition is that of self-criticism, whose origins lie in the tendency, noted above, of the child to internalize the verbal rebukes it has come to expect from its parents, which 'have first acquired reinforcement value as signals for the termination of its anticipatory anxiety following a transgression' (p. 188). Aronfreed goes on to suggest that, as the child matures, self-criticism comes to be regarded not as a stand-in for parental rebukes but as a self-regulative mechanism in its own right, affect-laden and intrinsically motivating. As in the delay of gratification model of self-control, the affect-conditioning picture of internalization envisages the older child, and the adult, as engaging in before-the-fact self-criticism in order to suppress improper behavior. One motive for doing so is the manifestly heteronomous desire to head off the anxiety and pain generated by parental punishments, verbal or physical. But Aronfreed, though firmly wedded to the general principles of conditioning and reinforcement, goes a step further and postulates that, once self-criticism has become a prospective mode of cognition as well as a retrospective one, it can also evolve into the motives of guilt and shame, which are the intrinsically motivating, affect-laden evaluative cognitions characteristic of morality.

In his application of the construct of anxiety to self-regulative behavior, Aronfreed explicitly distinguishes two basically different forms of self-regulation, only the second of which is specifically moral. The first comprises those forms of gratification-delay corresponding to what I earlier called *economic* evaluation. As we have seen, social learning theorists such as Mischel believe that the cognitive control of one's behavior consists in self-manipulative stratagems whose reflective cognition is only indirectly evaluative; primarily, it is either purely predictive (of long-term outcomes) or, at most, performative (self-directed threats or bribes proposed in the so-called performance contract). The second form of self-regulation distinguished by Aronfreed overlaps with the domain of moral judgment and conscience and so corresponds, in at least a rough way, to self-regulation by *ethical* evaluation. The latter sort of self-regulation is powered by anxiety just as much as the former sort of self-regulation is, but with this important difference: whereas in economic evaluation the self-manipulative motives for acting in accordance with one's cognitions are all varieties of fear, the motivational states associated with ethical evaluation are guilt and shame.

In this type of moral psychology, guilt and shame constitute the fundamental moral motives that, along with the morally neutral motive of fear, not only ensure compliance with internalized norms but also preserve the normative status of those norms. All three of these motives are described by Aronfreed as 'cognitive housings' for the nonspecific state of anxiety, with the latter concept serving in his theory as the rough equivalent of what I have called 'moral motivation.' His account of self-regulative motives and cognitions – unlike Rosenhan's account of altruism, Aronfreed's focuses more on self-reproach than on self-praise – is based on the supposition that some general adverse affective state, which he chooses to call 'anxiety,' underlies intangible payoffs as well as tangible ones. Just as a reinforcer is anything that increases the probability of a response, so the construct of anxiety here includes any psychological state avoided by the behaving organism. Researchers such as Aronfreed take the paradigm case of anxiety to be 'the generalized aversive state that is induced in a child by various forms of punishment' (1968b, p. 54; see also Aronfreed, 1968a; 1976). This specification leaves open just how tangible the punishments are, but we are invited to think first of tangible punishments – infliction of pain, withholding of prizes, etc. – and then of the punished child's corresponding feelings and aversions. Having thus established the construct's general boundaries of reference, the next move is usually to posit connections between the affect and what I have called intangible punishments and rewards, which are so very reinforcing not because they are intangible but only because they somehow involve large amounts of anxiety.

I said a moment ago that Aronfreed's construct of anxiety corresponds roughly to what I have called the concept of moral motivation, i.e., the tendency to take a moral point of view in the first place. I would now add that he has a constitutive rather than summary conception, using these terms in the manner explained in Chapter 1. However, this is not to say that Aronfreed thinks the typical moral agent has two phenomenologically distinct conations or even that the processes which fulfill these two functions have radically different structures. It is only to say that his internalization theory can be read coherently in terms of our moral motives/motivation distinction, which when all is said and done is a way of understanding his *theory*, not the moral experiences of the persons his theory is attempting to describe. What makes it possible for us to map the moral motivation/motives distinction onto Aronfreed's account of internalization is his differential account of anxiety as both (1) an unspecified aversive state and (2) a cognitively shaped affective experience. In the first of these characterizations, anxiety plays in his theory the role of what I am calling moral motivation: it is a necessary condition for any socialization whatever, including that which results (or consists) in the internalization of moral norms. In the second, it plays the role of moral motive: it is a sufficient condition for compliance with the cognized norms, with 'compliance' understood here as including both positive actions and negative ones, i.e., forbearances.

What Aronfreed actually says about 'nonspecific anxiety' is less interesting for our purposes than the fact that he explicitly relates the moral concern to a tension-reduction model. This is, of course, the same model that underlies his accounts of other behaviors, including learning behaviors. However, when we turn to those accounts we find that the two formally distinct notions of moral motivation and moral motive are blurred. Or rather, they are effectively collapsed into each other, since in his view a person acquires and maintains a conscience for the same reason that he or she formulates specific moral judgments and acts on them: to reduce anxiety. Aronfreed's view of conscience as a device for regulating one's affective states can be broken down into a few basic claims: (1) conscience is an inherently affective mode of self-cognition, (2) this self-cognition is, or can be readily reduced to, self-criticism, and (3) the affective value of such self-criticism is, or can be readily reduced to, the subject's aversion to anxiety, the prototype of which is the feeling state produced by punishment. The evaluative cognitions Aronfreed associates with moral conscience are those that have been elicited independently of external pressures such as external surveillance or the risk of punishment, which is to say that the evaluative cognitions identified as moral judgments are affective reactions to real or hypothetical breaches of internalized norms.

These norms are 'internalized' in two senses of that term, one weak and one strong, and it is not always clear which is central for Aronfreed. First of all, his view can be read as requiring – as a necessary but not sufficient condition for regarding an evaluative cognition as an ethical evaluation or moral judgment – that

what he calls the subject's 'reactions' (i.e., self-addressed evaluations) are motivated by anxiety attached to the 'intrinsic correlates
of the transgression itself.' This is a relatively weak sense of
'internalization' since it only attends to aspects or outcomes of
the *deed*. So reconstructed, Aronfreed's view is not very different,
if at all, from standard externalist theories, except that he con-
centrates on 'intrinsic' features, which are indispensable parts of
the action description as the idea of a death is for the notion of
murder (in contrast to extrinsic consequences or outcomes such
as the grief sustained by the victim's relatives and the punishment
inflicted by the court on the murderer). However, Aronfreed can
also be read with a more robust sense of 'internalization,' as
meaning norms themselves acquire intrinsic 'anxiety-reducing
value.' Under this reconstruction, his view requires – as a necessary condition for an evaluative 'reaction' to be counted as an
ethical evaluation or moral judgment – that it have been internalized in this stronger sense of internalization. The affective
load of moral cognition is, he tells us, attached 'directly to the
intrinsic correlates of the reactions, with the result that the
reactions themselves acquire some independent effectiveness in the resolution of a transgression' (1968b, p. 214).

We turn now to the nature of this 'independent effectiveness,'
that is, to the topic of how ethical evaluations, moral judgments,
evaluative cognitions, 'reactions,' etc., can be moral motives in
their own right, apart from any external reinforcements that
might be attached to behavioral compliance or noncompliance
with these cognitions. There is considerable diversity here. Moral
cognitions can be prescriptive or proscriptive, deontic or aretaic,
and of course directed to such widely different content domains
as sexual conduct and agroeconomic policy. Furthermore, a
universalized moral judgment looks very different from a judgment of self-reproach. The one is cool, impersonally general,
typically before-the-fact, whereas the other is emotionally charged,
particular to the point of being autobiographical, and typically
after-the-fact. But they all grip the agent in the same anxiety-
reducing way, reflecting Aronfreed's underlying tension-
reduction model of moral motivation. Regardless of their qualitative and structural differences, moral motives all have the same
quantitative design: the degree to which one is motivated by an
evaluative cognition 'is a function of the intensity of anxiety
which is mobilized by the intrinsic correlates of a...transgression'

(1968b, pp. 214–15). A moral judgment motivates because it is an 'internalized reaction to transgression,' or better, to certain constituent features of the action description of the transgression. The product of this reaction can be thought of positively or negatively, that is, as a commission or an omission, but whether compliance takes the form of an active deed or a forbearance, it is still self-regulated. Furthermore, just as the concept of negative actions has a counterfactual element – referring as it does not to the simple absence of action but also to the blocking of potential or nascent behaviors – so also does that of positive actions, at least those performed in accordance with internalized norms – since the latter acts are understood as *alternatives* to the suppressed act. Thus Aronfreed distinguishes two ways in which anxiety motivates compliance:

> When anxiety becomes directly attached to the intrinsic correlates of a punished act, [it] may interfere to some extent with the performance of an act, particularly if the anxiety is of high intensity. But the more important function of anxiety is to provide the motivation, and indirectly the reinforcement, for nonpunished behavioral alternatives to the punished act.
>
> (p. 55)

Of the various 'cognitive housings' that constitute nonspecific states of anxiety as motives, the two most important here are guilt and shame. Like fear, they can be keyed to individual acts or sets of acts, whose real or prospective performance occasions one or even all three of these motives, depending on how the agent has been socialized. Unlike fear, the moral motives of guilt and shame are not anticipations of punishments (tangible or intangible) administered by external sources (physical or social), but rather are anticipations of the negative affect that is generated from within the agent according to the conditioning mechanisms shaping his or her socialization experiences. The upshot of these experiences is that the agent not only acquires a set of standards for conduct but also learns to focus on certain aspects of acts that transgress those standards. When the focus is on the aspect of visibility, the moral motive evoked is shame; when the focus is on an action's harmful consequences for others, the subject experiences guilt, either prospectively or retrospectively.

This way of parsing the moral emotions is fairly common in the psychological literature (as well as in the anthropological studies of 'guilt and shame cultures' undertaken earlier in this century by Margaret Mead (1950) and Ruth Benedict (1946, 1958)), but for the sake of clarity we should note that it reverses the everyday reference of the terms 'shame' and 'guilt.' According to ordinary usage, which is the one favored by most philosophers who attempt to relate the two concepts,[4] 'shame' refers primarily to the affective and cognitive reaction to the failure to meet one's *own* ideals, whereas 'guilt' refers to the failure to meet the expectations of those with whom one feels bonded in some special way. So regarded, shame is akin to embarrassment, in that it can be attributed when there is no question in the agent's (or anyone else's) mind of specifically moral failure. Thus a man could be ashamed of his big nose, his poverty, his inability to pronounce German properly, and so on, without regarding these defects as shortfalls from moral ideals that are part of his plan of life (see Rawls, 1971, pp. 444-5; Tugendhat, in press). In contrast, the psychological usage adopted by Aronfreed specifies that the fear of exposure, ridicule, and chastisement by *others* is intrinsic to the concept of shame, with all internally administered chastisements relegated to the category of guilt.

However, regardless of whether we use the ordinary or reversed sense of the terms, the conceptual space between these pure types of guilt and shame is filled with many permutations and combinations. For instance, it follows from Aronfreed's description that many guilt-like reactions to transgression would, in certain social contexts, really be fear reactions, and vice versa. Thus reparation, apology, confession, even unspoken self-criticism can be thought of as mechanisms for warding off feared external threats rather than as ways to express or resolve one's guilt. Conversely, a certain punishment could seem dreadful not so much because of the fearsome physical pain it causes as because it dramatically illustrates the degree of harm the guilty person has done to others (or in the case of shame, the extent of one's social rejection). One point of overlap is especially interesting because it shows how the manipulative self-regulation involved in delay of gratification can combine with the evaluative self-regulation involved in self-reproach. A person's anticipation of being shamed or ridiculed can be regarded as a form of fear, since it 'represents a cognitive focus on an external source of anxiety' (Aronfreed, 1968b, p. 244). We must bear in mind that this case involves 'being shamed,' which is not quite the same thing as being ashamed. Of course, one typically feels shame while being shamed, so that the anticipation of a public humiliation will, so to speak, provide two negative experiences for the price of one. But the well-socialized agent would be motivated to avoid social transgressions even in the absence of fears of being shamed, since by hypothesis such a person has learned to shame him or herself, that is, to focus his or her own attention on aspects of the transgression that, if seen, would be generally disliked. As we can see from Mead's (1950) example of the Ojibwa whose shame would lead to suicide precisely because an act was not open to observation, the self-dispensed reinforcements of shame can be powerful indeed (see Aronfreed, 1968b, p. 249; J. Gilligan, 1976).

Because the two pictures of internalization that we have from reinforcement theorists such as Rosenhan and affect conditioning theorists such as Aronfreed assign a central role to those moral motives generally classifiable as 'self-reproach,' it is fair to say that the moral psychologies giving rise to these pictures take an internalist view on the relation between moral cognition and moral action. The model of self-regulation they rest on is, or at least aspires to be, a parapolitical one, since the values that provide the criteria for assessing first-order motivations are regarded as having authority in virtue of their own self-contained affectivity. Of course a person may fail to heed those values, but when they *are* heeded the values function executively, and not just as other vectors in the force-field. Nevertheless, although these internalization theorists' conception of conscience as a grid of shame and guilt feelings is more internalist in its metaethical perspective than are the outcome-oriented theories discussed in the last chapter, it is ambiguous on a crucial point of what might be called its affective epistemology.

This ambiguity is particularly striking in Aronfreed's work, most notably *Conduct and Conscience*. On the one hand, he sometimes speaks as though the affective load of guilt and shame (especially guilt) is produced by objective features of the subject's action – specifically the harm done to other persons. In such contexts, it seems as if intrinsic motivations are central to his model of self-regulation, which is why I said in the preceding paragraph that such an internalization theory seems to involve an internalist metaethical perspective. For instance, guilt is produced by evaluative cognitions that correspond to the moral principle of nonmalevolence, and this principle seems to derive its relevance from affiliative tendencies that are innate or at least functionally autonomous. Similarly, shame-producing evaluative cognitions are made possible by the subject's concern to preserve his or her social standing, a concern which apparently derives from affiliative tendencies that are not themselves extrinsically motivated.

On the other hand, Aronfreed's discussion often reduces the motivational force of evaluative cognitions to the subject's aversion toward the negative affect he or she associates with the violation of the moral principles in question. For Aronfreed, one is not anxious because of one's guilt or shame, but rather one feels guilt or shame precisely because one is anxious. Hence Aronfreed's attempt to associate affect directly with principles rather than outcomes is not as cognitive as it first appears. As Alston has pointed out, it leads us to the bizarre conclusion that 'the only way in which the adoption of a principle forbidding adultery can enter into the control of behavior is that negative affect has been associated with such acts'(1977, p. 95).[5]

Nonetheless, the second of these two interpretations of guilt and shame dominates the studies of internalization carried out by Aronfreed and those influenced by him. In it the moral life takes on a character of self-indulgence that is at fundamental odds with our ordinary, pretheoretical understanding of what morality is all about. That understanding has a tacitly internalist metaethical perspective, in that the feelings of guilt and shame are thought to be motivating, but *not* primarily because the agent seeks to escape their discomfort. The latter view is tantamount to the moral self-indulgence of F. C. Sharp's man 'who always rode in the street car with his eyes closed, because he could not bear to see ladies standing when he had a seat' (Sharp, 1928, p. 76) – a moral stance that is no less ridiculous now than it was back in the days of street cars and male gallantry. Viewed in this light, the moral domain envisioned in the reinforcement and affect-conditioning pictures of internalization loses its luster. Even worse, it loses its relevance as an action guide for anyone who accepts these pictures but continues to lead a reflective existence. I have already argued that externalist moral psychologies are self-effacing since the theorist who understands moral motivation exclusively in terms of the Principle of Universal Heteronomy forfeits his or her own moral self-respect and, conversely, finds the grounds for deep self-reproach utterly dissolved. I would now urge that a similar sort of self-effacement takes place when one reflects too closely on the internalization processes discussed above: once one's internalized moral motives are exposed as nothing more than an elaborate shield for the squeamishness illustrated by Sharp's man on the bus, they either lose their urgency or the moral agent/theorist loses his or her self-respect. If moral psychology is to resist these losses, it must hold out for a more deeply internalist conception of moral motives. This is much like waiting for Godot, in that as long as one stands within the frames of the foregoing reinforcement and affect-conditioning pictures of internalization, virtually nothing specific can be said about this conception ('If I knew who Godot was,' Beckett once said, 'I would have said so in the play'). From these standpoints, about all that can be said is that with such a conception evaluative cognitions would be seen to motivate primarily because they are expressions or symptoms of some other motivational process. Although this process is probably intensified by the subject's real or anticipated experiences of guilt- or shame-feelings, it is not identified with them or with any of the other disparate moral motives that effect our compliance to moral norms. In Beckett's play, there is no sense of progress as the tramps wait for Godot. But our spectrum metaphor is not so bleak: beyond the theories of internalization considered so far lie still other, more cognitive theories where one might hope a more determinate conception of moral motivation will emerge. The best-known of these is, of course, Freud's later psychoanalytic theory, to which we now turn.

The psychoanalytic picture of internalization

More than any of the moral psychologists discussed so far, the later Freud was directly concerned with the general question of why people care about being moral at all. (Since he was also more concerned with that question than his successors were, I shall focus on his own writings at the expense of post-Freudian psychoanalytic treatments of internalization, introjection, and identification.)[6] That moral motivation, rather than the compliance tendencies I have called moral motives, was a major theme in Freud's later work is borne out by his relative lack of interest in the standard philosophical puzzle of akrasia or weakness of will.

As Richard Wollheim has pointed out, for Freud the systematic discrepancy between an individual's moral code and his or her actual moral deeds 'simply reflects the different determinants or sources of, on the one hand, moral authority and, on the other, actual behavior' (1971, p. 227). Freud was much more interested in the often bewildering ways these two sorts of determinants are linked with each other than he was in the 'unremarkable' fact that they could be, and frequently were, separated in ordinary life.[7] But this does not mean that the later phases of psycho-analytic moral psychology retained the externalist metaethical perspective I previously ascribed to his earlier nonteleological notions of repression and cathexis. When Freud admitted teleological categories into his moral psychology, he almost certainly regarded the demands of conscience as capable of motivating their own compliance.

In this respect, the classic psychoanalytic picture of moral internalization is continuous with the internalization pictures already discussed, sharing as they do a common metaethical perspective. They all portray evaluative cognitions as not only internalized but also as sufficiently affect-laden to serve as motives for engaging in the moral behaviors corresponding to those cognitions. However, there are at least two enormous differences, which can be understood only within the context of Freud's larger account of the desires whereby the self is constituted. First of all, in the preceding pictures what was internalized was a rule, norm, or command. For Freud and his successors as well, the picture is quite different, since what is first internalized is not a norm but a whole person, or array of persons, with whom the moral subject *identifies* in such a way as to constitute the nucleus of his or her own moral motivation. Secondly, in the preceding pictures the internalized norms were thought of incrementally, as psychological reactions to logically arbitrary (if not purely situation-specific) requirements made by the social environment. Hence it was not necessary for those theorists to postulate a self-system having its own structure, personal boundaries, and internal intentionality. For Freud, on the other hand, the self is a highly structured system, whose inner conative forces shape whatever possibilities the external environment has for influencing the course of a person's psychological and social life.

To appreciate these two points, we should recall that psycho-analytic theory began with Freud's early discovery of libidinal desires, which constitute one specific instinctual region of the id that itself is but one specific part of the unconscious. (The three-way division of personality into id, ego, and superego was a relatively late development in Freud's thought (1923/1961)). Some years later he discovered a second instinctual region of the id: repressed aggressive desires (Freud, 1926/1959). It was not until *Civilization and Its Discontents* (1930/1961) that Freud spelled out the implications for moral psychology of his view that the interaction of life and death instincts is the basis for all human action. But even in this early period he tended to portray the instincts not as blind forces but as intentional agencies, which he described in personal categories. The earliest version of what he eventually called the superego was the 'censor,' first mentioned in *The Interpretation of Dreams* (1900/1958). As his thought progressed, this concept and that of the 'ego ideal' (Freud later claimed the terms were interchangeable) grew in importance, eventually being explained by him as the heir of the child's shattered Oedipus complex.

It is important to realize that in Freud's account the superego develops and internalizes with a fundamentally different rhythm than that which social learning theorists ascribe to the internalization of moral norms. In the latter case, internalization begins as soon as the child can respond to rewards and punishments. As we saw in the discussion of vicarious learning in the last chapter, a qualitative change in the internalization process supposedly takes place when the rewards and punishments begin to be filtered through the personae of models; however, this change does not constitute a structural transformation in the way the child organizes his or her social world. In contrast, Freud thought that the child is forced to reorganize everything: only by radically transforming his world could the child (Freud was thinking here primarily of boys) survive the crisis of discovering that the depth of his libidinal attachment to his mother is more than equaled by the extent of his father's power. The key to this reorganization is the child's discovery of the uses of fantasy. By imaginatively identifying himself with his father he 'becomes' that powerful figure by taking it into himself in a process referred to as *introjection*. In this way the child not only indirectly consummates his libidinal wishes but also keeps the rage of his real father from coming down in its full force. Prior to this intense point in his psychosexual history, there is nothing either distinctive or destructive about the child's sense of right and wrong: it is at most a loose collection of injunctions and attitudes learned in the ordinary course of things and of no special psychoanalytic or moral interest. But once the child has introjected the powerful, punitive, and ever watchful parental figures (Freud later expanded the story to include both parents, and eventually numerous other external figures), a *conscience* is in place, forming a third set of constraints bounding the ego (the other two being the constraints created by the boundary between it and the id and the boundary between it and the external world).

To summarize so far: in our juxtaposition of the psycho-analytic picture of internalization with the pictures drawn in conditioning-oriented socialization theories, we have seen that for Freud the affectivity of evaluative cognitions derives from certain personal features, themselves loaded with affective and motivational significance, that are associated with parents and other important external figures who are internalized – i.e., introjected – by the moral agent during childhood and beyond. Freud explains the 'demands of conscience' in terms that charac-terize our relations toward other persons – in particular, those persons whose own psychological states and dispositions toward us are authoritative. The severity of these demands, which he identifies with the superego, is 'simply a continuation of the severity of the external authority, to which it has succeeded and which it has in part replaced' (1930/1961, p. 74). The difference between submission to the demands of an external person and submission to those of the internalized figure is, Freud goes on to say, that in the former case one is thereby not only 'quits' with the authoritative figure but also rests assured of its continued love, whereas in the latter case one continues to live under the guilt-generating threat of a loss of love on the part of the internal figure, who – because internal – can see all one's unsavory wishes as well as one's unsavory deeds.

This is a very different sort of 'cognitive housing for anxiety' from any of the moral feelings discussed by Aronfreed or social learning theorists such as Rosenhan. For Freud, what is anticipated and dreaded at the hands of the superego is not an undifferentiated affective state but rather a specifically personal and interpersonal way in which that state comes about, namely, by being rejected or otherwise passed over by a significant other. Or more accurately:

it comes about by being rejected by the internal counterpart of that significant other, since we can live in fear of the loss of our parents' love long after their deaths.

Although Freud always described introjection as a defense mechanism, whose original purpose is that of protection from anxiety, we must bear in mind that the superego is the introjection of an external *person*, whose intentionality constitutes him or her as an authority as well as a menace. The so-called dynamic aspect of the superego is the subject's unconscious fear of punishment for the expression of those tendencies that, under one description or another, are the subject matter of moral judgments (e.g., sex, aggression, uncleanliness). Hence Freud observed wryly that 'the description of the pleasure principle as the watchman of our lives cannot be rejected' (1924/1961, p. 161). But we should not conclude from this deliberately understated observation that he reduced the fear of the loss of a parent's love to a 'bottom line' of anticipated physical chastisements. Freud recognized that the severity of one's superego does not correspond to the severity of one's upbringing: a child who has been raised by lenient parents can acquire a very strict conscience, simply by channeling its own aggression inward. Even so, the vehicle for this aggression is the parent – or more precisely, the introjected figure of the parent[8] – who, lenient or harsh, has been the principal authority in the child's life. Of course even the most lenient parent can sometimes be a menace. However, in Freud's account the external figure is a menace largely *because* of his or her authority: the child perceives itself as utterly dependent on this figure, who is in a position to block even the slightest quest for gratification the child might initiate. It would be more accurate still to say that the menace the child faces is an undifferentiated mix (undifferentiated to the child, that is) of authority and sheer power; hence when it is introjected as the superego, the menace appears in the guise of an internalized figure who is 'harsh, cruel and inexorable against the ego, which is in its charge' (1924/ 1961, p. 167). It harangues, criticizes, and punishes the child, all apart from any considerations about instrumental justifications that the norms in question might (but often do not) have.

The net effect of having confounded power and authority in this way is that the demands made by the superego are apprehended simultaneously as guides and goads. As we can see from the central role it assigns to deontic judgments, the psychoanalytic account of the emergence and functioning of the superego is worked out against an essentially Kantian moral backdrop, from which Freud's theory takes its own internalist metaethical perspective. It represents the 'oughts' spoken by the introjected figure as spoken with an authority whose motivational force is always given in advance, by the very conditions under which the introjecting fantasy occurs in the first place. Hence, Freud concluded, 'the categorical imperative of Kant is a direct inheritance from the Oedipus-complex' (Freud, 1924/1961, p. 167).

Summaries of Freud's theory of the superego often overlook this point, even those in otherwise sophisticated psychology textbooks or scholarly articles. As a result, the psychoanalytic picture of morality is presented as a trade-off between internal tranquility and external fear, made possible by an internalization process consisting in a cognitive legerdemain of identification and introjection. So put, morality is a burden we assume in order to forestall even greater burdens. It is only 'an internalized Danegeld' (Wollheim, 1984, p. 205), providing no positive fulfillment of any deeper needs and desires. But such an interpretation is grossly inadequate to Freud's own view; he in fact regarded morality as much more than a Danegeld, although his reasons for doing so changed over the years. As he wrote in 1924:

The situation is usually represented as though internalized social requirements were primary and the renunciation of instinct followed from them. This leaves the origin of the ethical sense unexplained. Actually, it seems to be the other way about. The original instinctual renunciation is subsequently enforced by external powers, thereby creating the ethical sense, which expresses itself in conscience and demands a further renunciation of instinct. [revised translation]
(1924/1961, p. 170; cf. Freud, 1923/1961, p. 54)

Up to the time of *Inhibitions, Symptoms and Anxiety* (1926/1959), he linked this 'original instinctual renunciation' to an abiding need for mastery over our sexual impulses, a view whose general outlines correspond to the hierarchical desire model described above. This view was reassembled by various neo-Freudians who claimed that the ego had its own irreducible instincts, one of which was the drive to self-mastery. But Freud himself was uneasy with the idea of a primitive urge or instinct to control one's erotic impulses, since eros is not merely a source of pleasure but, especially in its genital mode, the most important instantiation of pleasure (cf. 1926/1959, p. 91, n. 3). Accordingly, his earlier view of anxiety was that it arises when sexuality is repressed, and hence self-control is part of the causal explanation of anxiety rather than the other way around. But the story changed once Freud came to understand aggression as 'an original self-subsisting instinctual disposition in man' (1930/1961, p. 69). With this shift in his understanding of aggression came a new, morality-generating conception of anxiety, which Freud now regarded as the affective correlate of aggression. The negative quality of this affect creates a fundamental demand for the control of aggressive impulses, though not for the control of sexual ones except insofar as sex and aggression are interlocked. Because of this development in his view of anxiety, Freud's conception of the superego became much more subtle than is usually recognized: introjection is *consequent* upon projection, in the sense that before the child finds it necessary to identify with and internalize the menacing authority figure, the child has already transformed the external authority figure into a menacing one by projecting his own internal feelings of aggression onto that figure.

With this idea of an original, unchosen and largely unconscious projection, we arrive, at long last, at an unambiguously internalist conception of moral motives. What distinguishes such projection from other, nonmoralized dispositions such as envy or ennui is the aim, lodged deep in its intentionality, that it not go unrequited or at least not unnoticed. This aim moralizes aggression, bonding it conceptually (given the Freudian conception here described) to the fear of retaliation. By this I mean that it is inherent in the nature of aggression that the aggressor intends that his or her victims (including the original victim, the target of the original projection) *realize* that they have been aggressed upon. Accordingly, moral motivation has its origin in an original projection that temporarily relieves the child of the intolerable load of its own aggressive impulses but creates (in the child's own mind) the picture of a parent or other external figure who resents what has been done and who stands ready to retaliate against the child. When this picture is internalized, i.e., identified with and introjected in the form of a superego, the retaliatory power of the authority figure is enhanced by its complete access to the child's most secret thoughts and desires, as we have already noted. Hence one can feel guilty for even toying with the idea of attempting to resist the punitive demands of conscience, and so on.

Of course the rhythm of morality-generating projection and introjection is largely unconscious, as is evidenced by the therapeutic methods used when guilt has become pathological. On those occasions, the therapist seeks to expose the subterranean workings of the superego to the cooling air of conscious rationality, in hopes that doing so will attenuate the pressures that have come to bear on the ego from the superego. The therapeutic efforts of psychoanalysis are, as Freud put it in *The New Introductory Lectures*, intended

> to strengthen the ego, to make it more independent of the super-ego, to widen its field of perception and enlarge its organization, so that it can appropriate fresh portions of the id. Where id was, there ego shall be. It is a reclamation work of culture – not unlike the draining of the Zuider Zee.
>
> (1933/1964, p. 80)

But Freud never thought that therapeutic 'reclamation' could eliminate the superego altogether, nor that it should try to do so. Total self-transparency, as represented by the rationalistic ideal of an ego unmuddled by the id, is not only an impossible ideal but a self-defeating one: since the ego borrows its energies from the id, which it rides like a horse (1933/1964, p. 77), to eliminate the id would be for the rider to kill his horse in order to control it.

The classical objective of psychoanalytic therapy, then, is only to eliminate those infantile wishes that require an excessively severe superego. Once those wishes are eliminated, it is possible to bring the claims of the id, ego, and superego into a three-way balance, as exemplified by the 'erotic-obsessional-narcissistic' personality, which, like the just man in Plato's *Republic*, 'would be the absolute norm, the ideal harmony' (1931/1961, pp. 218–19). Commenting on this passage, de Sousa points out that it represents Freud's acknowledgment that the ego faces two kinds of reality: inner and outer (de Sousa, 1982, p. 159; cf. Freud, 1931/1961, p. 167). Since rationality, in its broad psychoanalytic sense, just *is* the ego's way of coping with reality, it follows that for Freud it was every bit as rational for one to accommodate the intrapsychic demands of id and superego as it was for one to take into account the natural laws of physics or the timeless principles of mathematic and logic. But he provides no grounds for assuming that these two sorts of coping can be reconciled, either in a person's own practice or in an overarching philosophical theory about the truth-relatedness of rationality.[9]

Indeed, there is reason to think that such a reconciliation is not only omitted from the Freudian account but impossible in principle, at least as far as a psychoanalytic theory of moral coping is concerned. I have already lamented the self-effacing nature of externalist moral psychologies, in which the theorist explains away his or her own moral motivation in the course of delineating its supposedly heteronomous structure. Similarly, earlier in the present chapter I complained that internalization pictures drawn within conditioning paradigms do not differentiate moral feelings from self-indulgence; consequently, in the standard social psychology accounts of moral socialization either the internalized norms lose their urgency as specifically moral claims or the fully reflective internalization theorist forfeits his or her own moral self-respect. Now we see that the same unwelcome result obtains in the case of the superego, which, though it functions as an introjected person rather than a repertoire of internalized norms, also must collapse as a *moral* force once it is recognized for the fantasy it is.

We may recall Parfit's (1984, ch. 1) argument to the effect that a theory is self-defeating if the outcome of taking it seriously is some state of affairs – be it an internal or external state – that must be counted bad or wrong on the theory's own terms. Even if Parfit is correct in adding that a self-defeating theory could nonetheless be true (insofar as the primary aim of a theory is to be true, not to be believed or to be liveable), it remains the case that a thoroughly Freudian view of one's own conscience would expose conscience's specifically moral pretensions as fraudulent; and on that account it would cease to be a truly moral psychology, though it might be some other sort of knowledge. In the aftermath of such an exposure the erstwhile moral psychologist might continue to be anxious for having acted or felt in certain 'wrong' ways, much as Dorothy and her friends continued to be influenced by the putative Wizard of Oz even after the curtain collapsed to reveal a rather silly old man. But once exposed, neither superego nor wizard have any purchase on one's loyalty or one's respect: words like 'right' and 'wrong' are then available for discourse only in the secondary, inverted-commas sense used by cultural anthropologists and other nonparticipating observers of moral discourse.

To put the matter another way, we may say that the superego functions effectively only to the extent that the subject fails to differentiate between his or her own self and the external figures who have been introjected. It may seem unduly harsh to speak of the identificatory process central to the psychoanalytic picture of internalization as a 'failure,' if only because it is precisely *because* children appreciate the otherness (the 'object-quality') of their parents that they form superegos in the first place. Freud's own work is not explicit on this point. However, the fact that he took as a condition for introjection the loss of a beloved object suggests that he always assumed that even in the earliest stages of superego-formation the child was already quite capable of subject–object differentiation. (In contrast to the child, the infant – who is immersed in an utterly undifferentiated world – has neither conscience nor need of one.) Post-Freudian psycho-analytic theorists have attempted to clarify the sense in which introjection, especially but not exclusively the introjection that creates the superego, is or centrally involves identification between self and other (see Loevinger, 1976; Meissner, 1981). They point out, rightly enough, that incorporation, introjection, and identification are separable concepts, although subsumed under the more general concept of internalization, and they go on to dispute the details of how these concepts differ. But there is no dispute over the classic psychoanalytic postulate that the child's solution to the problems posed by his own aggressive projections is a purely intrapsychic solution. That is, the child solves these problems in a way that is literally fantastic: by acting not upon the external world but only upon his repre-sentations of it and (most fundamentally) by forming a blithely unrealistic representation of his own relation to those representa-tions.

What makes such internal action successful (or, even when unsuccessful, at least sufficiently promising to have been worth trying) is the fact that there are *no epistemic constraints* on the sorts of beliefs and intentions one has toward one's internal world, beyond the constraints provided by the tension-reduction model itself within which all psychic functioning is conceived in psychoanalytic theory. In the economics of anxiety, the utility of a representation of, say, one's father as a haranguing internal voice is independent of the truth value of that representation. But probably no classical or neo-Freudian psychoanalytic theorist, and certainly not Freud himself, ever really denied that representations have objective truth value, since they can be tested against external reality with little or no effort on the subject's part. Why then, we cannot help but ask, does the Freudian subject not eventually advert to the fact that a given internal representation is true or false? The answer, which holds for later as well as earlier versions of psychoanalytic theory, is that representations such as that of the internal father figure are not so much semantic vehicles or cognitive mirrorings of an external world as they are intrapsychic power plays, effecting structural changes in one's very capacity to represent the world (or better, to cognize it). But with this answer psychoanalytic moral theorists take an epistemic stand toward their own internal representations as well as those of other persons, including not only the general array of 'others' but also specific clinical subjects such as Freud's Rat Man or Little Hans, whose consciences have been embalmed in case studies for our theoretical scrutiny. Once theorists take this epistemic stand, their conception of conscience can no longer be simply that of what Bertrand Russell called a wee small voice that tells you someone is looking. For such theorists the wee small voice may still be audible, but, when it is heard from an epistemic standpoint, it is accompanied by another voice that proclaims, in a stage-whisper, that in fact no one *really* is looking after all and that the wee small voice is only your own.

The self-manipulative trickery posited in the psychoanalytic account of the superego is, we should note, quite different from the imaginative activities involved in role-taking and imitative behavior, even though the difference is minimized by authors as diverse as Bandura (1986) and Kohlberg (1969/1984), who seem to regard the psychoanalytic constructs of identification and introjection more along the lines of 'willing suspension of disbelief' than as simple factual errors. Of course Freud did not actively encourage people to confound self and other. He was only too aware that the tendency toward this confusion is already quite well established in all of us, such that it needs no further boost from the psychoanalytic theorist or therapist. Futhermore, he knew from his clinical work how appallingly dysfunctional such confusion could be, especially in its psychotic manifestations (e.g., Freud, 1933/1964, pp. 16, 59, 153–4). But he never objected to it on straightforwardly epistemic grounds. That is, the raw fact that one is not, in external reality, one's father, mother, etc., never seems to have been offered as a reason not to identify internally with that person. As a therapist, Freud can be forgiven for being interested in the harmony of his patient's psychic life at the expense of its epistemic value. But as a moral psychologist, he cannot – if indeed we have a right to expect any theory of moral psychology to be not only true but also compatible with the desire to live a moral life.

Conclusion

To develop a truly adequate theory it is, I think, necessary to go beyond the conceptions of internalization discussed in this chapter, and to look at the far end of the spectrum for still more robustly cognitive models of moral self-regulation, in which moral reasons motivate because of their very reasonableness. These models may not themselves fully embody the internalist theory we are looking for. However, their very existence shows that it is possible to develop a view of moral motives and moral motivation more psychodynamic than those of internalization theorists such as Aronfreed and Rosenhan and yet more socially interactive than Freud's. It also shows that this can be done without throwing overboard their valid insights into the process by which morality becomes a profoundly personal concern. To this purpose, we must eschew the noncognitive biases of contemporary psychology and instead take cognitive and conative structures as givens, not in the sense of their being innate biological structures (though they may be that too) but rather as the organizational elements of the agent's personal experience. At the end of this book I shall try to flesh out the claim that it is because those structures organize the agent's personality, self-concept, and 'reason for going on' that they are the foundational structures of moral motivation. It seems likely that these constitutive cognitions and desires are empirical rather than transcendental structures, and hence form part of the subject matter of psychology as well as philosophy. If so, they can be presumed to include not only the relatively straightforward affiliative tendencies studied in social psychology and personality theory but also more problematic sorts of unconscious strivings as are charted in psychoanalytic theory. Then the affective features and motivating potential that internalization theorists such as Aronfreed correctly ascribe to 'evaluative cognitions' – moral ideals, values, and principles – could be thought of as deriving from the deep-seated strivings described by Freudian theorists. So conceived, moral cognitions are overridingly prescriptive self-regulators precisely because they articulate an agent's profoundly intimate, constitutive desires.

As we begin the next chapter the 'subtext' of this book – i.e., the theme underlying the exposition proper – takes a positive turn, in hopes of sketching out how to develop just such a conception. This will be in contrast to the relatively negative subtext of the present chapter, whose exposition was driven by the underlying aim of showing the limitations of internalization and psychoanalytic theories that reduce guilt and shame to the essentially noncognitive state of anxiety.

5

INTERNALIST MORAL PSYCHOLOGIES: COGNITIVE DEVELOPMENTAL THEORIES

If our review in the last two chapters concerning socialization and internalization theories shows anything about the requirements of psychological theory building, it is that moral psychology must take the subject's own viewpoint seriously. Instead of dismissing the evaluative cognitions of morality as rationalizations or (at best) epiphenomena of fundamentally irrational mental states, the theorist who truly wishes to understand moral experience must allow that the *reasons* behind normative judgments can be meaningful in their own terms, efficacious determinants of moral action, and crucial as explanatory elements in moral psychology. This is not to say that moral cognitions are unambiguous or to deny that they are often insincere or heavy with self-deception, but only to recognize that they are in principle available to the agent whose reasons and judgments they are – i.e., accessible by means of self-interpretation and communicable by means of self-reports and other sorts of verbal behavior, including that of moral argumentation. This phenomenological postulate is central in the theories we shall now examine, the cognitive developmental moral psychologies of Jean Piaget and Lawrence Kohlberg. Notwithstanding important differences in their approaches, they both believed that morality is inherently rational, not only in the sense that the moral significance of a situation is a highly cognitive construction but also in the sense that moral reasons are thought to have motivational efficacy *qua* reasons. In the cognitive developmentalist economy of moral self-regulation, values are not construed as expressions of fortuitous desires that one 'just has.' Unlike those Topsy-like desires or motives, which are themselves unmotivated by any cognitive processes, values are understood in cognitive developmental

109

theory as expressions of desires that are not only motivating but also motivated – and, furthermore, that these latter desires are motivated by rational considerations that can be classified and investigated in terms of their logical structures.[1]

For this reason, as well as because of its emphasis on the semantic dimension of evaluative cognition, the tradition represented by Piaget and Kohlberg stands at the (for now) most cognitive area of the moral psychology spectrum. I hasten to add that the metaphor of a spectrum is not meant to suggest there is a smooth continuity between the cognitive developmental approach to morality and the less cognitive approaches, such that they all could be regarded as 'cognitive' in the same sense but in different degrees. Many if not most of the moral psychologists and socialization theorists whom we have already reviewed employ categories such as 'cognitive' and 'evaluative cognition,' but as we have seen they use these categories to refer to verbal labels and, sometimes, to images and memories. In those theories cognition is thought of as 'a facilitator of associations' (Blasi, 1983, p. 181), invoked by their authors to render psychological explanations as versatile and general as the psychosocial behavior they are meant to account for. For cognitive developmentalists, however, cognition is thought of as 'understanding, construction of meanings, and coherent logical structures' (ibid.), enabling these theorists to differentiate actions having moral meaning from other, morally neutral actions.

The cognitive developmental view

Although both Piaget and Kohlberg wrote extensively about moral development, their metaethical perspectives are not always obvious. In particular, it is surprisingly difficult to discern their views about moral motives and moral motivation. Since neither author took these topics as explicit themes, it is necessary to reconstruct their theories so that their motivational suppositions show through, a task which calls for a certain amount of interpolation and guesswork. Even though Piaget interacted with his young subjects to the point of getting down on his hands and knees to play marbles with them, and Kohlberg participated in richly concrete sessions devoted to the self-governance of several 'just communities' established in schools and prisons, the primary object of their research was always the subjects' evaluative cognitions, not their actions or the motives behind their actions. They made no apology for this fact: as Piaget bluntly declared, it seemed necessary to 'make the best of it and try to examine, not the act, but simply the judgment of moral value' (1932/1965, p. 113). As in most of the research carried out within the cognitive developmental paradigm, they took as their unit of analysis the subject's verbalized judgment about morally right and wrong actions, with the subject's tendency to conform to those rules being only of secondary interest.

But let us not get ahead of ourselves. It is necessary first to get straight on a few of the main themes in the cognitive developmental literature on moral psychology before we can begin the trickier task of teasing out whatever distinctively motivational themes lie hidden between the lines of Piaget and Kohlberg's writings. The main themes relevant to our study can be gathered under three general headings: (1) the conception of developmental stages as *structures*, (2) the separating of moral development into distinct *stages*, either two (Piaget) or six (Kohlberg), and most important of all, (3) the *interiorization* process, in which concrete evaluations are transformed into verbalized moral judgments. After examining these themes in a general way, we shall turn to the more specific issue of how our distinction between moral motives and moral motivation is reflected, first in the work of Piaget and then in that of Kohlberg.

Structuralism: content vs. structure

In general, for cognitive developmentalists the phenomenological postulate mentioned at the outset of this chapter is inseparable from another, equally fundamental postulate, namely, that cognition and developmental change are to be understood *structurally*. That is, cognitive activity is organized in ways that transcend the specific features or contents of one's reasoning, being instead general, holistic structures that can be formally represented as logical systems. Exactly how these structures ought to be described, and whether there are different sorts of structures for different sorts of content domains (e.g., the moral, the physical, the aesthetic, the religious), is in dispute among cognitive developmentalists (e.g., Döbert, 1990; Puka, 1990). But as structuralists they agree that, whatever these structures might be, within each domain there is a hierarchical relationship among them, such that earlier stages of cognitive development are incorporated and transformed in the later stages, which earlier stages portend. Furthermore, progress from one cognitive stage to the next is a movement toward increasing logical stability or 'cognitive equilibrium' and hence proceeds through an invariant and irreversible sequence, though not necessarily one whose final stage is realized very often. Structures and their sequences are divined from the subject's verbal activities, usually those performed in an interview situation, and so in this sense cognitive structures are 'naturalistic' categories albeit not 'empirical' ones in the narrow, positivistic sense of the latter term. Their status is, therefore, epistemologically quite different from that of Kantian categories, which as synthetic a priori structures of thought were supposed to constitute the necessary conditions of any experience whatsoever. Even so, those writing in this tradition are quite correct in tracing their intellectual roots back to Kant, since they share his rationalistic view of the linkage of psychological processes with formal logic.

Because the present study is concerned with the motivational structure of morality rather than its reasoning structures, it would be distracting to go very deeply into the matter of cognitive developmental structuralism, though we cannot bypass it altogether. Suffice it to say here that, as far as morality is concerned, it is not always clear to what extent cognitive developmentalists have achieved their basic theoretical goal, that of charting logically cohesive structural stages. This is especially true of what is probably the best-known study of morality from a cognitive developmental perspective, Piaget's *The Moral Judgment of the Child* (1932/1965). This relatively early work employs structuralist categories – e.g., generalization, reciprocity, equality, equilibrium, intellectual egocentrism – that are central in his studies of such nonmoral modes of thinking as mathematical and scientific reasoning; but in order to understand that book as a structuralist account it is necessary to read back into it ideas about social and moral cognition that Piaget did not develop until much later in his life, after he was clearer in his own mind about the details of his structuralist paradigm (see Piaget, 1960, 1970). In those later works, moral judgment was discussed incidentally and as a purely logical operation, i.e., apart from the judgment's evaluative contents and the social circumstances evoking it. But in his earlier study, the form and contents of evaluative cognition are not separated from each other, with the result that Piaget's focus there slides back and forth between the intellectual and the motivational dimensions. This is true, though to a lesser extent, in the work of Kohlberg as well. It would, therefore, be a mistake to think that because the motivational dimension of morality is not a logical structure, it is irrelevant to the cognitive developmental moral psychologies of Piaget and Kohlberg. For all their differences, both authors shared a fundamental belief that social reciprocity as well as logical reciprocity is at stake in moral cognition, and that positive social feelings as well as a sense of purely intellectual satisfaction are the hallmarks of a successful resolution of conflict.

The moral stages: heteronomy vs. autonomy

Cognitive developmental moral psychology thus links the development of moral judgment directly to the quality of the child's social interactions. Piaget and Kohlberg believed that the general direction of this development process is toward greater self-determination, though they differed as to the nature and number of its stages. Piaget described moral development as comprising two stages of moral judgment, whereas Kohlberg expanded the sequence to six. Both accounts portray each stage as having its own characteristic social perceptions, its own structural features, and its characteristic moral feelings and motives. Following Kant's lead, Piaget called the first of his two stages a morality of *heteronomy*, since it is characterized by deference to external – usually parental – authority. Accordingly, Piaget's second stage is a morality of *autonomy*, since in it mutual respect and co-operativeness – especially among peers – are dominant. Unlike Kohlberg and many other cognitive moral developmentalists, Piaget did not think the transition to the higher moral stage was especially difficult or rare. On the contrary, he thought that under normal conditions it takes place spontaneously in early adolescence, when the child comes to realize that his or her current view of moral rules provides no way to resolve the more complex problems of cooperation that arise when it is with peers, rather than parents, that the child has to interact.

These two moralities are modes of social interaction as well as structures of moral reasoning, which is reason enough not to regard them as pure structures. Piaget himself minimized the nonstructural qualities of the two moralities,[2] and often suggested that the social dimension and the cognitive (structural) dimension of moral judgment were concurrent 'aspects' of a single psychosocial reality. For instance, he declared: 'Whether we describe the facts in terms of social morphology or from the point of view of consciousness (and the two languages are, we repeat, parallel and not contradictory), it is impossible to reduce the effects of cooperation to those of constraint and unilateral respect' (1932/1965, p. 108). But it is significant that he went on a few lines later to refer to heteronomy and autonomy as 'clusters of moral facts' rather than as logically coherent patterns of judgment. It is for this reason that Kohlberg and others later compared the two Piagetian stages to Weber's (1949) notion of 'ideal types,' in which certain 'content themes' are clustered together. (A 'bootstrapping' methodology is used to establish types: the content themes are initially clustered because they appear to the researcher as having prima facie similarity or relatedness, and finally because empirical investigation reveals them to be statistically correlated with each other.)[3] At this point an underlying 'structure' is postulated and given a heuristic label such as 'heteronomy': however, this is not a structure in Piaget's narrow sense of logical form but rather a theoretical construct devised in order to account for the fact that the clustered elements – which may include content-related considerations as well as logical-structural features – cluster together in spite of there not being any logical relationships among them (as would be the case if they were true structural stages). Of course, the fact that there are no logical relationships *among* the elements does not preclude the possibility of such relationships existing *within*, or simply *as*, some of the elements. This is surely the case in Piaget's so-called 'two moralities,' whose defining characteristics include structures of reasoning such as reciprocity (or, in heteronomy, the equally structural specification of non-reciprocity), as well as cognitive contents such as the subject's belief in the sacredness of rules, respect for parents, and legal literalism.

Kohlberg began his career with a dissertation (1958) that was originally designed to take up where Piaget left off, by tracing the progressive development of autonomy during adolescence. However, because Piaget's stages had confounded content and structural features, Kohlberg found that differences in moral reasoning were more aptly represented by a six-stage model, which he then spent the next three decades refining. The stages were grouped into three levels, corresponding to three so-called sociomoral perspectives whereby the subject understands his or her relationship to society and its rules. These perspectives are the concrete-individual perspective (Stages 1 and 2), the member-of-society perspective (Stages 3 and 4), and the prior-to-society perspective (Stages 5 and 6). The first two stages are 'preconventional' in that they are not constituted by any special awareness of social conventions as such: the judgments of an action's rightness are keyed entirely to the punishments or rewards associated with that action. But we must note that even at this very early level of cognitive development the child is actively discriminating between right and wrong, which as we have seen is a second-order evaluative activity and not a wanton drifting in the direction set by one's strongest first-order desires. (Kohlberg occasionally spoke of this sort of nonevaluative drifting as an altogether nonmoral or amoral 'Stage 0.') In the normal course of childhood experience, the fact and importance of social conventions emerge fairly early, typically around age 9 or 10. The child has a stake in being a 'good boy' or 'nice girl' (Stage 3), labels used by Kohlberg to indicate that the child relates to other individuals, especially significant others such as parents, in ways that are conditioned by social expectations that he or she shares with those individuals. These expectations are often couched in moral language, since the roles constituted by these expectations can have a seriousness equal to any duties that might be found at a higher stage of cognitive development. Indeed, children are not the only ones for whom these roles are of enormous moral significance: the loyalties and other bonds between a man and his aging parent, a mistress and her servant, or feudal lords and their vassals, are enduring themes in Eastern and Western literature. As the set of roles becomes greater and more complex, the need emerges for a more comprehensive perspective from which conflicting demands can be sorted out. This higher perspective (Stage 4) is one in which the social system is understood as a whole: thus a boy caught in a tug of war between his promises to his brother and his obligations to his father is led to ask what course of action will be best for the family considered as a holistic system, a patriot who is upset about the hate-filled war his country is fighting will consider challenging its legality in the federal courts, and so on. But the final criteria of rightness may not be conventional even in this relatively sophisticated sense. In that case, moral justifications are 'postconventional,' either because they look at the transhistorical requirements of a utility-oriented social contract (Stage 5) or the even more abstract, totally ahistorical requirements of a justice-oriented system of principles having to do with fairness, respect for persons, and mutual dialogue (Stage 6).[4]

Interiorization: concrete vs. verbal evaluation

Epistemologically, the single most important theme in cognitive-developmental moral psychology is a process that Piaget called the 'interiorization' of moral judgment. Kohlberg called it the 'one-track assumption' to indicate that, instead of there being two separate developmental tracks, moral judgment 'arises out of moral action itself' (Kohlberg and Candee, 1984, p. 506). This idea is a hallmark of most if not all of the cognitive developmental theory done in the Piagetian tradition, although in Kohlberg's work it is somewhat modified, as we shall see below. Certainly it dominates all aspects of Piaget's work, and finds its fullest expression in his treatments of scientific and prescientific thinking. Regardless of whether the content-domain is that of morality, mathematics, or whatever, before verbal (reflective, symbol-laden) thinking can take place 'within' the individual, there must have been *action* – a purposive exchange 'between' the individual and the environment. Unlike emotivist theories of moral judgment, in which moral cognition is the expression of utterly noncognitive conations and affective dispositions, according to the cognitive developmentalists' interiorization model what is expressed in the verbal judgment is (to the extent that the action is purposive) itself a cognition, albeit a nonverbal one. As the philosopher John Macmurray (1957) has shown in a somewhat different line of argument, the self as subject is a derivative of the self as agent.[5] The preverbal but nonetheless action-guiding concrete judgment is concomitant with the action itself, but the interiorization or verbalization is not. There can be a time-lag of weeks, perhaps years, between concrete and verbal thinking, especially when the judgments are moral judgments and even more especially when they are autonomous moral judgments.[6] It is worth quoting Piaget at length on this point:

Now it may be that there is correlation between verbal or theoretical judgment and the concrete evaluations that operate in action (independently of whether these evaluations are followed up by real decisions). We have often noted that in the intellectual field the child's verbal thinking consists of a progressive coming into consciousness, or conscious realization of schemas that have been built up by action. In such cases verbal thought simply lags behind concrete thought, since the former has to reconstruct symbolically and on a new plane operations that have already taken place on the preceding level. Old difficulties, which have been overcome on the plane of action will therefore reappear or merely survive on the verbal plane. There is a time-lag between the concrete phases and the verbal phases of one and the same process.

(1932/1965, p. 117)

Applying this general idea to morality, Piaget concluded that 'in the moral sphere there is simply a time-lag between the child's concrete evaluations and his theoretical judgment of value, the latter being an adequate and progressive conscious realization of the former' (ibid.). Kohlberg expanded on this theme by claiming that the idea of interiorization does not rule out the possibility of a two-way causation along the single track that runs between moral judgment and action. Piaget himself tended to emphasize the movement from action to thought, the so-called *pris de conscience*, unlike Kohlberg, who claimed, 'A new moral judgment may guide new behavior while the performance of a new behavior may lead one to construct a new moral judgment' (Kohlberg and Candee, 1984, p. 506).[7]

To their credit, Piaget and Kohlberg both clearly recognized that not all verbalized moral judgments (especially those expressed in an interview situation) are interiorizations of the individual's concrete evaluations, since a person might be perfectly sincere and yet think, as did some of the children Piaget interviewed, that 'what is expected of him is a moral lecture rather than an original reflection' (1932/1965, p. 118). In such cases there is a gap between what one says and one's actual moral values, so that it is possible to consider effective moral thought separately from that verbal morality which 'appears whenever the child is called upon to judge other people's actions

117

that do not interest him directly or to give voice to general principles regarding his own conduct independently of his actual deeds' (p. 174). Even so, it is important to recognize that the gap in question is not understood in cognitive developmental theory as a manifestation of rationalization or ego defense. It takes as the normal case of moral cognition that in which verbalized judgments are true interiorizations of concrete action-solutions: the former are articulations rather than rationalizations, since no deception of self or others is involved. Nor are the verbalizations mere disguises for fundamentally irrational urges, since the concrete judgments are rational even though they are preverbal. (Of course cognitive-affective phenomena such as self-deception, rationalization, and ego defense are not defined out of existence by the cognitive developmental account of interiorization. The point here is just that within this account such phenomena would count as aberrations, not as prototypes of the interiorization process.)

Piaget's moral psychology

Let us now turn from the general themes of cognitive developmental theory to the underlying motivational postulates of Piaget's moral psychology, beginning with two broad contrasts between it and the moral psychologies already considered. One is the contrast with internalization theories, in which the ontogenesis of the moral point of view is radically different from Piaget's conception of moral motivation. The other is the contrast with standard social learning theory accounts of moral socialization, whose metaethical perspective is straightforwardly externalist and hence incompatible with Piaget's somewhat elusive conception (as I interpret it) of how moral motives work. Taken together these two contrasts encapsulate Piaget's somewhat meandering discussion of moral heteronomy and autonomy, especially his critique of Durkheim's inability to move beyond a purely heteronomous notion of morality. Using that critique as a textual reference point, let us briefly consider the first contrast, with internalization theory, which sets the stage for what I shall later say about moral motivation. It also leads us back to the second contrast, with social learning theorists, a discussion that will in its turn set the stage for my later remarks about moral motives, as well as recall what was just said about interiorization.

(1) To introduce his notion of a heteronomous stage of morality, Piaget adopted the expository strategy of situating his own social interactionist account of morality *vis-à-vis* the internalization theory then prevailing – Durkheim's account of the acquisition of moral norms. He was frequently quite deferential to Durkheim, whose influence was then at its peak and who apparently anticipated many of the later ideas of internalization. But unlike Durkheim, Piaget was not an internalization theorist at all. Although he spoke of moral rules as 'interiorized' – which as we just saw means 'verbalized,' not 'internalized' – Piaget understood socialization not as a process of 'taking in' extant social norms but rather as a process of 'constructing' norms in the course of accommodating oneself to increasingly complex social situations. In this respect his notion of socialization is fundamentally different from Durkheim's (or, for that matter, that of any moral psychologist we have discussed so far). Unlike Piaget, Durkheim held that morality consists of rules that not only transcend individual interests but also have a so-called sacredness independent of their social utility. Thus he wrote in *L'Education Morale*: 'Any collective habit almost inevitably presents a certain moral character' (cited in Piaget, 1932/1965, p. 344). But although Durkheim himself was much more interested in the social origins of moral norms than he was in their psychological origins, it is clear that he and Piaget had this much in common: both thought that the grip which moral values have on the individual is originally a function of the *respect* the individual has for the group or for the authority figures representing the group. In this regard their views stand in common contrast to the other views of moral internalization that we have considered, in which the bonds of responsibility and obedience were assumed to be products of the same socialization processes that produce other, more specific moral values. The main difference was that, whereas for Durkheim the individual remains in their grip throughout adulthood, for Piaget heteronomy is normally a temporary phase, albeit one of critical importance. For Durkheim, the difference between constraint and cooperation is one of degree or explicitness, in that more complex social hierarchies replace brute coercion with increasingly subtle forms of social pressure. For Piaget, though, the difference between heteronomy and autonomy involves two qualitatively different forms of social interaction – respect for adult authority and reciprocity among peers – in the

same way that it involves two qualitatively different sorts of cognition and also (as we shall see at the end of this section) two qualitatively different sorts of *affectivity* (using that term in the broad continental sense to cover not only emotions and affects but also 'feelings' operating as motivations).[8]

(2) With certain qualifications, Piaget understood the relationship between moral judgments and moral motives from an internalist metaethical perspective. On that account his perspective was radically different from the perspective of the socialization theories we examined earlier.[9] Here again the contrast is illustrated by Piaget's own comparison of his approach with that of Durkheim, whose metaethical perspective was an unambiguously externalist interpretation of the relationship between moral judgments and moral motives. Furthermore, as an externalist (and perhaps also because he was a sociologist, not a psychologist) Durkheim himself felt no need to explore either the psychological ontogenesis of moral motivation or its conceptual architecture. He provided no useful account of how internalization takes place, beyond certain insightful but essentially negative claims about the irreducibility of social phenomena to psychological ones and some rather less satisfying, vaguely metaphysical speculations about the 'group mind' that instills moral attitudes in the individual. Obviously, in these respects Durkheim's views were worlds apart from the hard-nosed empirical assertions of contemporary social learning theorists. However, they were developed from the same general metaethical perspective – the externalist standpoint, from which moral rules are viewed as inevitably associated with punitive sanctions and as completely group- or culture-specific so far as their contents are concerned.

Moral psychology took a critically important metaethical turn, therefore, when Piaget replaced Durkheim's externalist account of socialized agency with his own implicitly internalist account of moral heteronomy and moral autonomy as motivationally charged processes of social cognition. For Piaget, what was distinctive about moral autonomy was its perception of the social world as a network of peers, in which reciprocity and justice function as principles of both cognitive and social equilibrium. And what was distinctive for Piaget about the less developed, heteronomous moral stage was not its mindless conformity to collective norms but rather a quite different (albeit equally negative) cognitive feature: its confusion of moral rules with physical laws. This confusion gives rise to other attitudes, such as an almost religious attitude of awe before powerful and sacred authority figures, rigidity in interpreting the rules, and so on. But although in Piaget's view it stands toward such attitudes as their cause, the confusion of moral and physical laws is itself considered to be the effect, rather than the cause, of two other cognitive limitations. These are the child's inability to distinguish between subjective and objective aspects of his or her experience, and the child's related inability to distinguish between his or her own perspective and those of other persons. These two sorts of inabilities, Piaget reminds us over and over again, are themselves purely cognitive limitations. However, they not only limit the way one verbally cognizes or *represents* the world; they also determine the scope of the pretheoretical thought that directs action without necessarily representing it to oneself. And this distinction, between what Piaget called 'verbal thought' and 'active or concrete thought' (1932/1965, p. 114), is of the utmost importance to my reconstruction of Piaget's views of moral motives and moral motivation.

Moral motives and moral motivation

This reconstruction begins with the following warning: it is important not to confuse with each other the three key distinctions I have used to summarize cognitive developmental moral psychology, namely, the distinctions between structure and content, heteronomy and autonomy, and concrete and verbal judgment. It is especially necessary to be alert to the difference between the second and third distinctions, which together form a four-cell matrix, such that autonomous moral judgments and heteronomous ones each have a concrete phase and a verbal phase.

With this warning in mind, we can ask whether there is a place in Piagetian moral psychology for our philosophical distinction between moral motives and moral motivation. In the other moral psychologies we have considered, the answer to this question was either No or Barely, owing to their minimal cognitive commitments. However, in the present case, the answer seems to be Yes, although it is a qualified and tentative one. It is qualified because the distinction is less evident in some contexts than others, and it is tentative because reconstructing the motivational framework of Piaget's moral psychology involves so much guesswork on our parts. For instance, at the beginning of *Moral Judgment* Piaget draws a distinction between 'the practice or application of rules' and 'the consciousness of rules' (pp. 27–8). At first glance, this seems to correspond to the moral motives/ motivation distinction, but in fact it does not. It is much closer to the distinction between ethics and metaethics, since by 'consciousness of rules' Piaget seems to mean a metacognition the child has about the linguistic status of his or her own evaluations, according to which they are understood first as simple descriptive propositions, then as sacred unalterable prescriptions, and finally as mutually constructed cooperative arrangements. The remarks he makes about the child's progress through these three phases of rule-consciousness are relevant here, since he seems to regard a person's moral self-understanding as an affective state of 'moral feelings' as well as an intellectual achievement. But (to illustrate the need for guesswork) the cognitive status of the construct 'moral feeling' is by no means clear here or in any of his other discussions of affectivity. We shall take up this problem in a moment, but first let us pursue the more basic question of whether, and how, the distinction between moral motives and moral motivations can be mapped onto the Piagetian account of moral development. Keeping in mind Piaget's notion of interiorization, let us first consider concrete evaluations, and subsequently turn to their verbalized counterparts, the moral judgments articulated by his interviewees.

(1) In the first case, that of concrete moral judgment (made at either of the two stages of moral development), there is little or no suggestion of any desire on Piaget's part to maintain a conceptual difference between the two functions of conscience as moral motivation and moral motive. In saying this I do not mean to imply that he has a summary conception of conscience, as do reinforcement-oriented moral psychologists for whom there is no formal distinction between the functions of moral motives and motivation. Rather, he seems to have collapsed them into each other in such a way that, in spite of their formal difference, these two concepts are *materially coincident* at the concrete level of action. The same general conditions that – when felt, perceived, or otherwise preverbally cognized – cause the Piagetian subject to make (concrete) moral judgments in the first place also are thought to motivate him or her to act on those judgments. More specifically: given Piaget's general view of the relation between

preverbal thought and action, it follows for him that regardless of whether the moral agent is a heteronomous or autonomous thinker, the relevant motive/motivation is the agent's own need – or better, the felt need – to make an action-guiding choice in some sort of social situation. If the social situation – or better, the perceived social situation – is one of fundamental dependence and inferiority *vis-à-vis* parents and other authorities, then the agent's general problematic is that of getting along with those powerful figures, which of course includes the subordinate problem of interacting with less powerful others (e.g., other children) in ways that are demanded or permitted by the authorities. If, on the other hand, the social situation in question is one of fundamental equality *vis-à-vis* the other relevant actors, then the general problematic is that of getting along with those others in a cooperative way – which of course includes the subordinate problem of acting for one's private ends in a way that does not itself damage those modes of cooperation that have already been established. But whether the social situation is one of dependence or equality, within this account it is necessarily the case that *compliance with one's (concrete) moral judgment is motivated by the very conditions of (social) disequilibrium that prompt one to engage in evaluative cognition in the first place.* I say 'necessarily the case' quite deliberately here, to indicate that within the theoretical, term-defining context of Piaget's moral psychology, it is analytically true (i.e., tautologous) that concrete judgments are responses to the same felt needs that subsequently motivate the subject to act on those judgments. What is *not* necessarily the case, though, is that the latter motives are always decisive, since a motive is only a *tendency* to act, not a guarantee. (Hence the parenthetical note inserted by Piaget into the long passage cited above, where he remarks that concrete evaluations are to be described in his study 'independently of whether these evaluations are followed up by real decisions.')

(2) The matter is considerably different in the second case, which is that of verbalized moral judgment (again, considered at either of the developmental stages, heteronomy or autonomy). Insofar as Piaget's account of moral verbalization can be read as part of his more general view that cognitive stages are increasingly equilibrated structures, there seems good reason to separate, materially as well as formally, the function of moral motives from that of moral motivation, even though Piaget himself never

felt the need to make that point in so many words. What leads the morally cognizant Piagetian subject to go on to formulate his or her concrete evaluations as verbal moral judgments is, I suggest, primarily a desire for *cognitive* equilibrium rather than a desire for social equilibrium. Since cognitive equilibrium is achieved by better thinking, not by doing, a conceptual gap exists here that was not present in concrete evaluation. That is, it is not logically incoherent to suppose that moral judgments are interiorized and verbalized through a purely cognitive striving that does not itself motivate behavioral compliance with those judgments – which is to say, through a moral motivation that does not function as a moral motive. It does not follow formally from the simple proposition that one is inclined to *verbalize* one's concrete evaluations (i.e., has moral motivation) that one is also inclined to *act on those verbalizations* (i.e., has moral motives). We are led, therefore, to the unexpected conclusion that, notwithstanding his debts to Kant, Piaget was committed to an *externalist* view of the relationship between even the most sincere verbal moral judgment and the corresponding action, insofar as those judgments can exist and be considered apart from concrete evaluations. There is, of course, an indirect and probabilistic linkage here, in that – as we saw in the last paragraph – it *does* follow from Piaget's postulated correlation between concrete thought and action that one tends to act on one's concrete evaluations, and – as we saw still a bit further back – interiorized moral judgments are by definition the verbal representations of those concrete evaluations. Even so, this linkage not only is indirect but also has too much play or conceptual slippage to warrant any tight conceptual claims of the sort in question. Interiorization is essentially retrospective: one can with perfect logical consistency continue to hold moral beliefs even after the concrete action-tendencies that originally gave rise to them have withered away. Piaget said language was able to conserve objects and values 'not present perceptually' (1962, p. 124), but what is thereby conserved is their impersonal intelligibility, not their personally felt urgency. For the latter, one must re-enter, vicariously at least, the action situation from which the concrete moral judgments originally emerged.

Another reason for refusing to postulate, either on Piaget's behalf or our own, that verbalized judgments must always coincide with concrete judgments is the fruitful tension that often exists between the concrete and abstract moments of moral thinking. As Rawls has argued in a different context (1971, pp. 20–1, 46–51), the reflective person finds it necessary constantly to cross-check intuition and moral principle with each other, and to modify each of them accordingly – which again suggests a discrepancy between the deliverances of concrete and verbalized moral judgment, and hence a difference, or at least the logical possibility of a difference, in the manner and direction they motivate the agent making these judgments.[10] Of course to argue for the logical possibility of such a difference is not the same as arguing that such differences always exist or are in fact prominent in the experience of real-life moral agents. Piaget, who presumably never read Rawls, seemed to think that sincere moral verbalizations are usually in concord with one's preverbal intuitions, whereas Rawls (who did read Piaget) sees such equilibrium as an ideal that is probably never realized. But this is a separate issue, and does not affect the conclusion about Piaget's view of the relationship between thought and language that seems to follow from what has just been said, namely, the conclusion that his moral psychology provides no basis for presuming that verbalized moral judgments (no matter how sincerely they are made) are the same as the original preverbal evaluations, either in their contents or in their motivating properties.

To this conclusion I would add another, to which we shall return shortly: that although the metaethical perspective under-lying Piaget's account of verbal judgments is externalist, his account of concrete moral judgments proceeds from a specific type of internalist perspective, which I called 'causal internalism' in Chapter 1 (see also Wren, 1990). As we have seen, for Piaget concrete judgments are causes, in that they have the power to move the subject into action, action which is only later reprised in verbal but causally ineffective (nonmotivating) judgments. The most famous philosophical example of causal internalism is of course Kant himself, who regarded as moral only those actions performed 'out of duty,' i.e., those whose causal ante-cedents include a verbalized judgment equivalent to 'This is the morally right thing to do.' But despite Piaget's frequent dec-larations of affinity with Kant in other matters, when it comes to metaethics there is a huge difference between their respective causal internalisms. Unlike Kantian moral reasons, Piagetian nonverbal cognitions do not motivate by dint of their rational elegance or transcendental status (how rationally elegant or transcendental can a purely nonverbal cognition be?) but because of an altogether different sort of rational quality. This latter quality, ascribed to all moral judgments but especially those involving rights-claims, is the equilibrating promise that certain evaluative cognitions purport to have for the moral subject whose deepest need is (in Piaget's view) for stable interaction with the environment, especially the social environment.

Affectivity and moral motives

Throughout the book *Moral Judgment*, Piaget used the term 'feelings' to denote the modes of respect characteristic of the two moral stages. Heteronomy, we are told, is based on 'feelings of awe' for certain key individuals, and autonomy is based on 'feelings of solidarity' toward one's peers. To explain the first sort of feelings, he elaborated on the difference between his idea of a 'feeling of unilateral respect' and Durkheim's idea of a 'feeling of respect for the group as such.' To explain the second sort of feelings, he transformed the idea of logical reciprocity into an affective, other-regarding desire, writing that autonomy appears 'when mutual respect is strong enough to make the individual feel from within the desire to treat others as he himself would be treated' (1932/1965, p. 196). These morally toned feelings grow out of more general, premoral affective notions of sympathy, antipathy, and even 'vindictiveness' that make up the affective base for moral socialization, whose end product is the sense of justice as mutual fairness. From these considerations, Piaget drew the following conclusion about the early awakening of the child's conscience, which to this philosopher's ear actually sounds more like Hume than Kant: 'The play of sympathy and antipathy is a sufficient cause for practical reason to become conscious of reciprocity' (Piaget, 1932/1965, p. 230).

The role of moral feelings is even more pronounced in Piaget's later writings on affectivity, where he actually defined morality as 'an apparatus of conservation of affective values, by means of obligations' (1962, p. 138). There he argued that cognitive processes, especially those involving conservation, have close analogues in the affective field, such that feelings (like perceptions) are carried over from one set of circumstances to another. At the beginning, we are told, the infant's feelings are altogether transitory, since there are no semantic vehicles to preserve them when the situation that originally provoked them changes. As infancy turns into childhood, affective and cognitive reaction patterns or 'schemata' come into being which, though not themselves representational, somehow ensure that ideas and feelings evoked in previous situations are re-invoked when similar situations occur. But it is only after the child is verbally competent and established within a domestic web of linguistically transmitted Do's and Don't's that affective conservation is possible. 'For example,' Piaget wrote, 'when you examine the moral feeling of a six- or seven-year-old child, you find that he is perfectly sensible to certain orders and rules imposed by the parents, and shows the beginning of moral feelings' (1962, p. 136). But these are very rudimentary conservations, Piaget hastened to observe, since for such children, 'when the parents are gone, these rules or orders are not obeyed.'

Regardless of whether the notion of affective conservation provides us with a useful key to six- and seven-year-old backsliding, Piaget's larger point seems indisputable: moral feelings become richer as the child grows older. They also become more numerous, a point not stressed in his earlier work. After the child has begun to have moral feelings, we are told, there arise 'new feelings in the field of moral feelings,' the most important of which is an emergent 'feeling of justice.' Finally, Piaget attributed to the young adolescent a new set of moral sentiments, which he called *ideological* feelings: 'These feelings are not attached to particular persons or only to material realities but attached to social realities and to essentially ideal realities, such as feelings about one's country, about humanitarianism or social ideals, and religious feelings' (1962, p. 137).

Such remarks make it clear that Piaget did not regard morality as a purely cognitive enterprise. His characterization of morality as an apparatus for affective conservation is reminiscent of Schopenhauer's notion of morality as a reservoir of feelings or McDougall's idea that morality was built up out of increasingly other-regarding sentiments. But for most contemporary English-speaking philosophers, the first historical comparison to come to mind will be with Hume and other eighteenth-century moral sense theorists, for whom the primary moral motivation for taking the moral point of view was some other-regarding sentiment such as sympathy, and the primary moral motives were those which articulate these sentiments. Hence it is more than a little tempting, at least for a reader not already predisposed by the secondary literature portraying Piaget as a thoroughgoing Kantian, to read him as taking a Humean slant on the matter of moral motivation. After all, such a reader might suppose, it is because Piaget thought we have other-regarding feelings that he believed we regularly deem questions of fair distribution, etc., worth raising.

If Piaget had systematically pursued this line of reasoning, which the reader will recognize from Chapter 1 as the 'expressive internalist perspective,' his moral psychology would have been less rationalistic. But in fact he did not, and so there seems little point in trying to reconstruct his views, especially those presented in *Moral Judgment*, as constituting some sort of incipient moral sense theory. For all his attention to moral feelings, he refused to regard sympathy or any other affective tendencies or sentiments as an antecedent condition or basis for taking the moral point of view. It is true that he believed affectivity is relevant to morality, but only regarding the passage from moral judgment to moral *action* (i.e., the area of moral motives), not the preservation and development of conscientiousness itself (i.e., the area of moral motivation). Furthermore, because of his strong cognitivist belief that without an intellectual apprehension of *rules*, feelings are bereft of any sense of right and wrong, Piaget insisted that unless they are cognitively regulated, sentiments 'will rest only upon individual sympathy or antipathy and will thus remain arbitrary' (p. 230). Along with Kant (1785/1959, p. 16), Piaget believed that since the power of an empirically grounded feeling to determine a person's action is contingent on fortuitous circumstances, such a feeling cannot be in itself either moral or immoral.

Hence it is not surprising that, at the end of his long book on moral judgment, Piaget distanced himself from Durkheim by claiming, in alliance with Kant, that (mature) morality is characterized by a 'higher and purely immanent feeling of obligation, *which is the product of rational necessity*' (p. 370, italics added). This remark makes it clear that Piaget's concept of moral motives was rationalistic in the extreme, especially but not exclusively in his characterizations of the higher moral stage. That is, his underlying metaethical perspective was that of 'causal internalism,' which I have defined as an internalist perspective that regards an evaluative cognition sufficient in itself to move the agent to perform the deed in question. Thus we are faced with a discrepancy between this perspective and the externalism that a few pages back I attributed to Piaget's view of verbalized moral judgments. One way to account for this discrepancy is to postulate that he has either forgotten about the gap between concrete evaluations and verbalized judgments or else decided to ignore it in the context of this quotation, which concerns higher-staged moral thinking. However, since I have just insisted on the conceptual importance of recognizing this gap, a more plausible as well as more charitable interpretation would be that when he speaks here of 'rational necessity,' his reference is to the accommodation–assimilation strategy characteristic of preverbal thinking. But regardless of which exegesis we adopt, the question remains: Why did Piaget persist in calling the awareness of one's obligation a *feeling*?

The ultimate answer to this question reaches deep into the architecture of Piagetian psychology, to reveal a dualism whose own internal problems and instabilities I shall not dwell on here. We saw above that he tended to think of the social and cognitive dimensions of moral judgment as concurrent aspects of a single reality. This way of putting the matter presents him as a double-aspect theorist, whose psychological theory can be compared to the monism of Spinoza in which there is only one metaphysical reality, unknown to us except through its two co-terminal aspects of mind and matter. However, that comparison is less apt when we turn to Piaget's discussions of the parallelism between the cognitive and affective dimensions. Here a different (but equally problematic) deep-level resemblance suggests itself, namely, a resemblance to Leibniz's pre-established harmony between the course of mental events and that of physical nature. In his Sorbonne Lectures and elsewhere (1954/1981, 1962, 1967), Piaget displayed great agility in keeping the cognitive and affective domains separate but parallel. However, precisely because it is a parallelism and not a convergence, his theory seems unable to produce a theoretically useful synthesis or resolution of the gap between affectivity and intelligence, especially in regard to our interest in the compliance motives that mediate between moral judgment and moral action.[11] It seems safe enough to nominate as moral motives relatively specific 'feelings' such as gratitude, loyalty, and the other affective orientations cited by Piaget, especially the feelings of unilateral and mutual respect. But this does nothing to sharpen the reference of his phrase 'a higher and purely immanent feeling of motivation,' even though the context makes it clear that he regards this feeling as the moral motive *par excellence*.

And so we are pushed to the rather disappointing conclusion that Piaget has nothing new to say about the affective structure or the cognitive content of moral motives, though, as we saw a few pages back, his account of their interpersonal function is promising, especially as regards cooperative activity. To speak of moral motives as 'feelings' does no harm, but it does not do much good either, so long as one is limited to a neo-Leibnizian view of affectivity and cognition as independent parallel psychological domains. Within such a view there are no constraints on whether a term like 'feelings' is to be interpreted as designating an affective state ('feelings of gratitude'), or a state of cognitive attention ('feelings of mutuality'), or a generalized interest that combines both ('feelings of respect'). The simplest and best approach to Piaget's uses of the term 'feelings' is, I believe, to refuse to regard it as a technical term, and instead to be content with the unanalyzed examples of moral motives Piaget provides in the course of talking about moral feelings.

Self-regulation and moral motivation

Fortunately, Piaget's discussions about affectivity are more suggestive for the issue of moral motivation than they are for moral motives. The Piagetian key for unlocking the question of why people care about morality in the first place is not his ambiguous notion of moral feelings, including feelings of respect, but rather his often-repeated claim that conscience develops as a way of preserving and promoting *equilibrium*. Now, as we have seen, there are different kinds of equilibrium, for instance: a social harmony of wills; a psychological balance of intrapersonal states of desire, need, self-concept, etc.; or a biological accommodation of the organism to its environment. But the kind of equilibrium most central to Piaget's cognitive developmental theory is the coherence of a system of thinking, which involves internal logical consistency and (when thinking is about the world) comprehensive, effective understanding of the environment. In Piaget's view, all human development is continually directed toward increasing equilibrium, and this direction is self-direction or, as he later came to call it, *autoregulation*. Since the prefix 'auto' is often used to connote automaticity, I shall usually replace Piaget's term with the one I have been using up to now, 'self-regulation,' when the discussion refers to his idea of human autoregulation. As he was fond of pointing out, human auto-/self-regulation is unlike the autoregulation of noncognitive systems such as thermostats and biological organisms, since it is a semantic process rather than an interplay of causal forces or a self-manipulative method of delayed gratification. Furthermore, our self-regulation does not stabilize once equilibrium has been established with the environment; since there are always new ways of representing and controlling the actual and possible worlds, human self-regulation tends toward optimal, adaptive equilibrium in a process that Piaget sometimes called 'equilibration' (Piaget, 1971, pp. 10–13; see Flanagan, 1984, pp. 136–44).

Another way to differentiate human self-regulation from autoregulation of nonhuman systems is to point out how the former relies on what Piaget called *decentration*: the lifting of oneself out of the immediate field of experience so that the egocentrism of the previous stage gives way to a new, increasingly sophisticated differentiation between one's own, here-and-now point of view and those of other persons and for other contexts. A crucial part of the child's cognitive development is the ability to resolve perceptual conflicts by decentrating from the perceptual experience itself; this relatively advanced form of decentrating is called 'conservation' because the subject manages to preserve and assimilate certain otherwise unassimilable perceptions by subordinating them to a system of logical transformations. Such a decentration amounts to what we might call a *metaperception* of the relationships between immediately present but illusory perceptions and other, hypothetical ones. In more Piagetian terminology: decentration conserves meanings through reversibility, and thereby resolves cognitive conflict. This account of cognitive conflict resolution is well known, at least in its broad outline. What is less well known is that Piaget gave an analogous account of the resolution of affective conflicts, especially moral ones, in which the paramechanical notion of 'will power' is replaced by a concept of decentration that corresponds in its essential points to the parapolitical notion of desires introduced above, in which

131

higher order desires have authority over those lower in one's motivational hierarchy.

The first thing to note about Piaget's account of moral decentration is that it repudiates the energy model of motivation exemplified by Freud's cathexis theory. By way of reconstructing Piaget's view, we can say that 'will' is not a burst of psychic energy but rather an organizational structure, and hence is what philosophers would call a formal cause rather than an efficient cause. Piaget used the term 'will' in much the same way that the term 'higher-order desire' was used above to refer to a metamotivation aimed at the configuration, or reconfiguration, of already-existing tendencies or motives. What he called the 'pseudo-problem' of will as a mysterious new force competing in an already burgeoning force-field arises only if we erroneously think of action-tendencies or desires as absolute quantities, such that the only way to make a lesser quantity prevail over a greater one is to add to it. In Piaget's decentration model, however, the competing tendencies have their respective strengths *in virtue of their cognitive contexts*. By changing the contexts within which the tendencies are experienced, their motivational rankings *vis-à-vis* each other can be altered without introducing any new quantities. Thus Piaget concluded:

> Therefore, the act of will consists here simply in relying upon a decentration, upon something which is exactly analogous to the reversibility of the intellectual operation and which consists in subordinating the actual value, the desire, to a larger scale of values, the value of the engagement that I have undertaken, the value of the work. From the moment that I react according to my ordinary scale of values, from the moment that I include my actual desire in the permanent scale of values, the conflict is resolved and the initially strong tendency becomes the weaker one.
>
> (1962, p. 143)

Now the obvious objection to this conclusion is that decentration is itself an exercise that requires an additional force: one must, circularly, have will in order to decentrate. Piaget took notice of this objection, but his rejoinder was surprisingly weak. Decentration is indeed a force, he replied, but one that results directly from the permanent scale of values which Piaget eventually identified with having will. If these values are strong, then decentration occurs, regulating the subject's affective tendencies in the way just described, all without the need for any new force. But, he claimed, if these values are weak or incoherent, the flat fact is: 'There will be no will' (1962, p. 145).

Unfortunately, Piaget has not done away with the additional force problem at all. If will is a meaningfully superordinate function, it must be distinguishable from the values it conserves. Otherwise we are back to the old force field model of conflict resolution, with the term 'will' now used as a shorthand device referring to whatever the moral struggle's resultant motivational vector turns out to be. Of course, one could posit some independent source of energy for the will, as did Fichte, Schopenhauer, and Freud. Or one could go to the other extreme and just collapse the distinction between cognitive and affective conservation altogether, by understanding the decentration which Piaget called 'will' as a purely intellectual act of redirecting one's attention. However, Piaget has explicitly disavowed both of these alternatives, saying of his notion of decentration:

> But I would like to specify that this is not an intellectualistic interpretation of will, but an affective operation, by which I mean that it is not enough to remember, to know, to understand. If I am at my desk and recall my obligations, which I invoke simply through intelligence, and the satisfaction that I will have when I finish this work, my desire will not change as long as my understanding is only through intelligence. To decentrate the domain of will is not to invoke memories through the intelligence, but to revive permanent values, that is to say, to reanimate permanent values, to feel them, which means that it is an affective operation and not an intelligent one.
>
> (1962, p. 144)

Here again Piaget's discussion loses its edge by invoking the spongy category of 'feeling' as well as other ill-defined terms and metaphors. What it means to 'revive' or 'reanimate' permanent values, not to mention what it means to be a *value* in the first place, is never explained, either in his *Moral Judgment* or any of his later works. Some appeal to our intuitions in these matters is, I concede, probably inevitable, but Piaget fails to gather these intuitions into either a heuristic model or an explanatory hypothesis about the self-regulatory function of moral motivation.

Furthermore, there is no suggestion by Piaget that either the so-called permanent values or the operation of will has an epistemic dimension whereby one's values or will can be praised or derided as true or false. This is part of a more general weakness of Piaget's constructivism, namely, that it replaces truth values with what might be called accommodation values, and hence the desire to know the world is replaced by the desire to get along with it (cf. Blasi, 1983; Flanagan, 1984, pp. 146–8). In spite of its location at the end of the cognitive–noncognitive spectrum as well as its focus on issues of justice and fairness, Piaget's moral psychology is a long way from the classical philosophical notion of moral objectivity, according to which one steps outside one's own shoes and even outside the world as a whole, taking what Nagel (1986) has called a 'view from nowhere.'

Nevertheless, what Piaget said about moral judgment and affectivity seems more congruent with the hierarchical model of self-regulation proposed in the present study than do any of the other moral psychologies we have looked at so far. Like the other authors we have examined, he has offered no explicit account of why people care enough about the moral domain to engage in evaluative cognition about issues such as justice, and so we can only extrapolate his tacit conception of moral motivation from what he has actually said. But from his discussions of autonomy, autoregulation, decentration, and affective conservation, we can tease out the general outlines of the idea that morality plays a superordinate role in regard to first-order desires as well as to the feelings associated with those desires. In sum, I believe we can ascribe to Piaget a hierarchical conception of moral motivation as a special kind of metamotivation, as well as a metaethical conception of morality as internally motivational and autonomous. He construed this metamotivation as an intellectual striving toward an equilibration that is essentially cognitive and only contingently related to the agent's historically conditioned sense of self. Paradoxically, it was not until Kohlberg had exploited the full range of cognitive possibilities in Piaget's moral rationalism that the connection between moral motivation and self-realization became a theme in its own right within cognitive developmental moral psychology.

Kohlberg's moral psychology

It is probably the case that no modern moral psychologist has had a philosophical breadth equal to Kohlberg's. He was a careful student of the classical works in ethics – Plato, Aristotle, Kant, Mill – as well as the contemporary works of G. H. Mead, Hare, Rawls, Habermas, and others. The use he made of these sources is sometimes quite problematic, even though he thought of himself more as incorporating their diverse ideas than as mounting a philosophical critique or revision of them. For instance, he left it to others to construct philosophical arguments against authors like Foot, MacIntyre, or Williams, with whom he was not in basic intellectual sympathy. That itself was an appropriate division of labor, since his own audience and expertise were primarily in the social and behavioral sciences. But it is likely that Kohlberg was too trusting of academic philosophy in general as well as of that part with which he was most sympathetic, and that he mistook shortlived patches of homogeneity in the literature of moral philosophy for consensus or even resolution of deep and probably intractable problems.

Whatever the reason, Kohlberg was clearly unique in the way he used the work of academic philosophers as a map for charting the psychological terrain of moral development. He even wrote two articles entitled 'The Young Child as a Philosopher' (1979) and 'The Adolescent as a Philosopher' (Kohlberg and Gilligan, 1971), which argued that children and adolescents have the same fundamental need to make sense of their moral lives that professional philosophers do. Furthermore, he believed that the concepts and cognitive operations that provide this sense also have a motivational grip on the child and the adult that the child becomes: that is, not only do moral cognitions cause moral actions, but they do so at the verbal as well as preverbal level, and in virtue of their perceived rationality. In this respect, then, Kohlberg provides us with one of the rare examples of a moral psychologist who takes a causal internalist metaethical perspective not only with regard to preverbal moral judgments (as we just saw, Piaget also did this) but also toward fully verbalized moral judgments. He said, often and more explicitly than Piaget ever did, that it is the cognitive features of moral evaluations rather than the affect associated with those evaluations (or sometimes, when speaking more cautiously: *in addition* to such affect) that lead to behavioral compliance with the evaluations when they are truly the agent's own moral beliefs.

However, Kohlberg also said many other things about the motivational dimension of morality, some of which suggest that his metaethical perspective is not completely caught in the above-mentioned label 'causal internalist.' One of his favorite themes is that morality involves intrinsic motivations such as mastery strivings or effectance motivations, which supports my contention that he is a causal internalist. But sometimes, especially in connection with the lower stages, he seems to lapse into an externalist perspective on moral motives. At still other times, especially in connection with the higher stages, he reveals an internalist perspective that goes far beyond the intellectualism of Piaget's causal internalism, claiming in tones more reminiscent of American pragmatism than Kantian rationalism that moral responsiveness supposes a dialogal disposition inherent in human subjectivity. In what follows we shall first consider the externalist interpretation of Kohlberg, which I shall use as a foil for uncovering his true view of the nature of moral motives, namely, his causal internalism. Finally, we shall take up the still more elusive matter of his view of moral motivation.

Kohlberg's putative externalism

Kohlberg is often represented (even by those most sympathetic with his robustly cognitive view of morality and moral development) as having an externalist view of how individual moral actions are motivated. Perhaps it is inevitable that commentators whose own academic training was in reinforcement-dominated psychology departments would tend to interpret Kohlbergian stage labels such as 'punishment orientation' and 'instrumental hedonism' in this way.[12] But Kohlberg himself bears some responsibility for this misunderstanding, since he occasionally described the early stages of moral reasoning in punishment–reward terminology. It is, I think, important to examine those descriptions somewhat closely, not so much out of a concern for the historical record (slips of the pen are not our interest here) as because doing so will reveal the range and dialectical character of his cognitivism. Accordingly, I shall try to show that the apparent externalism in his accounts of the moral stages is not really a metaethical perspective at all but only an artifact of Kohlberg's efforts to present his highly cognitive ideas in categories familiar to the American psychology establishment of the 1960s.

Perhaps the most remarkable illustration of Kohlberg's putative externalism is the list of 'motives for engaging in moral action' he once used to explicate his six stages. It was developed as part of his subsequently discarded Aspect Scoring system, explained at length in his seminal essay 'Stage and Sequence' (1969/1984). I shall refer to it as the Kohlberg-Rest list, as it originally appeared in a dissertation by James Rest (1969), a student of Kohlberg's. It runs as follows (italics added):

MOTIVES FOR ENGAGING IN MORAL ACTION

Stage 1. Action *motivated by avoidance of punishment*. ('Conscience' is *irrational fear* of punishment.)

Stage 2. Action *motivated by desire for reward or benefit*. Possible guilt reactions are ignored and punishment viewed in a pragmatic manner. (Differentiates own fear, pleasure, or pain from punishment consequences.)

Stage 3. Action motivated by *anticipation of disapproval of others*, actual or imagined-hypothetical (e.g., guilt). (Differentiation of disapproval from punishment, fear, and pain.)

Stage 4. Action motivated by *anticipation of dishonor*, i.e., institutionalized blame for failure of duty, and by guilt over concrete harm done to others. (Differentiates formal dishonor from informal disapproval. Differentiates guilt for bad consequences from disapproval.)

Stage 5. Concern about maintaining respect of equals and of the community (assuming their respect is based on reason rather than emotions). Concern about own self-respect, i.e., to avoid judging self as irrational, inconsistent, nonpurposive. (Discriminates between institutionalized blame and community disrespect or self-respect.)

Stage 6. Concern about self-condemnation for violating one's own principles. (Differentiates between community respect and self-respect. Differentiates between self-respect for general achieving rationality and self-respect for maintaining moral principles.)

(Kohlberg, 1969/1984, pp. 52–3)

It should be evident that the foregoing descriptions of Stages 1 and 2 take the same externalist perspective that was criticized two chapters back, in our discussion of social learning theory and other theories of moral socialization. Similarly, the descriptions of Stages 3 and 4 take the same metaethical perspective that emerged in the last chapter's discussion of various internalization theories – a perspective whose internalism is more rhetorical than logical. The descriptions of Stages 5 and 6 are not so problematic, at least as far as their metaethical perspective is concerned.[13] However, taken as a group the six Kohlberg-Rest stage descriptions present a general picture that is something of a metaethical compromise, in that moral judgments are represented in crudely externalist terms at the beginning of the developmental sequence, and only gradually assume an internalist character as the child matures.

Regardless of whether they are composed by Kohlberg or by his expositors, accounts of moral motives such as the Kohlberg-Rest list are strikingly discrepant with his other motivational and metaethical views. Of course, even if those accounts truly represented Kohlberg's basic conception of how moral motives work, we would not be justified in ascribing an externalist metaethical perspective to Kohlberg himself but only to the preconventional and conventional persons who are the subjects of his research. Whether or not such an ascription is correct, it would not affect the much trickier question of how seriously the underdeveloped perspectives of such agents should be taken by the metaethicist attempting to discover the meaning of terms like 'moral.' But secondly, and much more importantly, the list gives a badly distorted picture of what Kohlberg really thought moral motives were for the subjects themselves. The distortion is especially great at the preconventional level, which is turned into a stock example of the Principle of Universal Heteronomy. This impression is furthered by some of Kohlberg's early remarks (e.g., in his dissertation) about the difference between his first moral stage and that of Piaget. He rejected Piaget's idea that the most important characteristic of heteronomous moral judgments is the 'awe' with which the child regards his or her parents. Kohlberg's view may seem at first glance to be much more in line with mainstream American socialization theory, in that he believes the principal consideration is not the sacredness of the parents but their power, even their sheer physical size. On closer inspection, however, his view seems to be even farther from the mainstream than Piaget's was.

Kohlberg thought that before parents or other authority figures are respected, they must be regarded as representatives of something beyond themselves, a regard that supposes a much greater cognitive-moral maturity on the part of the child than Piaget acknowledged. Thus the responses Piaget interpreted as indications of respect for the 'sacredness' of one's parents were interpreted by Kohlberg as 'indicating *cognitive* naïveté, independent of emotional overevaluation' (1958 (cited in Kohlberg, 1984, p. 658), italics added). The same holds for the sacredness of the rules issued by the parents: instead of being regarded by the young child as independent entities, as Piaget's theory of 'moral realism' claimed, rules are understood by the child within a context of punishment and reward. Thus Kohlberg believed that although the Stage 1 subject has a primitive sense of right and wrong, he or she is unable to differentiate between moral rightness and other sorts of rightness, all of which are rolled together in a single rationale. It is because Kohlberg usually described it as a hedonic rationale that he appears to have conceived the child's moral motives noncognitively, i.e., in externalist terms.

Kohlberg's causal internalism

However, careful examination of his writings reveals a much different metaethical base as well as a correspondingly different conception of the nature of human action. Kohlberg's alternative to Piaget's account of moral motives is not the externalist Principle of Universal Heteronomy but rather an internalist view of 'projective' conformity motivation originally put forth by James Mark Baldwin and reclaimed a half-century later in Kohlberg's own dissertation. As he there paraphrased Baldwin:

> [At Stage 1] judgments of bad are made in terms of physical properties and consequences of action rather than in terms of psychological intentions or functional appropriateness to some norm. [Stage 1 is] manifested in objective responsibility,

in physicalistic definitions of lies, and in the belief that punishment is a physically automatic response to deviance (immanent justice and expiative, rather than restitutive or reforming, punishment).

(1958 (cited in Kohlberg, 1984, p. 658))

Twenty-six years later Kohlberg made the same point rather more clearly, when he issued an extended description of the moral stages remarkable for its precision and detail even though it does not depart in any basic way from what he had been saying all along. At Stage 1, he wrote,

the moral significance of an action, its goodness or badness, is seen as a real, inherent, unchanging quality of the act, just as color and mass are seen as inherent qualities of objects.... *Punishment is seen as important in that it is identified with a bad action rather than because the actor is attempting pragmatically to avoid negative consequences to him- or herself.*

(1984, p. 624, italics added)

Such characterizations make it clear that Piaget's notion of moral realism as a reification of rules is replaced in Kohlberg's Stage 1 by a realism of moral qualities. The latter sort of realism is reflected in the causal internalist assumption that the Stage 1 child receives a moral motive to perform an action from his or her moral judgment – which at this stage is the judgment that parentally defined labels or rules apply to the action in question. In making this assumption Kohlberg took a giant step away from reinforcement-oriented accounts of moral education, and moved only a little way from Piaget's original idea of a moral realism that is internalist despite its cognitive limits – the lack of mediating concepts such as intention or personal desert, the failure to realize that dilemmas exist because there are multiple perspectives, etc. Similarly, although Kohlberg did not accept Piaget's interpretation of heteronomy as an awe-filled compound of love and fear in the face of adult authority, the major difference between them on this point is that Kohlberg thought the characteristics determining an adult's authority or power are 'physical properties,' not that he reduced the child's concept of authority to the concept of brute power. Elementary though they are, the reasoning and moral motives at Stage 1 are nonetheless qualitatively different from the extrinsically motivated evaluations that pass as moral evaluation in less cognitive paradigms, as the italicized portion of the last citation indicates.

Similar sketches can be made of Kohlberg's other moral stages, thus countering the ostensibly externalist themes in the Kohlberg-Rest list of moral motives. But they can be drawn more rapidly, building on the internalist redescription of Stage 1 just given. Thus Stage 2, which Kohlberg regarded as an early but genuine form of Piagetian moral autonomy (because what makes something right or wrong is there defined, not by authority, but by the demands of cooperation among equals), is distorted in the Kohlberg-Rest list, where it is described as 'motivated by desire for reward or benefit.' The key idea, rather, is that thanks to an emergent awareness of multiple perspectives, the Stage 2 subject recognizes that each person has his or her own interests and that these can collide with those of others unless some sort of traffic management is set up in the form of moral rules or norms of noninterference. That these interests are usually represented hedonically is not an intrinsic part of the logic of Stage 2; it is only important that rightness is understood as that which allows one to pursue one's own interests in a field populated with other interest-pursuing agents. Since the norms at this stage are 'standards for regulating action which are thought to be satisfying to the needs or interests of individual selves' (1984, p. 626), the individual's motivation for complying with the norms is provided by the needs or interests they facilitate. Or at least that is what would happen in the romantic case of a society in which no conflicts ever arise except those which can be resolved by simple coordination of projects, adding perhaps that from each individual's perspective, the delays in gratification and other overhead costs incurred by such ideally successful coordination are minimal.

Stages 3 and 4 are also distorted in the Kohlberg-Rest list of moral motives, which represents actions at those stages as motivated by anticipation of disapproval, either on the part of individuals or by the group. Such characterizations do not sit well with what Kohlberg said elsewhere about Stage 3, for instance, that the shared norms not only are behavioral standards but also specify the kind of motives a 'good boy' or 'nice girl' (or good role-occupant of any other sort) has. Typically, these role-constituted motives are other-regarding, prosocial, and hence involve interpersonal trust and social approval. But Kohlberg's central motivational idea at Stage 3 is that the agent acts out of

141

these motives, loyalty or gratitude for example, *and is thereby approved*, not that he or she wins approval and is thereby motivated to be loyal or grateful. Otherwise Kohlberg would have had the same theoretical embarrassment as the theorists whom he elsewhere (e.g., 1969/1984) criticized, on grounds similar to those I invoked in the last chapter, for putting the cart before the horse in the matters of guilt and shame. The same reasoning holds for Stage 4, except that here the subject takes the perspective of a generalized member of some society or group. He or she is aware that even good Stage 3 persons can find themselves in practical conflict with each other, and hence the informally shared norms at that stage must be systematized, all in order to ensure the common good. The fundamental moral motive at this stage is not the 'anticipation of dishonor,' as the Kohlberg-Rest list has it, but rather the desire 'to avoid disagreement and disorder' (1984, p. 632). Since the very notion of moral rightness at this stage is that of social cooperation, it follows that Kohlberg's moralconventional agent will to some extent be motivated by the very considerations that lead him or her to judge a course of action as the right one. And this conclusion, once again, reveals the causal internalist metaethical perspective from which Kohlberg usually discussed moral cognition.

Finally, although the descriptions on the Kohlberg-Rest list of the two postconventional stages, 5 and 6, are not as egregiously externalist as the others, a corrective word or two may be needed here also. By stipulating their respective moral motives to be the concerns for maintaining respect of others and of oneself, the Kohlberg-Rest list appears to postulate a rather unadmirable narcissism at the heart of the moral life. Indeed, this paradox is not limited to Kohlberg's account of principled thinking, since it tends to show up whenever one inquires about the motivational springs of deontological morality. However, as other philosophers (see Williams, 1976) have pointed out, the supposed paradox of moral narcissism is not a true paradox at all but only an *ad hoc* abuse of deontological and other self-regarding modes of normative thinking. As for the unfortunate list we have been considering, it suffices here to note that its self-regarding language is more than compensated for elsewhere by the non-narcissistic descriptions that Kohlberg usually gave of the two highest stages, even though those descriptions underwent considerable revisions over the years. Stage 5, we are told on numerous occasions (e.g.,

Kohlberg, 1984, pp. 634–8), can have either human welfare or human rights as its primary focus; but in either case the relevant moral motive would be some form of benevolence, in the sense of an intrinsically motivating concern for the interests of others. Benevolence is also the motivational base for Stage 6, at least in Kohlberg's final formulation (Kohlberg, Boyd, and Levine, 1990), since the difference between the two highest stages has to do with the degree of self-consciousness with which principles are formulated, not with their criteria of rightness or their motivational engagement.

These considerations should lay the ghost of externalism to rest as far as Kohlberg's six stages are concerned, though we have yet to sort out the details of the internalism they embody. For most of his career, Kohlberg confined himself on this matter to cryptic Platonic statements to the effect that moral actions are determined by 'the knowledge of the Good which lies behind them' (1970, p. 79). It was only in the later period of his work, from the beginning of the 1980s or so, that Kohlberg systematically investigated the question of how moral judgments cause moral actions. In the course of addressing that question, he developed his problematic construct of 'responsibility judgments,' to which we now turn.

Responsibility judgments and moral motives

Although his original focus was on cognitive structures, not on motives or actions, Kohlberg was struck by the numerous empirical findings that people differ in fairly regular ways as to their willingness to translate moral judgments into action (see Blasi, 1980, for a comprehensive review of these studies). To account for these regularities, he supplemented his original view that interiorized moral judgments are intrinsically motivational with a claim that looked beyond the verbalized moral judgment *per se*, focusing instead on the 'space' between the evaluative cognition and the decision to act. In doing so, Kohlberg parted company with those cognitive moral psychologists (e.g., Loevinger, 1976) who, like Baldwin, had assumed that moral judgment, motivation, and outward action form a unity that can be assessed in one blow by means of projective tests or some other sort of personality evaluation instrument (see Kohlberg and Candee, 1984, p. 508). Their view was probably a reaction to the work of social learning theorists and other noncognitive moral psychologists who had filled the space in question with utterly nonmoral variables such as anxiety or learned expectancies. As Brown and Herrnstein made clear in the passages cited earlier, these variables do not mediate, directly or indirectly, between specifically moral judgments and moral actions but rather constitute a completely distinct 'second road.'

Hence it would have been natural for Kohlberg, who not only held a strong general belief in the power of rational thinking to cause actions but specifically rejected the two-road theory, to have allied himself with these other cognitive moral psychologists. But in fact he did not. Instead he declared that although he remained within the structuralist tradition, his preferred strategy was to 'assess judgment and conduct separately and then ask questions about the relations between the two' (ibid.). To answer these questions, he postulated a new mode of moral cognition, the responsibility judgment:

> The prediction from stages or principles to action requires that we take account of intermediary judgments that an individual makes. One does not act directly on principles, one acts on specific content judgments engendered by those principles. We hypothesize that moral principles or 'structures of moral reasoning' lead to two more specific judgments, one a judgment of deontic choice, the other a judgment of responsibility. The first is a deontic decision function, a judgment of what is right. The second is a follow-through function, a judgment of responsibility to act on what one has judged to be right.
>
> (Kohlberg and Candee, 1984, p. 517)

This passage is revealing for several reasons. It makes a point usually overlooked in discussions of the higher stages, namely, that moral principles are not themselves moral judgments (and we may add, not moral motives). Also, it reminds us that when Kohlberg spoke of moral judgments, what he had in mind was the rather sharply delimited class of *deontic* evaluations – that is, judgments about the rightness of actions as such, as distinguished from judgments about the goodness of their outcomes or the character of the agents. But most revealing of all is his characterization of the responsibility judgment as a 'follow-through function.' This phrase suggests that responsibility judgments only intensify the intrinsic motivational power of their corresponding moral/deontic judgments, an idea that reiterates the internalist view of moral judgments as inherently prescriptive, that is, as logically signifying an incipient commitment to action. In this sense, then, responsibility judgments supervene upon deontic ones. But this is only a suggestion, not a developed thesis, and it is by no means always prominent or even operative throughout Kohlberg's writings, including the essay from which the preceding passage was taken and which is our principal source concerning his theory of responsibility judgments.

That essay brings together a variety of ideas that do not always fit well with each other but are nonetheless relevant to our present topic. For brevity's sake I shall single out just a few of these ideas, beginning with what I take to be the heart of Kohlberg's own mature view, the idea that responsibility judgments normally operate in tandem with moral judgments. He apparently continued to believe that it is possible for deontic judgments by themselves to cause action, i.e., to function as moral motives, but he also held that often, especially in difficult situations, they motivate only to the extent that they are accompanied or 'followed through' by judgments of responsibility. Throughout this book we have understood internalism as the metaethical view that moral judgments are logically connected to moral motives, and causal internalism as the more specific view that this connection is a causal one. So considered, sincerely made moral judgments provide moral motives. However, in the light of Kohlberg's discussion of responsibility, I should add that in the last sentence 'moral judgment' denotes any morally referenced evaluative cognition and can be thought of either as a deontic judgment, a responsibility judgment, or the two judgments taken as a whole, depending on the sort of moral struggle that is involved.

As Kohlberg noted, his idea of responsibility as a followthrough function is in contrast with Gilligan's (1982) nowfamous conception of responsibility as an *alternative* to reasoning about justice and other sorts of objective judgments.[14] He also contrasted it with Brown and Herrnstein's externalist conception of moral action as explainable by completely nonmoral variables.[15] Kohlberg postulated responsibility judgment as an explanatory variable that is itself moral but which behavioral scientists could use to account for the obvious fact that moral motives differ in strength. To explain individual differences in the readiness and manner with which people move from their moral/deontic judgments to action, he looked for patterns amid those differences. In this latter task he seems to have been quite successful. Under the high-sounding label 'monotonic relationship' Kohlberg presented an array of data which I shall here summarize by saying that people at higher stages of moral thinking are more inclined than others are to act on their judgments, which is to say they are more inclined to follow through on their deontic judgments by making the corresponding responsibility judgments. Or, to use an equally high-sounding philosophical term, we could say that he found akrasia (moral weakness) to be inversely correlated with cognitive stage development.

Assuming that his data, derived from quite diverse laboratory and naturalistic studies, are accurate, the obvious question is: *Why* do higher stage reasoners have more effective moral motives, that is, tend to take their reasoning more seriously? An answer to this question would not only reveal Kohlberg's conception of moral motives but also lead us to his conception of moral motivation, that is, the 'moral care' that brings people to ask moral questions in the first place. Unfortunately for the simplicity of our exposition, Kohlberg offers two separate answers to this question. Both are closely tied to core features of the moral domain described briefly in the opening chapter. The first answer, which is a direct expression of Kohlberg's enduring rationalism, explains the efficacy of moral motives in terms of universalizability, which is itself an index of that feature of morality described in Chapter 1 as impartiality or objectivity. The second, which also manifests his rationalism but leads beyond it to a theory of the self, explains their efficacy in terms of what I have called the executive feature of morality. Both of these answers, but especially the first, display great confidence in the action-determining power of the intellect. They suppose that the standard case of moral judgment has rational qualities that not only equilibrate but also motivate: that they dispose the individual not only to make a deontic evaluation but also to ratify that evaluation in an action-determining judgment of responsibility. The metaethical framework for this supposition is, of course, that of causal internalism, which is bred in the bone of Kohlberg's moral psychology.

In the first answer, Kohlberg outlines a stagewise conception of objective thinking about morality that incorporates the twin features of universalizability and prescriptivity, adapted from the metaethical writings of Hare (1952, 1963) and Frankena (1965, 1973). In a nutshell, Kohlberg's claim here is that the monotonic relationship found in the moral domain between personal consistency and cognitive development can be traced back to these formal features, in that increased cognitive adequacy in moral reasoning leaves the subject with fewer loopholes. As subjects move to higher stages their thinking becomes increasingly universalizable, reversible, etc. – in short, increasingly adequate as objective thinking. The range of applicability attributed to deontic judgments becomes wider and wider, with correspondingly less leeway remaining outside that range wherein the subject can make an exception of him or herself. Thus Kohlberg seems to consider akrasia more of a cognitive lapse than a weakness of the will, though he does distinguish it from the psychoanalytic construct of denial and other sorts of defense whose function is to block the consciousness of wrongdoing (Kohlberg and Candee, 1984, p. 532). His stress on the cognitive dimension is hardly surprising. Well before Kohlberg wrote about the category of a responsibility judgment, he insisted that, because 'moral judgment dispositions influence actions through being stable cognitive dispositions, not through the affective changes with which they are associated...you follow moral principles in a situation because you feel they correctly define that situation' (1971, pp. 230–1). If we recall that the logical features of universalizability, reversibility, and so on comprise fairly advanced cognitive operations, it becomes clear from this first answer that Kohlberg shared Piaget's view that people are not only inclined to *cognize* in the most logical and hence most objective manner available to them but also to *act* in a way that to them seems most logical and objective. But why they are so inclined is the very question we are trying to answer, and so this first answer does not advance our discussion of moral motives. Taken by itself, Kohlberg's rationalistic account of moral responsibility, considered either positively as a moral motive or negatively as akrasia, is circular.

However, his second answer is not circular, though it too is profoundly rationalistic. Kohlberg thought responsibility judgments are moral motives because he associated them with the executive or self-regulative features of morality in a way that constitutes 'the positive conception of responsibility' (Kohlberg and Candee, 1984, p. 533). Monotonicity between stage and action could be explained as 'the growth of a positive idea of moral freedom or autonomy with each stage' – an idea which, he went on to say, involves on the part of the subject 'a metaphysical stand, or a stand on the nature of human nature, with regard to the metaphysical issues of free will versus determinism' (ibid.). Exactly why Kohlberg characterized his second answer as a *positive* conception is not clear (what was negative about the first answer?), but there seems little doubt that with this explanation we move away from purely formal structures of reasoning to more existential considerations about the personality of the moral reasoner. Although Kohlberg did not spell out this last point in so many words, his so-called positive conception sees responsibility as the ability to invest oneself in the moral task at hand. For Kohlberg as well as for higher-stage subjects themselves, moral judgments are regarded as the expressions of one's freedom and power to regulate one's own motivational system in terms of those desires, hopes, and values deemed most central to one's life. Put simply, the thought that a moral judgment is *my own* judgment makes it a moral motive for me.

This Kohlbergian claim has a ring of truth to it, in my view, but it is not without its own problems when we look at the whole sequence of moral stages. Since the higher the stage, the more independent one is from the bondage of individuating circumstances (even, at the highest stages, those of one's own moral tradition), Kohlberg found it theoretically appropriate and empirically predictive that cognitively higher subjects are less likely than lower subjects to act contrary to their own moral judgments (see ibid., pp. 533–4). As already noted, Kohlberg used the term *autonomy* to describe the 'freedom and power' involved in his positive conception of responsibility, but this usage points to a problem that goes beyond his choice of words. If the greater responsibility of higher-stage subjects is attributed to the autonomy of their moral reasoning, where does this leave lower stage moral reasoners? We seem to be back to the externalism of the crude Kohlberg-Rest list of moral motives, in which lower-stage subjects are moved solely by the prospect of punishments and rewards apart from any thoughts about their appropriateness. My own view is that Kohlberg was right to emphasize the relationship between responsibility judgments and one's sense of self, but his suggestion that autonomy itself constitutes a moral motive needs to be considered more carefully before we can make sense out of his second answer to the question of why higher-stage reasoners tend to take their reasoning more seriously than do those at the lower stages.

Autonomy and cognitive competence

Leaving aside the rest of the extensive philosophical and psychological literature on autonomy, we should recognize the ambiguity of that concept within cognitive moral development theory. As Kohlberg himself observed, his own use of the term differs from Piaget's: the child moves into what Piaget called autonomous morality as early as Kohlberg's Stage 2, though it is not until Stage 5 or 6 that full autonomy is attained. Because Piaget's research was with younger children, it is not surprising that he did not portray the breakthrough into moral autonomy as an especially stunning or subtle cognitive achievement. Kohlberg, in contrast, usually did, representing autonomy as a state or disposition of critical reflection.

So considered, autonomy is a matter of 'thinking for oneself.' Kohlberg sometimes said that it was one of several features of morality that lie midway between content and form (Kohlberg, Levine, and Hewer, 1983/1984, pp. 251–3), but this is a bit misleading. He understood autonomy as an attribute of one's cognitive activity, closely tied to those structuralist features such as reversibility and reciprocity that find their philosophical expression in Kant's Categorical Imperative. Consequently, autonomy takes on a much more formal and rationalistic character in Kohlberg's theory of moral stages than in Piaget's: the prior-to-society moral perspective characteristic of Stages 5 and 6 transcends not only the specific tasks and value-contents the historical agent must deal with but even the social arrangements and speech situations within which the agent's commitments and beliefs arise. In unmistakably Kantian tones, Kohlberg described the perspective of principled thinking as 'that of *any rational individual* recognizing the nature of morality or the fact that persons are ends in themselves and must be treated as such' (1976, p. 35, italics added). Autonomy thus had as its principal meaning in Kohlberg's work a capacity for critical reflection that creates cognitive independence from individuating circumstances, such that one can take the objective, agent-neutral perspective of 'any rational individual.' As a cognitive category, it does *not* mean strong will, self-reliance, or any other personality trait. Furthermore, unlike Piaget's notion of autonomy, it does not directly refer to the way one interacts with one's peers, which would be a matter of content,[16] but only to the structural characteristic of how one organizes and deploys moral reasons *per se*.

Admittedly, one can also find statements made by Kohlberg outlining another, more content-oriented notion of autonomy. That notion, foreshadowed in his 1958 dissertation, also supposes that autonomy is reliably exhibited in moral verbalizations (typically, taken from the same interviews that are scored for moral stages), but takes nonverbal or 'intuitive' moral thinking into account as well, and can be read as characterizing moral motives and motivation as well as verbalized moral cognition. The underlying nonstructuralist conception of autonomy seems to be something on the order of an aggregate moral virtue combining such executive virtues as courage and conscientiousness, as developed by Kohlberg in a different context much earlier in his career (1969/1984).[17] Later, following Weber's notion of ideal types, he called this sort of autonomy a *moral type* (1984, pp. 652ff.; see also Tappan, Kohlberg, *et al.*, 1987). (Heteronomy, in this context, is not a concept in its own right but is only the negation of autonomy. Hence none of the richness of Piaget's descriptions of heteronomy is to be found in Kohlberg's description of the heteronomous moral type.) Drawing liberally from Piaget as well as from Kant and Baldwin, Kohlberg clustered together nine conceptually different but intuitively interlinked concepts, established construct validity by the 'bootstrapping' method described above, and employed them as criteria for application of the type-category 'autonomy.' These criteria,[18] which we need not discuss here, range over a variety of personality variables, from cognitive structures to social sensibilities and value orientations.

But even though the criteria for this revised conception of autonomy are represented by Kohlberg as a mixture of content and structural features, his basic idea remains essentially cognitive – and yet just as inexplicably action-oriented as before. The criteria he clustered together were selected to mark the extent to which a person's moral *reasoning* (not the ensuing action) is 'free from external constraints and influences,' since it uses 'justifications that reflect respect for the dignity and autonomy of the actors in the dilemmas without regard for emotional or egocentric considerations' (Tappan, Kohlberg, *et al.*, 1987). In short, Kohlberg's autonomous types not only think for themselves, they also take or at least think they are taking an objective point of view. In their moral judgments they try 'to get it right,' even though they differ on what getting it right means. But why does this sort of moral thinking get translated into action significantly more often than nonautonomous moral thinking does? Once again, we seem to be no closer to an account of how moral motives motivate.

The truth of the matter, I believe, is that Kohlberg's extensive discussions in the 1980s of responsibility judgments and autonomy have little to add to what he said in 1969 concerning the intrinsic desires people have for mastery, effectance, and interesting experience – all of which he gathered under the rubric 'primary competence motivation.' In his long essay 'Stage and Sequence,' he developed this theme in the context of imitative learning, but it applies just as well to other contexts such as self-esteem, internalization, and the passage from thought to action. For instance, commenting on the 'motivational forces' involved in reality judgments ranging from physical conservation to moral decisions, he described these forces as 'general "drive-neutral" motives of effectance, or competence, which orient the child both toward *cognitive adaptation to a structured reality* and toward the maintenance of *self-esteem*' (1969/1984, p. 116, italics added). Thus self-esteem is produced by social approval because such approval signifies to the agent that he or she is competent in some respect, such as the cognitive competence involved in moral judgment making. Similarly, to act on one's moral judgment signifies to the agent (and others whose opinions matter) that he or she has judged competently, which is to say has adapted cognitively to a structured reality or, as I put it less tendentiously a moment ago, has managed 'to get it right.'

Years later, Kohlberg reiterated this point in an extended discussion of the social self theories of Baldwin, Mead, and Vygotsky (Hart, Kohlberg, and Wertsch, 1987). Harking back to his earlier essay, he claimed that at the lower stages a subject relies on models to clarify 'how he [or she] is doing' (p. 233). At the higher stages, the validating feedback about one's competence is provided not by models society has established but by one's ideal self, which can thereby 'prescribe obedience resulting in a sense of obligation in situations in which current societal norms are violated' (ibid., p. 246). But in either case the fundamental motivational concept is that of competence motivation; only the cognitive and social channeling is different.

The postulate that competence motivation is the motor of practical reasoning seems to me correct as far as it goes, which is indeed much farther than the social learning accounts of modeling go. This postulate led Kohlberg to represent the discrimination between right and wrong as a primitive normative structure of action, one that for normally developing persons exists even at the earliest stages of cognitive development. This insight, which we first met in the course of analyzing the Kohlberg-Rest list of moral motives, is perhaps Kohlberg's most important single idea. But it falls disappointingly short of explaining how it is that this almost universal discrimination can function as a moral motive. What is needed, I would argue, is some way to expand the competence postulate so that it includes not only cognitive capacities but also noncognitive, or better, *personal* competencies. To be fair, we should note that Kohlberg's construct of responsibility judgment was deeply influenced by Blasi's (1983) work on personal consistency, and that Kohlberg explicitly referred to that work in a way that suggests fundamental agreement with Blasi (Kohlberg and Candee, 1984, p. 578; see his discussions of ego development in Kohlberg, 1973, 1981/1984, and Snarey, Kohlberg, and Noam, 1987). For Blasi, responsibility is the awareness 'that an action evaluated as moral is also judged to be *strictly necessary* for the individual, though external constraints are absent' (1983, p. 198). That is, for Blasi what is distinctive about a responsibility judgment is not so much its application of a general rule to a determinate situation as the attendant conviction that an action is necessary for one as an existent individual. By 'necessary' here Blasi means something like 'necessary to one's sense of self' or perhaps better, 'necessary to one's *present* personal identity,' as when Luther cried '*Ich kann nicht anders.*' Despite his familiarity with Blasi's work, Kohlberg never fully appreciated the differences between it and his own conception of responsibility judgment. In the absence of any textual evidence to the contrary, we are left with the conclusion that Kohlberg's structuralist conviction that moral reasoning has its own cognitive incentives prevented him from systematically exploring the possibility that when one makes the responsibility judgment that X is the 'only' thing to do, the 'only-ness' is a function of a sense of self that includes, but is much more than, cognitive competence.[19]

Kohlberg's conception of moral motivation

As we just saw, primary competence motivation was a conspicuous theme throughout Kohlberg's work even though it has often not been emphasized by his commentators (and often enough not by Kohlberg either). In such contexts as imitative learning, competence motivation seems to function as what in this book I have been calling moral motive, but as far as I can tell it also functions in Kohlberg's general theory as what I have been calling moral motivation. There is no single reason why one asks the question 'What should I do?' but there may well be a single reason (or at least a relatively small and well defined set of reasons) why in the course of answering that question one takes the moral point of view. We have seen that Kohlberg felt that curiosity strivings and mastery or effectance strivings form a unity (competence motivation), such that in the presence of interpersonal problems such as scarcity of food or other resources, the deep-seated desire we have for cognitive competence is transmuted into a desire for moral competence. That is, we want 'to get it right,' and to do so at what seems to us the most cognitively adequate level of reasoning.

I therefore suggest that for Kohlberg the general tendency to process reality in moral terms was always a form of competence motivation. However, as with the tendency to put one's deontic judgments into action, it is likely that he also felt this general tendency manifests itself differently in different individuals. His own research along with that of Rest and others (cited in Kohlberg and Candee, 1984, pp. 538–9) led him to admit that some people may be more sensitive to the moral issues inherent in a situation than others are, even though they may not be especially sophisticated or skillful at untangling those issues. The data corresponding to this last claim are not uniform, but their general pattern corresponds to what common sense would have predicted, namely, that such individual differences do exist and that they correlate roughly with other variables such as intelligence, education, and stage of justice reasoning. Kohlberg was aware of these data, as well as of the general distinction between interpreting a situation as containing a moral issue and formulating a moral judgment about what should be done. However, he failed to distinguish between the two corresponding types of individual differences (degrees of moral sensitivity and degrees of consistency between one's deontic judgments and actions), and this failure hobbles his discussion of the so-called monotonic relationship between judgment and action. Even so, the distinction itself seems consistent with what he has said elsewhere about the moral point of view as well as about the efficacy of moral cognition.

Conclusion

Kohlberg's account of why people care about morality incorporates Piaget's views on perspective taking and other forms of social interaction, but it goes beyond them. Kohlberg thought of moral motives as responsibility judgments, and moral motivation as a fundamental cognitive striving, as explained in his discussion of primary competence motivation. He saw – correctly, in my view – that objective thinking in morality as elsewhere satisfies a deep personal need, but he explained this fact by a model of self, derived from Baldwin and Mead, that seems to be unduly cognitive in that reason-giving is supposedly an end in itself. Throughout his many books and articles, this and other aspects of the justification game are discussed by Kohlberg as though they were solipsistic exercises or, if that is too strong, as though one engages in moral reasoning by, and for, oneself alone. However, it may not be necessary to take such a lofty cognitive approach to moral psychology in order to preserve Kohlberg's insight that objective thinking is a core feature of subjectivity itself as well as of the moral domain. To my knowledge no psychological Prometheus has successfully carried this insight from the high cognitive plateaus of Baldwin and Piaget back down to the richer atmosphere of desires, needs, affectivity, and other persons, but that does not mean it has not been tried (Blasi has come close). Nor – as I shall argue in the final chapter – does it mean that it cannot be done.

6

SOME PHILOSOPHICAL
SPECULATIONS

The previous chapter leaves us with little doubt that cognitive developmental theory usually has an internalist perspective on moral motivation, no matter how problematic that perspective might sometimes be. Kohlberg quite accurately identified himself with Plato's view that to see the Good is to choose it. Admittedly, his discussion of responsibility judgments does not fit well with this internalist perspective, for it suggests that deontic moral judgments in themselves may not be capable of motivating one to act morally. But I think the idea of a responsibility judgment *can* be incorporated into an internalist metaethic, once we recognize that the so-called moral judgments discussed in the cognitive developmental literature are not quite the same semantic vehicles as the propositions or moral beliefs that internalist moral philosophers have analyzed. The moral judgments discussed by psychologists such as Piaget and Kohlberg are verbalizations that have been elicited in an interview situation. The moral protagonist whose problem is examined in the course of these interviews is nearly always a third party, and a hypothetical one at that – such as the famous Heinz, whose wife will die of cancer unless he steals a drug from an unsympathetic druggist. However, it seems plausible that when a moral judgment is formulated *in vivo*, rather than, say, in an interview about Heinz's dilemma, the usual reason it is formulated at all is simply that the agent cares in a personal and nontheoretical way about the answer. Thus it is hardly surprising that the agent is prepared to pass from moral judgment to moral action, i.e., that considered moral reasons are moral motives.

In this respect, an *in vivo* moral judgment about the requirements of justice, duty, human rights, etc., is logically and

155

metaethically coordinate with other common but powerful normative judgments, regardless of whether one's moral taxonomy includes them as part of the moral domain, such as the judgment that a given course of action is what human welfare requires, what God's Will requires, what one's personal flourishing requires, and so on. No matter how they are labeled, characteristic to all these beliefs is the sense of practical urgency that typically accompanies them and which, in the eyes of those who adopt an internalist perspective, is considered a logically necessary component of all sincere moral judgments. That is, these judgments have practical urgency when they are the products of a reflective process stimulated by a live situation, where the urge to ask questions such as 'Is X the thing to do?' arises from within the agent. In contrast, when normative judgments are elicited in an interview situation, or in some comparably removed situation such as a Sunday school class or a moralizing discussion with one's parents or peers, the desire to ask the question 'Is X the thing to do?' arises from without. It may not be inevitable in such cases that the subject adopt the observer's standpoint, in which value terms are used in the 'inverted commas sense' mentioned in the first chapter. However, there is nothing unnatural about speaking in this way. Indeed, the inverted commas sense is often the most appropriate way to use evaluative terms, even though the appropriateness of taking an observer's standpoint in those dialogal situations does not constitute grounds for adopting the externalist perspective as one's metaethical view. Even when the person being interviewed (or otherwise provoked to consider normative issues vicariously) proves capable of reasoning at the higher stages of cognitive development, the moral judgments expressed may have no personal urgency for the speaker. However, this is improbable since most people functioning at those higher cognitive stages also function at higher ego-developmental stages, as is seen in Kohlberg's discovery of the monotonic relationship between stage level and degree of personal consistency. This point is also supported by other work on self-identity done by psychologists like Blasi, Lind, and Noam, as well as philosophers like Frankfurt and Taylor, whose hierarchical conceptions of human motivation were noted earlier in these pages.

In other words, the fact that within the cognitive developmental paradigm moral judgments have recently been so conceptualized that they are not in themselves motivational but rather must be complemented by a responsibility judgment only indicates that moral judgments are often formulated as answers to questions that the subject does not personally care about. That conceptualization does not imply that moral judgments are of their very nature inert, and so the externalist perspective receives no support from the apparent consensus on the part of latter-day cognitive developmentalists that moral judgments need to be mediated by responsibility judgments. Indeed, the internalist perspective gets a new insight, albeit not a knock-down argument for its own correctness, when we reflect on the conditions that lead people in real life to care in the first place about getting straight on matters of right and wrong. In what follows I shall make a few speculations about these conditions, considered under the rubrics of autonomy and self-interpretation.

Autonomy reconsidered

Earlier in this book I referred to Frankfurt's well-known hier-archical model of higher-order desires and motivations, by which he meant desires that take other desires as their objects. I suggested that this scheme can be used as a model of moral psychology, though I have not tried to work out its details in this book or to defend its philosophically controversial aspects. Within the general framework provided by that model, I would propose the following related idea as a working postulate or heuristic device for future work in moral psychology. Although moral motives such as benevolence and fidelity operate at the first level of motivation (where moral action takes place), it is because they are endorsed at the second level that they are differentiated from ordinary, nonmoral desires. Unlike unregulated bursts of affection and other desires whose occurrences, directions, and outward effects depend on no antecedent identification with the agent's will, moral motives (along with the states of affairs that are their objects) are invested with value in the ongoing process of moral judgment, reason-giving, and less verbal forms of evaluative cognition that constitutes conscience.

But this does not explain what leads the agent to endorse some desires and to repudiate others, or at least to regard them as morally irrelevant. Hence I have introduced the idea of moral motivation as still another working postulate or heuristic device, in hope of seeing how far it can take us. This is the idea, touched on at various points in the previous chapters, that there is some deep-level concern or set of concerns that leads a person to engage in the evaluative cognitions characteristic of morality. If there is any such general tendency, it is probably best envisioned as an overarching, intrinsic albeit not innate motivation to take an executive point of view on one's otherwise unintegrated and unvalued action-tendencies. As I have already said, what I have in mind corresponds roughly to what is often meant by the term 'conscientiousness' (though that term is also used to refer to specific virtues, such as the disposition to keep one's promises). In some cases this tendency is experienced as a form of freedom, in others as a form of bondage. When it is experienced as freedom, moral motivation is properly characterized as a form of *autonomy*, since the agent is directing his or her life in the most fundamental way possible, namely, by making certain motives his or her 'will.' (When it is experienced as a form of bondage, moral motivation is properly characterized as a more or less acceptable form of *heteronomy*, as we saw earlier in connection with the noncognitive approaches to socialization theory.)

We saw in the last chapter that Kohlberg understood the full development of autonomy to consist in a life regulated by principles that have themselves been subjected to critical reflection. However, while I would not want to deny the intellectual or moral worth of such a life, I am not so sure that critical reflection *per se* is what makes moral motivation autonomous. After all, critical reflection is itself an ideal whose acquisition is a contingent and largely fortuitous process, one which for historical, political, and other reasons is unavailable to the vast majority of moral agents no matter how well-intentioned they might be. Consequently, instead of thinking of critical reflection as an intrinsically valuable quality that *makes* a life (or a cognitive process) autonomous, I would like to propose that the autonomy associated with morality is itself generated by some other cherished thing or quality that is *disclosed* in the course of such reflection, adding perhaps that it can *only* be disclosed in that way. Exactly what it is that is disclosed remains to be seen, but we may suppose that it is in some sense one's 'true' or 'real' self and the relation which that self has with its social world. In this reconstruction of the notion of moral autonomy, critical reflection reveals the source of one's autonomy to be some pre-established feature of the self whereby one identifies with certain normative principles as 'one's own.' This feature, which may not be reducible to exclusively cognitive or conative categories, is by hypothesis not the object of an antecedent choice although over time it may be modified by the choices that one makes. It is, to use Taylor's phrase, the subject's 'deepest unstructured sense of what is important,' which critical reflection does not so much create as bring to definition (1976, p. 297).

In other words, I am suggesting that the fully autonomous agent is one who identifies with certain normative principles or values because of the way they articulate his or her 'own' inchoate sense of what is important. Why it is that one identifies with these rather than other typically moral motives, principles, values, ideals, and so on is presumably an empirical question that is best answered within the context of the subject's own personal history, though it would be premature to rule out the possibility that some such motives, etc., are universal structures that anyone would identify with who fully understood his or her own psychological makeup. But why one identifies with *some* moral motives, etc., rather than none at all is not so much an empirical question as it is a problem of theory construction. Of those psychological theories of socialization that are sufficiently cognitive to allow the question of moral motivation to take shape at all, none so far seems to have appreciated the possibilities of the neo-Humean (expressive internalist) idea that we are disposed to make moral judgments and to live by them primarily because they articulate even more basic personal dispositions, and because they do so in a way that integrates those dispositions with each other as well as with the demands of the external world. Within the theoretical scaffolding provided by this idea, the notion of what I shall call a *basic desire* functions as a special case of what is usually called intrinsic motivation. As such it contrasts with the alternative model of extrinsic motivation, in which desires are expectations of independently specifiable affective states. Like its biological counterparts, physiological drives, a basic desire is not an expectation but a tendency, and a quite imperious one at that.

It is important to remember that the basicness involved here is a functional category, which leaves the content of the basic desires as yet unspecified. That we must, for analytical purposes, start somewhere does not entail that there is some particular place from which we must always start, as Danto (1973, p. 33) once pointed out in connection with Bertrand Russell's doctrine of basic propositions. That is, the hierarchical model of moral motivation does not commit us to a theory about which desires are basic, any more than the claim that everyone has some parent commits us to the claim that there is some person who is the parent of everyone. All that is involved is the idea that there are *some* desires that define us to ourselves. These constitute our personal identity, not only in the detached theoretical sense of providing us with ways of describing our personalities but also in the immanently practical sense of giving point to our lives. They are, in a word, the central reason that someone living at the higher stages of ego-development regards death as an evil. As Williams (1976, p. 207) puts it:

> Some desires are admittedly contingent on the prospect of one's being alive; but not all desires can be in that sense conditional. For it is possible to imagine a person rationally contemplating suicide, in the face of some predicted evil; and if he desires to go on in life, then he is propelled forward into it by some desire (however general or inchoate) which cannot operate conditionally on his being alive, since it settles the question of whether he is going to be alive.

These desires, Williams goes on to say, are 'categorical' in that they do not depend on the assumption of one's own existence but rather serve to prevent that assumption's being questioned, or to answer the question if it is ever raised. To be sure, this is an important insight. But keeping in mind Danto's maxim about starting points, we must be careful not to jump from Williams's quite plausible philosophical proposition to the empirically unwarranted but often held position that everyone's personality rests on the same set of basic or – as I shall also call them – *constitutive desires.* Even so, there may be considerable commonality in this regard. Many interesting personality theories set up typologies based on categorical desires, e.g., Sullivan's list of 'syndromes,' Adler's 'styles of life,' Freud's 'character types,' and Gilligan's 'voices.' We need not subscribe to a strict nomothetic model of personality in order to use these or other typologies, since they can be used in what Allport (1961, pp. 257–361; 1962) calls morphogenic studies of personality, in which concepts such as 'trusting' are employed whose application is not confined in principle to only one person although the patterns of application are (cf. Maddi, 1972 p. 395; Harré and Secord, 1972, pp. 276–7). Hence although constitutive desires are not universal constituents of personality, neither are they *sui generis*, only capable of entering into purely ideographic or biographic accounts.

Motivation and self-interpretation

Unfortunately, such commonality is of little relevance to any moral agent trying to comprehend the motivational base of his or her ideals and second-order evaluations, since it treats deep-level desires and aspirations as simply given. The reality is otherwise: their efficacy as psychic forces is inextricably tied to the interpretation the agent puts on them – and so on him or herself – in the articulative process referred to a few paragraphs back. To articulate what I have called constitutive desires is not to describe them the way one describes a table as brown or a line of mountains as jagged but rather 'to shape our sense of what we desire or what we hold in a certain way' (Taylor, 1977, p. 126). A reinterpretation of, say, the desire to be in control of one's self (such that self-control is now understood as a prudential strategy instead of as a matter of honor or dignity) alters the desire even though in one sense its object, self-control, remains the same.

Once moral motivation is understood in this way, it is possible to make sense of the purchase that evaluative cognitions such as moral principles and ideals have on us. In moral motivation the desire-component of evaluative cognition is not just any desire, it is not just a very strong desire, and it is not just a desire whose fulfillment promises maximal affective payoff. It is a 'heart's desire,' or less sentimentally, a desire without which the agent's life would lose its point. It is powerful, not because it overwhelms by its strength (whatever that might mean) but because in some sense yet to be examined it *is* the agent. Unlike other desires and aspirations that might find their way into an aesthetically pleasing self-representation (i.e., nonmoral ideals such as Mittyesque pictures of oneself as awesomely suave, unmatchably clever, etc.), this sort of desire constitutes the moral agent's 'identity,' using that term in the way ego development psychologists like Erikson, Loewald, and Loevinger have (see also Frankfurt, in press).

By now it should be apparent that the constitutive desires making up the conative component in moral motivation are themselves first-order desires, not second-order ones. Constitutive desires such as the desire to affiliate or achieve (McClelland's (1951, 1961) nAff and nAch) do not have other desires as their objects. For all their generality and plasticity, they are orientations of a world-engaging subject, not self-regarding volitions of a solipsistic entelechy. Perhaps there is no reason in principle why any sort of want – nAff, nAch, or any other n's or desires – cannot establish one's deep-level sense of what is most important and, consequently, be articulated as an ego ideal. However, it seems likely that person-oriented desires will dominate an agent's roster of constitutive desires, because of their special associations with the crucial ego-formative experiences of childhood and afterwards. It is of course no easy matter to ascertain when a motivational set is so entwined with a person's sense of self that it is morally charged. As the medievals knew only too well, discernment of spirits is as difficult a task as it is important.

In this regard, one ego ideal stands out from all the rest as an especially important moral ideal, that of *reasonableness*. The cognitive features of morality studied so extensively by psychologists and philosophers are, I think, all grounded in this ideal, for it accounts for why people bother to *justify* their actions and motivations to others as well as to themselves. Like all linguistic transactions, reason-giving presupposes intersubjective grounds of relevance. There have been extensive epistemological discussions about what makes some cognitive structures count for speaker and hearer alike as truths and, beyond that, as justifications. What is usually only hinted at in these discussions is the possibility of a subject's refusing to play the reason-giving game altogether. Such refusals are neither uncommon nor abnormal when specific games are proposed, e.g., justifying a decision to marry. The typical way of making such a refusal is to supply a pseudo-answer like 'Because I wanted to' when queried for an account of one's action, though the blunter reply 'None of your business' also works on many occasions. But as the philosopher Fingarette (1967, p. 37) has observed, there is something ominously odd about such a refusal when it amounts to the refusal to enter into any reason-giving communication whatsoever:

> If an individual will not play a game with us, we can still fall back on the intelligible framework of everyday life outside that game. But what if he will not enter life's fray itself in the spirit in which we enter it? To face such a person, such a

reality (and not merely to think it) is to experience a deep anxiety; a queasy helplessness moves in our soul.

In the same vein, Gauld and Shotter (1977, pp. 192–3) have described the anxiety pervading the converse situation: that of an individual who cannot justify (however speciously) his actions:

> The point we are trying to make here is that in ordinary everyday life people have, if they want to do anything, to be able to justify it to others. If they cannot, then...they have lost that attribute which gives them autonomy in relation to others, the ability to reject criticism and to show that their actions do in fact accord with the values and interests agreed to by all in their society. *To be unable to justify oneself is to risk being an outcast, a non-person; it is to lose one's personhood.* (Italics added)

It is primarily the business of the psychology of personality, not philosophy, to delineate the affiliative tendencies and other pro-social dispositions that constitute the conative foundations of what might be loosely called the drive-to-justificatory-discourse. But it is necessary here to recognize the great importance we spontaneously assign to interpersonal reason-giving and, by extension, the *intra*personal reason-giving that takes place in the internal forum of an agent's conscience and is an integral part of moral self-regulation. This importance is one of *moral seriousness*, in the sense that failure to give reasons for one's actions can be a moral failure, an irresponsibility that is itself a form of contempt for those who share one's world. Following Jürgen Habermas (1984, 1990), I would argue that the fundamental procedures or conditions of human communication are continuous with the moral norms that make interpersonal life possible, especially the norm of respect for persons. (It is worth noting that Kohlberg thought Habermas's 'discourse ethics' was fully compatible with his constructivist view of moral autonomy (Kohlberg, Levine, and Hewer, 1983/1984; Kohlberg, Boyd, and Levine, 1990).)

As I have presented the matter here, the antecedent identification of oneself with the ideal of reasonableness and related ideals and values such as fairmindedness, nonarbitrariness, and so on makes it possible for evaluative cognitions such as the rules of distributive justice to incarnate themselves as moral motives, in the manner described by deontological moralists

163

such as Kant and cognitive developmentalists such as Kohlberg and Piaget. In turn, these rational ideals are rooted in certain primitive tendencies such as a standing aversion to the prospect of being ostracized for refusing to engage in the practice of justifying one's actions. These are perhaps the most important of the identity-constituting tendencies I have collectively identified as 'basic desires.'

However, I should point out that this is only one of several ways of representing moral motivation within the general formula: 'Basic desires produce moral motivation via ego ideals.' For instance, the personal roots of one's ideal of being a reasonable person might be mastery strivings, not desires for affiliation. It might even be the case that people are naturally hardwired to be logotropic, such that they have ingrained propensities (of varying strengths) to follow the most formally consistent rules of conduct, much as when Hercule Poirot entered a room he felt a need to straighten any pictures that were hanging out of line. Even in this latter, rather unlikely case, I would suggest that what generates the ideal of reasonableness is an antecedent tendency or basic desire, one which is relevant and motivationally significant on extra-logical grounds.

Which of these representations is the best hypothesis for studying the moral motivation of the contemporary ethical worlds (including perhaps non-Western ones) is a psychological question that can be appropriately introduced in a theoretical study like this one but cannot be answered without empirical investigation. Furthermore, similar hypotheses can be proposed for other ideals besides those of reasonableness. Basic desires for the well-being of others may underlie the ideals of benevolence and justice (and their corresponding deontological principles), basic mastery strivings may be the conative deep structures that are displayed as temperance and courage, and so on. The story is undoubtedly extremely complicated, since there is no reason to expect a one-to-one correspondence between basic desires and specific moral ideals or principles. Thus affiliative tendencies (which are probably best thought of in the plural) might be articulated as justice ideals/principles in one context and as loyalty ideals/principles in another, and both justice and loyalty may articulate other primitive tendencies as well. Furthermore, we may expect moral actions will often be overdetermined by several complementary ideals, as well as by intermediate tendencies and articulations that should be included in any ethical account: thus one tendency can itself be an expression of another, deeper tendency, and some principles or ideals are derived from other ones. Finally, we should note that not all moral ideals or principles are authentic self-articulations, even though they might be heavily laden with affect as well as with respectability. Ideals can be cognized by the agent who conforms to them as general social practices having nothing to do with his or her own personality structure. Thus one whose socialization has been entirely a matter of external inducements may regard the ideals represented in the Boy Scout Law as correct recipes for social acceptability, but not as integral to his or her own self-concept. To take on the urgency of a *moral* ideal, a norm must be one's 'own' in the special sense just described.

I have tried to show in the last few pages that morality, even cognitivist, juridical morality, can be thought of as a mode of evaluation whose criteria are ideals articulating the agent's deepest sense of what is important, the identity-constituting desires. But if these desires are as indeterminate as I have suggested, the greatest moral struggle would seem to be that of self-interpretation, not that of resisting temptation, despite what nearly all moralists, philosophers, and psychologists have supposed. Furthermore, temptations may themselves be of the second order, a point which philosophers are wont to overstress (casting the moral struggle as between prudential and moral forms of self-regulation), just as psychologists are wont to overlook it (casting the moral struggle as between conflicting first-order tendencies). In any event, it seems undeniable that self-interpretation is an important type of moral cognition, just as decisive for living well as our social interpretations are. Hence moral psychology is more cognitive than even cognitive developmentalists suppose, since the subject matter of moral psychology turns out to be something far more subtle, and far less objective, than observable behaviors, collective socialization practices, or moral judgment structures. Rilke once wrote, 'We are not very reliably at home in the interpreted world,' an idea that applies perfectly to the moral world within. To his idea I would add another, that for morality as for everything else, the interpreted world is the only one we have. Perhaps we care so deeply about the adequacy of our moral cognitions because we somehow know both ideas are true.

NOTES

1 Moral motives and moral motivation

1 I have found the category 'social psychology' especially hard to work with, since for some professional psychologists it refers to the psychological processes characteristic of groups rather than of individuals, whereas for others it simply refers to the study of social interactions between individuals. However, in either case social psychology includes the processes whereby individuals are socialized into groups, and hence the acquisition of moral and other social norms (see Gergen and Gergen, 1981). In the present study I shall reserve the term 'socialization theory' for this sort of research, which is actually a blend of social and developmental psychology.

2 Thus Russell believed that a national entity such as England was a logical construction out of entities such as its nationals, and hence that facts about England can be expressed more 'ultimately' though often less conveniently by a set of statements about Englishmen, etc. (see Russell, 1905/1956, 1921).

3 '"When *I* use a word, it means just what I choose it to mean – neither more nor less." "The question is," said Alice, "whether you *can* make words mean different things." "The question is," said Humpty Dumpty, "which is to be master – that's all."'

4 Note that 'function-oriented' is used here without the behavioristic connotations of 'functionalism,' as the latter term was used earlier in this century in the bitter psychological debates between the partisans of introspection and phenomenology (structuralists) and those who eschewed any such attempts to get inside the black box of the mind (functionalists).

5 But we do not say that one acts out of temperance, courage, etc., which suggests that purely executive virtues are not best thought of as moral motives.

6 In his classic philosophical study *The Concept of Motivation* (1958), R. S. Peters drew a distinction between 'motives' and 'motivation' that associated the former term with reasons for action and the latter with nonrational determinants such as drives. While not wanting to

167

deny Peters's basic point that reasons are other than drives, etc., I should note that my own use of the two terms 'motive' and 'motivation' is altogether different from his.

7 True, such 'motivational realism' is often laden with qualifications, and with good reason, given the studies by Hartshorne and May (1928–30) showing the extent to which seemingly established virtues such as honesty wax and wane depending on situational factors. The notion of moral motives as personality variables is alive and well in the psychological literature of the 1990s, in spite of social learning theory's now-largely-spent blasts (especially Mischel, 1968) against personality theories based on the supposition of cross-situational dispositions. True, there is a lingering wariness among psychologists concerning especially broad motivational dispositions such as 'obedience' or 'reverence,' but for the most part their wariness is based not in their nominalist sympathies but rather their suspicions that such categories are not so much moral motives as screens behind which people hide in order to rationalize improper and even atrocious behavior.

8 It may seem a mistake to omit from this list other-regarding features, such as concern for the well-being of others. After all, the Golden Rule is the paradigm of morality for many, perhaps most people (at least in Western cultures). But if it is the case that human existence is inherently interpersonal, then care, altruism, etc., can be seen as matters of supreme importance or seriousness, and on that last account deemed part of the moral domain. I shall make this point below, but only cryptically. The classic discussion of the arguments for and against building other-regardingness into the formal concept of morality is found in Frankena (1958).

2   The Principle of Universal Heteronomy

1 The following are now regarded as classics in the psychology of moral socialization: Whiting and Child (1953); Bandura and Walters (1963); Miller and Swanson (1960); Berkowitz (1964); Sears, Rau, and Alpert (1965); Aronfreed (1968b); Hoffman (1970a, 1970b). Some of the more prominent later works are Rushton (1980), Bandura (1986); and Eisenberg, Rekowski, and Staub (1989).

2 This way of putting the matter mixes two quite different sorts of technical jargon: strictly speaking reinforcements operate as causes, not goals, whereas motives are teleological (goal-oriented) categories. But this difference does not seem important in the present context. Insofar as reinforcement theory can take on the task of moral psychology in explaining why people act in certain ways denominated as 'moral' rather than in other ways, it has an implicit notion of what I am here calling moral motives. (The problems of mixing motivational and reinforcement categories have been discussed in Ferguson (1976), Maddi (1972), and elsewhere.)

3 In what follows we shall deal primarily with the gap between the

historical foundations of socialization theory and its self-proclaimed cognitivism; for a careful and technical discussion of the comparable gap between its would-be cognitivism and its actual experimental practices, see Lind, 1985, esp. ch. 4.

4 'For such an observer, deviations by a member of the group from normal conduct will be a sign that hostile reaction is likely to follow, and nothing more. His view will be like the view of one who, having observed the working of a traffic signal in a busy street for some time, limits himself to saying that when the light turns red there is a high probability that the traffic will stop. He treats the light merely as a natural *sign that* people will behave in certain ways, as clouds are a *sign that* rain will come. In so doing he will miss out a whole dimension of the social life of those whom he is watching, since for them the red light is not merely a sign that others will stop: they look upon it as a *signal for* them to stop, and so a reason for stopping in conformity to rules which make stopping when the light is red a standard of behavior and an obligation. To mention this is to bring into account the way in which the group regards its own behavior' (Hart, 1961, pp. 87–8).

5 Thus Robert Hogan once proposed to an audience of moral psychologists Malcolm X's dictum that 'doing good is a hustle too.' For all their other differences, Hogan and Malcolm X both illustrate the tendency which most of us have to feel relieved when we discover that moral prophets, saints, and heroes really aren't so lofty after all. (Hogan's remarks were delivered at the Florida International University Conference on Morality and Moral Education, Miami Beach, December, 1981.)

6 The phrase 'reflective equilibrium' is from Rawls (1971, p. 20). However, he uses the term to refer to the balance between one's intuitions about justice and one's considered judgments about justice, rather than the balance between one's philosophical and psychological theories about morality.

7 Although the difference between moral beliefs and factual beliefs is one of the more bitterly contested issues in current philosophical literature, the contending accounts all share the common-sense intuition that each of these sorts of beliefs is in some central way liable to assessment, be it a binary assessment such as 'right-or-wrong' and 'true-or-false,' or graduated assessments such as 'appropriate-or-inappropriate' and 'adequate-or-inadequate.' To keep the present discussion from getting any more complicated than it has to be, I shall use 'true' as the general term of assessment for factual beliefs and 'right' as the general term of assessment for moral beliefs, without intending to suggest that other terms (e.g., 'good,' 'coherent,' or 'well-founded') might not do just as well if not better for either type of belief.

8 Sidgwick writes: 'Thus, on Utilitarian principles, it may be right to do and privately recommend, under certain circumstances, what it would not be right to advocate openly,' and so 'the doctrine that esoteric morality is expedient should itself be kept esoteric' (1907/

1962, pp. 489–90). For further discussion of these passages and some of Sidgwick's other views, see Parfit (1984, ch. 1) and Williams (1982, 1985).

3 Externalist moral psychologies: socialization theories

1 This point was made earlier in this century by the emotivist philosopher C. L. Stevenson, who developed a semitechnical moral psychology that anticipated the contagion theory described here. See Stevenson, 1944, esp. pp. 8–11.

2 The first of these ways looks at the strengths of tendencies. Hours of deprivation time, voltages of deterrent electrical shocks, frequency of repetition, and other indirect quantifications of drive strength, or its auxiliary concept habit strength, have been used as units for measuring strengths of tendencies. For instance, to study the phenomenon of conflicting motivations toward the same object, Miller (1948a, 1951) and later Brown (1957) equipped rats with little harnesses attached to apparatuses that measured in units of physical force how strongly the rats were pulling toward the goal box. He then correlated this measurement with a measurement of distance from the goal (or in subsequent experiments by Brown, the 'temporal distance') and so determined the strengths of the approach and avoidance tendencies, i.e., fear and hunger. Because both sorts of tendency were involved at the same time – the rats feared getting shocked as they approached the desired food – and because each tendency had a different gradient or rate of increase, it was necessary to infer their separate strengths indirectly by a fairly elaborate procedure, but the basic idea was simply that of attaching empirically established cardinal values to desires.

The second way to conceive a desire's strength looks at expected utilities. An early cognitivist reaction to drive theory approaches, even relatively sophisticated ones such as Miller's, replaced the push of drive with the pull of expectancies (Tolman, 1951). It attempted to rank desires by calculating the values of their respective contents along some common scale, harking back to Bentham's hedonic calculus. With the discovery of 'pleasure centers' in the brain that are electrically stimulated (Olds and Milner, 1954), the dream of quantifying the desirability of an object seemed less fantastic than it did to Bentham's early critics (Mill, 1838/1950). True, most empirical research on the desirability-characterization of objects has continued to regard expectancy or 'incentive' as a behavioral-peripheralist category, much as Tolman considered reinforcement a performance variable, rather than to regard it as a neurological-centralist one. Even so, attempts to quantify desirability continued in motivation theory (cf. Young, 1961; Cofer and Appley, 1964; Ferguson, 1976), although the units tended to be so indirectly connected to observable measures that it is sometimes problematic whether they are truly quantitative or mere preference-orderings, i.e., whether they are objective, cardinal values or subjective, ordinal ones.

3 Not everyone would agree with this assessment. Rapaport (1960) reconstructed the whole of psychoanalytic theory in terms of Freud's earlier tension-reduction conception of drives, Pribram (1962, p. 445) called the emphasis on cathexis in 'The Project' an uncanny stroke of luck or genius, and Solomon (1974, p. 52) followed Pribram by praising that work as sophisticated by modern philosophical as well as neurological standards. Such applause seems to me excessive, though W. D. Hart may have been justified in saying 'we have not yet got the right to deprecate Freud's energic models in the way it is now fashionable to do' (1982, p. 198).

4 Regarding Freud's failure to note this distinction, see Holt (1967), as well as Loevinger (1976, p. 327).

5 In the present context, 'truth' can be understood not only in the narrow, correspondence sense of the term but also in the functionally equivalent senses that term carries in coherence and constructivist epistemologies. Some other locution, such as 'cognitive appropriateness,' would probably be a better generic term here than 'truth,' were it not that cognate locutions (such as 'truth-making') would then have to be replaced by clumsy and distracting bits of newly minted jargon.

6 In an interesting philosophical analysis Foot (1978) argues that what makes approval or disapproval meaningful is the belief that it is given by someone who has some socially constituted role as well as some rational grounds for (dis)approving. Such a person has or represents *authority*, broadly construed, and hence speaks in a voice that is something other than his or her own personal response.

7 But it does have limits. The term 'self-regulation' is *not* used in these pages to refer to what Piaget (1971) and others have called 'autoregulation,' which is a systems theoretic category roughly equivalent to that of homeostasis. That is, systems are autoregulating because they contain mechanisms that correct deviations from certain reference points, such as the temperature setting on a thermostat. Psychologists taken with systems theory sometimes use the term 'self-regulating' to indicate that a psychological process has subsidiary processes for its own maintenance, but this is not the way the term is used here. In the psychological processes of self-regulation that I have in mind, what is regulated is not the process, but the subject's own *self*. Similarly, by 'self-referential' I mean: referring to the self. If, in the course of regulating (or referring to) the self, some cognitive process is also regulated (or referred to), that is all well and good, but this is incidental to the sense in which I employ these reflexive locutions.

8 Something analogous to self-regulation is involved in such delays, viz., coping strategies to deal with the frustration that could otherwise be intolerable. These strategies have been studied recently (e.g., Miller and Karniol, 1976) as well as long ago by Freud (1911/1958), who speculated that the prototype of coping with an externally imposed delay was that of the infant who 'binds the time' between

nursings by generating hallucinations and wish fulfillment imagery of his mother's breast. However, whether or not the infant's case is prototypical of adult ways of coping with externally imposed delay, it seems unmistakably and radically different from moral coping in that the infant is not the author of the delay.

9 And presumably the short-term reward as well, though this point seems to have been overlooked by the theorists in question.

10 'The use of the term "contract" should not be construed to imply more than a convenient analogy. Its purpose is to facilitate a rudimentary conceptual organization and hypothesis generation by borrowing from an area that has already integrated the relationships between standards, performance criteria and payoff conditions for many social practices' (Kanfer and Karoly, 1972, p. 408).

4 Internalist moral psychologies: internalization theories

1 It should go without saying that to insist on the logical possibility of action is not to say that action will always take place. This is so not only because the agent's motivation may not be strong enough to prevail over other action-tendencies, but also because sometimes forbearance rather than overt behavior is the appropriate thing to do. This rather banal point is easily overlooked for the simple reason that very often nothing needs to be done beyond endorsing and identifying with certain motives that I have. For instance, in the course of second-order reflection I recognize that some first-order desire d of mine, say that my child be sheltered, is not only without serious competition in my repertoire of desires but is also a noble, morally worthy one. I do nothing in my regard by way of self-control because no extra intervention is needed: I already have d as my strongest first-order desire, and am prepared to act on it, having found upon evaluating it that it is just the kind of desire I want to have.

2 Or more often, behavior-modification, with the intrapsychic chips falling where they may.

3 We may note in passing that this is not the only way that one's interest can be drawn away from the outcomes of first-order desires. An experimenter such as Wundt might be more concerned with measurable or phenomenological qualities of his own desires (their frequency, intensity, duration, etc.) than with their contents. Or an autobiographer such as Virginia Woolf might be concerned with some quality of her motivations whereby they would make interesting reading. Like the experimenter's interest in motivational qualities, the autobiographer's interest reveals the general possibility of attending to a desire without focusing on the desired object, i.e., on its anticipated outcome. It is obvious, though, that the concern in each of these cases is not a truly second-order motivation for the simple reason that their respective modes of self-study do not involve self-evaluation.

4 E.g., Rawls (1971), Richards (1971), Williams (1973), and G. Taylor (1985).

5 Needless to say, the affective association in question can be acquired vicariously, as Alston well knows. Neither he nor Aronfreed should be read as presenting us with the ludicrous caricature of moral education as commencing with overt transgressions: as though, say, sexual values were best taught by starting with a few robustly distressful acts of adultery designed to set the affective stage required for the virtue of chastity.

6 Meissner's *Internalization in Psychoanalysis* (1981) provides a good overview of recent work on the topic, especially the debate between Lernberg and Kohut. Whatever use clinicians might be able to make of the numerous studies written by other ego theorists, especially during the 1930s and again in the 1960s, there is little that relates to the present study. Exceptions (in addition to Meissner) are the works of Klein, Loewald, Erikson, and Loevinger, which develop the topic of ego ideals. See also the essays on morality and ego functions contained in Noam and Wren (in press).

7 The reference here is to Freud's (1916/1957) discussion of persons who are 'criminals from a sense of guilt,' i.e., whose noncompliance to moral standards is actually *produced by* guilt rather than the other way around.

8 In his *New Introductory Lectures* (1933/1964), Freud notes that the superego of the child is not really built up on the model of the parents themselves but rather on that of their own superegos. As parents, they are 'glad to be able now to identify themselves fully with their own parents who in the past laid such severe restrictions upon them' (p. 67). In this way the moral tradition is perpetuated: the same contents are taken over from one generation's superego to that of the next generation.

9 Thus de Sousa concludes, 'Freud's theory provides no procedure for regulating these balances, and no hint as to how one might construct a fully unified and integrated notion of rationality' (1982, p. 161).

5   Internalist moral psychologies: cognitive development theories

1 The distinction between motivated and unmotivated desires goes back to Aristotle's *Nicomachean Ethics*, 3:3; cf. Nagel, 1970, pp. 29 ff., and Harman, 1977, pp. 44 ff.

2 Though he was more cognizant of it than the majority of those psychologists and educators who have written summaries of his theory of moral development. See Piaget, 1932/1965, pp. 84–6, 284.

3 Kohlberg (1958) was the first to use the ideal typological approach to reconstruct Piaget's two moralities as types rather than stages. As he and his colleagues recently characterized it, this approach involves 'simultaneous willingness to select out and stress empirical consistencies that can be coherently interpreted, and willingness to revise

and reform principles of observation and interpretation as new empirical patterns seem to emerge' (Tappan, Kohlberg, *et al.*, 1987).

4 Kohlberg occasionally discussed the possibility of a still higher perspective in which one takes the point of view of the cosmos. Although he sometimes called this perspective a 'stage' (Stage 7), it does not seem to be a new structural whole. For other reasons that this 'stage' is not usually included to the usual six-member list, see Kohlberg, Levine, and Hewer, 1983/1984, pp. 249–50.

5 Piaget's conception of agency does not include any inherent reference to other persons. For Macmurray, however, 'the self as agent' (the title of the first volume of his Gifford lectures (1957)) necessarily acts in a field of other 'persons in relation' (the title of the second volume (1961)). James Youniss (1980, 1984) has expanded the cognitive developmental paradigm to include Macmurray's categories.

6 For instance, Piaget thought that it normally took about a year for an 'effectively' autonomous child or young adolescent to become verbally conscious of the idea of autonomy (1932/1965, p. 119).

7 It is interesting to compare this essay with an earlier version that was subsequently published in Kurtines and Gewirtz (1984), especially concerning a passage that I cited a few lines back. In that essay Kohlberg described himself as 'following Jean Piaget,' in whose view 'moral judgment arises out of moral action itself, although there is no single causal direction' (p. 53). In the later version, the reference to Piaget is omitted and the judgment-to-action direction gets more attention: 'In our view, moral judgment development both causes moral action and arises out of moral action itself' (Kohlberg and Candee, 1984, pp. 505–6).

8 Among continental psychologists 'affectivity' (or sometimes just 'affect') refers to something much more dynamic and conative than the feeling states described in most Anglo-American psychological theories of affect. Thus Theodore Mischel (1971, p. 317) wrote, 'Piaget uses "affect" in a very broad sense, to cover feelings, emotions, desires, needs, interests, values, and will, just as he uses "intelligence" broadly to cover all sorts of cognitive structures.'

9 Although Piaget uses the term 'heteronomous' to characterize the first moral stage, his sense of the term is quite different from the mechanistic sense involved in my earlier characterization of externalist moral psychologies as dominated by the Principle of Universal Heteronomy.

10 Rawls's own discussion (1971, pp. 17–22) of this cross-checking process applies most obviously to autonomous moral thinking, but the same general point also holds for heteronomous moral thinking, i.e., that it is by no means necessary that the motives for compliance with one's concrete valuations carry over as tendencies to act on their verbalized counterparts. A rigidly heteronomous child might, for instance, verbally judge that it is always wrong to lie, even if the intention is harmless (telling a joke) or positively beneficent (trying to protect a friend). Let us suppose, in line with the general thesis of metaethical internalism, that this child's verbal judgment somehow

carries with it at least a glimmer of readiness to refrain from lying regardless of the circumstances, i.e., an across-the-board desire to act in accordance with that uncompromising moral judgment. Nevertheless, no matter how compatible or mutually supportive these dispositions might be in the order of execution, this general compliance readiness (moral motive) is conceptually quite different from the cognitive-affective dispositions that lead the heteronomous child to make – and obey – those preverbal judgments that precede his or her verbal judgments, e.g., 'Lying is always wrong.' The underlying, concrete evaluation may very well be much less rigid than the verbalized judgment even when it is just as strongly felt. It is fueled by the child's background awareness that, say, mother and father trust me, will be disappointed or angry if I lie, and so on – in short, by the awareness that a primary social bond would be imperiled by lying. In contrast, the verbal judgment is a result of the background concrete awareness that even occasional lying does not make sense, that it does not fit into the heteronomous child's authority-constituted social worldview, etc.

11 Describing the momentary rush of excitement that accompanied the translation of the Sorbonne Lectures which appeared shortly after Piaget's death, one especially alert commentator observed: 'As one reads the translation, however, the excited feelings soon die out ... the long-awaited breakthrough can hardly be considered as the missing theoretical link' (Sprintall, 1986, p. 147).

12 However, psychologists are not the only ones who interpret Kohlberg in this way. Cf. Kleinberger, 1982, pp. 153–4.

13 Even so, the description of Stage 5 seems at first glance rather close to the externalist social approval models of Rosenhan, Aronfreed, and Freud, characterized as it is by the so-called 'concern about maintaining the respect of equals and the community.' But the externalist overtones of this idea are offset by Kohlberg's assumption that this respect 'is based on reason.' It should also be noted that the descriptions of these last two stages were superseded by Kohlberg's later formulations, especially in his final statement of Stage 6 (Kohlberg, Boyd, and Levine, 1990).

14 Kohlberg's discussions elsewhere (esp. Kohlberg, Levine, and Hewer, 1983/1984, pp. 361ff.) of Gilligan's concept of care are not entirely satisfactory as far as his interpretation of her work is concerned. However, this does not affect the present point, which is that her use of the term 'responsibility' is quite other than Kohlberg's, since for her it is not a 'follow-through' concept but rather the heart of an alternative morality.

15 Brown and Herrnstein (1975, p. 289) argued that, even if moral judgments are postulated as having some motivational impact (which they doubt), in cases where people make the same moral judgments, differences in behavior are due to purely nonmoral considerations.

16 Piaget understood autonomy as conceptually interchangeable with mutual respect, which he defined as 'the state of equilibrium

towards which unilateral respect is tending when differences between child and adult, younger and older are becoming effaced; just as cooperation is the form of equilibrium to which constraint is tending in the same circumstances' (1932/1965, p. 96).

17 See also the short discussion of Galon's notion of responsibility as a second-order disposition (Kohlberg and Candee, 1984).

18 The titles of these criteria are: Freedom, Mutual Respect, Reversibility, Constructivism, Hierarchy, Intrinsicalness, Prescriptivity, Universality, and Choice. As Kohlberg and his associates explain, the first four of these criteria are derived directly from Piaget. An extended description of the criteria and the method for combining them as a psychological measurement of 'autonomy' is provided in the appendix to Kohlberg's scoring manual (Tappan, Kohlberg, *et al.*, 1987).

19 Toward the end of his life Kohlberg seemed to have become increasingly aware of this point, which he nonetheless continued to address in terms of competence strivings. See the posthumously published essays in Kohlberg, 1987, especially chapters 6–8.

REFERENCES

Akamatsu, T. J., and Farudi, P. A. (1978). Effects of model status and juvenile offender type on the imitation of self-reward criteria. *Journal of Consulting and Clinical Psychology* 46:187–8.

Allport, G. W. (1961). *Pattern and Growth in Personality*. New York: Holt, Rinehart & Winston.

Allport, G. W. (1962). The general and the unique in psychological science. *Journal of Personality* 30:405–22.

Alston, W. (1977). Self-intervention and the structure of motivation. In T. Mischel (ed.), *The Self*. New York: Rowman & Littlefield.

Amacher, P. (1965). Freud's neurological education and its influence on psychoanalytic theory. *Psychological Issues* 4 (4, Whole no. 16).

Anscombe, G. E. M. (1963). *Intention*. Oxford: Blackwell.

Aristotle (1954). *Nicomachean Ethics* (W. D. Ross, trans.). Oxford: Oxford University Press.

Aronfreed, J. (1964). The origins of self-criticism. *Psychological Review* 71:193–218.

Aronfreed, J. (1968a). The concept of internalization. In D. A. Goslin and D. C. Glass (eds), *Handbook of Socialization Theory*. New York: Rand-McNally.

Aronfreed, J. (1968b). *Conduct and Conscience: The Socialization of Internalized Control over Behavior*. New York: Academic Press.

Aronfreed, J. (1971). Some problems for a theory of the acquisition of conscience. In C. M. Beck, B. S. Crittenden, and E. V. Sullivan (eds), *Moral Education: Interdisciplinary Approaches*. Toronto: University of Toronto Press.

Aronfreed, J. (1976). Moral development from the standpoint of a general psychological theory. In T. Lickona (ed.), *Moral Development and Behavior*. New York: Holt, Rinehart & Winston.

Aronfreed, J., and Paskal, V. (1965). Altruism, empathy, and the conditioning of positive affect. Unpublished manuscript, University of Pennsylvania.

Ashby, W. R. (1968). Principles of the self-organizing system. In W. Buckley (ed.), *Modern Systems Research for the Behavioral Scientist*. Chicago: Aldine.

Atkinson, J. W., and Reitman, W. (1958). Performance as a function of motive strength and expectancy of goal-attainment. In J. Atkinson (ed.), *Motives in Fantasy, Action and Society.* New York: Van Nostrand.

Bandura, A. (1965). Influence of models' reinforcement contingencies on the acquisition of imitative responses. *Journal of Personality and Social Psychology* 1:589–95.

Bandura, A. (1969). *Principles of Behavior Modification.* New York: Holt, Rinehart & Winston.

Bandura, A. (1971a). Analysis of modeling processes. In A. Bandura (ed.), *Psychological Modeling: Conflicting Theories.* Chicago: Aldine-Atherton.

Bandura, A. (1971b). Vicarious and self-reinforcement processes. In R. Glaser (ed.), *The Nature of Reinforcement.* New York: Academic Press.

Bandura, A. (1977). *Social Learning Theory.* Englewood Cliffs, NJ: Prentice-Hall.

Bandura, A. (1986). *Social Foundations of Thought and Action.* Englewood Cliffs, NJ: Prentice-Hall.

Bandura, A., and Mischel, W. (1965). Modification of self-imposed delay of reward through exposure to live and symbolic models. *Journal of Personality and Social Psychology* 2:698–705.

Bandura, A., and Walters, R. H. (1963). *Social Learning and Personality Development.* New York: Holt, Rinehart & Winston.

Benedict, R. (1946). *The Chrysanthemum and the Sword.* Boston: Houghton Mifflin.

Benedict, R. (1958). *Patterns of Culture.* New York: New American Library.

Bentham, J. (1834/1983). *Deontology* (ed. A. Goldworth). Oxford: Oxford University Press.

Berger, S. M. (1962). Conditioning through vicarious instigation. *Psychological Review* 69:450–66.

Berkowitz, L. (1964). *Development of Motives and Values in a Child.* New York: Basic Books.

Berkowitz, L., and Geen, R. G. (1966). Film violence and the cue properties of available targets. *Journal of Personality and Social Psychology* 3:525–30.

Bixenstine, V. E. (1956). Secondary drive as a neutralizer of time in integrative problem-solving. *Journal of Comparative and Physiological Psychology* 49:161–6.

Blasi, A. (1980). Bridging moral cognition and moral action: A critical review of the literature. *Psychological Bulletin* 88:1–45.

Blasi, A. (1983). Moral cognition and moral action: A theoretical perspective. *Developmental Review* 3:178–210.

Brandt, R. B. (1979). *A Theory of the Good and the Right.* Oxford: Oxford University Press.

Brehm, J. W. (1960). Attitudinal consequences of commitment to unpleasant behavior. *Journal of Abnormal and Social Psychology* 60:379–83.

Brewer, W. F. (1974). There is no convincing evidence for operant or classical conditioning in adult humans. In W. B. Weimer (ed.), *Cognition and the Symbolic Processes.* Hillsdale, NJ: Erlbaum.

Brink, D. O. (1989). *Moral Realism and the Foundations of Ethics.* Cambridge: Cambridge University Press.

Brown, J. S. (1957). Principles of intrapersonal conflict. *Conflict Resolution* 1:135–54.

Brown, R., and Herrnstein, R. J. (1975). *Psychology*. Boston: Little, Brown.

Bryan, J. H. (1971). Model affect and children's imitative altruism. *Child Development* 42:2061–5.

Burton, R. V. (1963). Generality of honesty reconsidered. *Psychological Review* 70:481–99.

Butler, J. (1726/1983). *Five Sermons Preached at the Rolls Chapel and A Dissertation upon the Nature of Virtue* (ed. S. Darwall). Indianapolis: Hackett.

Byrne, D. (1971). *The Attraction Paradigm*. New York: Academic Press.

Byrne, D., and Byrne, L. A. (1977). *Exploring Human Sexuality*. New York: Harper & Row.

Casey, W., and Burton, R. (1986). The social-learning theory approach. In G. Sapp (ed.), *Handbook of Moral Development: Models, Processes, Techniques, and Research*. Birmingham, AL: Religious Education Press.

Cautela, J. (1971). Covert conditioning. In A. Jacobs and L. Sachs (eds), *The Psychology of Private Events*. New York: Academic Press.

Cofer, C. N., and Appley, M. H. (1964). *Motivation: Theory and Research*. New York: Wiley.

Danto, A. (1973). *Analytical Philosophy of Action*. Cambridge: Cambridge University Press.

de Sousa, R. B. (1982). Norms and the normal. In R. Wollheim and J. Hopkins (eds), *Philosophical Essays on Freud*. Cambridge: Cambridge University Press.

Dember, W. N. (1974). Motivation and the cognitive revolution. *American Psychologist* 29:161–8.

DePalma, D. (1975). Research and theory of moral development: A comment. In D. DePalma and J. Foley (eds), *Moral Development: Current Theory and Research*. Hillsdale, NJ: Lawrence Erlbaum.

Döbert, R. (1990). Against the neglect of 'content' in the moral theories of Kohlberg and Habermas: Implications for the relativism–universalism controversy. In T. Wren (ed.), *The Moral Domain: Essays in the Ongoing Discussion between Philosophy and the Social Sciences*. Cambridge, MA: MIT Press.

Eisenberg, N., Rekowski, J., and Staub, I. (eds) (1989). *Social and Moral Values: Individual and Societal Perspectives*. Hillsdale, NJ: Lawrence Erlbaum.

Eysenck, H. J. (1970). A dimensional system of psychodiagnostics. In A. R. Mahrer (ed.), *New Approaches to Personality Classification*. New York: Columbia University Press.

Eysenck, H. J. (1976). The biology of morality. In T. Lickona (ed.), *Moral Development and Behavior: Theory, Research, and Social Issues*. New York: Holt, Rinehart & Winston.

Falk, W. D. (1947–8). 'Ought' and motivation. *Proceedings of the Aristotelian Society* 43:111–38.

Ferguson, E. (1976). *Motivation: An Experimental Approach*. New York: Holt, Rinehart & Winston.

Ferster, C. B. (1953). Sustained behavior under delayed reinforcement. *Journal of Experimental Psychology* 45:218–24.

Ferster, C. B., and Hammer, C. (1965). Variables determining the effects of delay in reinforcement. *Journal of the Experimental Analysis of Behavior* 8: 243–54.

Festinger, L. (1957). *A Theory of Cognitive Dissonance.* Stanford: Stanford University Press.

Festinger, L., and Freedman, J. (1964). Dissonance reduction and moral values. In P. Worchel and D. Byrne (eds), *Personality Change.* New York: Wiley.

Fingarette, H. (1967). *On Responsibility.* New York: Basic Books.

Flanagan, O. (1984). *The Science of the Mind.* Cambridge, MA: Bradford Books/MIT Press.

Foot, P. (1978). Approval and disapproval. In P. Foot, *Virtues and Vices and Other Essays in Moral Philosophy.* Berkeley: University of California Press.

Frankena, W. (1958). Obligation and motivation in recent moral philosophy. In A. I. Melden (ed.), *Essays in Moral Philosophy.* Seattle: University of Washington Press.

Frankena, W. (1965). Recent conceptions of morality. In H. Castaneda and G. Nakhnikian (eds), *Morality and the Language of Conduct.* Detroit: Wayne State University Press.

Frankena, W. (1973). *Ethics.* Englewood Cliffs, NJ: Prentice-Hall.

Frankfurt, H. (1988a). Freedom of the will and the concept of a person. In H. Frankfurt, *The Importance of What We Care About: Philosophical Essays.* Cambridge: Cambridge University Press. (Originally published in *The Journal of Philosophy* 68 (1971), 5–20.)

Frankfurt, H. (1988b). The importance of what we care about. In H. Frankfurt, *The Importance of What We Care About: Philosophical Essays.* Cambridge: Cambridge University Press. (Originally published in *Synthese* 53 (1982), 257–72.)

Frankfurt, H. (In press). On the necessity of ideals. In G. Noam and T. Wren, *Morality and the Self.* Cambridge, MA: MIT Press.

Freud, S. (1895/1950). Project for a scientific psychology. In J. Strachey (ed.), *The Standard Edition of the Complete Psychological Works of Sigmund Freud* (vol. 21). London: Hogarth.

Freud, S. (1900/1958). *The Interpretation of Dreams.* In J. Strachey (ed.), *The Standard Edition of the Complete Psychological Works of Sigmund Freud* (vols 4–5). London: Hogarth.

Freud, S. (1911/1958). Formulations on the two principles of mental functioning. In J. Strachey (ed.), *The Standard Edition of the Complete Psychological Works of Sigmund Freud* (vol. 12). London: Hogarth.

Freud, S. (1915/1957). Repression. In J. Strachey (ed.), *The Standard Edition of the Complete Psychological Works of Sigmund Freud* (vol. 14). London: Hogarth.

Freud, S. (1916/1957). Some character types met with in psychoanalytic work. In J. Strachey (ed.), *The Standard Edition of the Complete Psychological Works of Sigmund Freud* (vol. 14). London: Hogarth.

Freud, S. (1923/1961). *The Ego and the Id.* In J. Strachey (ed.), *The*

Standard Edition of the Complete Psychological Works of Sigmund Freud (vol. 19). London: Hogarth.

Freud, S. (1924/1961). The economic problem of masochism. In J. Strachey (ed.), *The Standard Edition of the Complete Psychological Works of Sigmund Freud* (vol. 19). London: Hogarth.

Freud, S. (1926/1959). *Inhibitions, Symptoms and Anxiety.* In J. Strachey (ed.), *The Standard Edition of the Complete Psychological Works of Sigmund Freud* (vol. 20). London: Hogarth.

Freud, S. (1930/1961). *Civilization and Its Discontents.* In J. Strachey (ed.), *The Standard Edition of the Complete Psychological Works of Sigmund Freud* (vol. 21). London: Hogarth.

Freud, S. (1931/1961). Libidinal types. In J. Strachey (ed.), *The Standard Edition of the Complete Psychological Works of Sigmund Freud* (vol. 21). London: Hogarth.

Freud, S. (1933/1964). *New Introductory Lectures on Psychoanalysis.* In J. Strachey (ed.), *The Standard Edition of the Complete Psychological Works of Sigmund Freud* (vol. 22). London: Hogarth.

Gauld, A., and Shotter, J. (1977). *Human Action and Its Psychological Investigation.* Boston: Routledge & Kegan Paul.

Geen, R. G. (1978). Some effects of observation violence on the behavior of the observer. In B. A. Maher (ed.), *Progress in Experimental Personality Research.* New York: Academic Press.

Gergen, K. J., and Gergen, M. M. (1981). *Social Psychology.* New York: Harcourt Brace Jovanovich.

Gillespie, N. (ed.) (1986). Moral realism: Spindell Conference 1985. *Southern Journal of Philosophy* 24 (supplement).

Gilligan, C. (1982). *In a Different Voice: Psychological Theory and Women's Development.* Cambridge, MA: Harvard University Press.

Gilligan, J. (1976). Beyond morality: Psychoanalytic reflections on shame, guilt, and love. In T. Lickona (ed.), *Moral Development and Behavior: Theory, Research, and Social Issues.* New York: Holt, Rinehart & Winston.

Habermas, J. (1984). *The Theory of Communicative Action. Vol. 1: Reason and the Rationalization of Society* (T. McCarthy, trans.). Boston: Beacon Press.

Habermas, J. (1990). Justice and solidarity: On the discussion concerning Stage 6. In T. Wren (ed.), *The Moral Domain: Essays in the Ongoing Discussion between Philosophy and the Social Sciences.* Cambridge, MA: MIT Press.

Hare, R. M. (1952). *The Language of Morals.* Oxford: Oxford University Press.

Hare, R. M. (1963). *Freedom and Reason.* Oxford: Oxford University Press.

Harman, G. (1977). *The Nature of Morality.* Oxford: Oxford University Press.

Harré, R. (1980). *Social Being: A Theory for Social Psychology.* Totowa, NJ: Littlefield, Adams.

Harré, R. (1984). *Personal Being: A Theory for Individual Psychology.* Cambridge, MA: Harvard University Press.

Harré, R., and Secord, P. (1972). *The Explanation of Social Behaviour.* Oxford: Basil Blackwell.

Hart, D., Kohlberg, L., and Wertsch, J. (1987). The developmental social-self theories of James Mark Baldwin, George Herbert Mead, and Lev Semenovich Vygotsky. In L. Kohlberg (ed.), *Child Psychology and Childhood Education: A Cognitive-Developmental View.* New York: Longman.

Hart, H. L. A. (1961). *The Concept of Law.* Oxford: Clarendon Press.

Hart, W. D. (1982). Models of repression. In R. Wollheim and J. Hopkins (eds), *Philosophical Essays on Freud.* Cambridge: Cambridge University Press.

Hartshorne, H., and May, M. A. (1928–30). *Studies in the Nature of Character: Vol. 1. Studies in Deceit; Vol. 2. Studies in Service and Self-Control; Vol. 3. Studies in Organization of Character.* New York: Macmillan.

Heckhausen, N., and Weiner, B. (1972). The emergence of a cognitive psychology of motivation. In P. C. Dodwell (ed.), *New Horizons in Psychology* 2. Harmondsworth: Penguin.

Heider, F. (1958). *The Psychology of Interpersonal Relations.* New York: Wiley.

Herrnstein, R. J. (1966). Superstition: A corollary of the principles of operant conditioning. In W. K. Honig (ed.), *Operant Behavior: Areas of Research and Application.* New York: Appleton-Century-Crofts.

Hoffman, M. L. (1970a). Moral development. In P. H. Mussen (ed.), *Carmichael's Manual of Child Psychology* (vol. 2, 3rd ed.). New York: Wiley.

Hoffman, M. L. (1970b). Conscience, personality, and socialization techniques. *Human Development* 13:90–126.

Hoffman, M. L. (1976). Empathy, role-taking, guilt, and development of altruistic motives. In T. Lickona (ed.), *Moral Development and Behavior: Theory, Research, and Social Issues.* New York: Holt, Rinehart & Winston.

Hogan, R. (1973). Moral conduct and moral character: A psychological perspective. *Psychological Bulletin* 79:217–32.

Holt, R. R. (1965). A review of some of Freud's biological assumptions and their influence on his theories. In N. S. Greenfield and W. C. Lewis (eds), *Psychoanalysis and Current Biological Thought.* Madison: University of Wisconsin Press.

Holt, R. R. (1967). Beyond vitalism and mechanism: Freud's concept of psychic energy. In J. H. Masserman (ed.), *Science and Psychoanalysis.* New York: Grune & Stratton.

Kanfer, F. H. (1970). Self-regulation: Research, issues, and speculations. In C. Neuringer and J. Michael (eds), *Behavior Modification in Clinical Psychology.* New York: Appleton-Century-Crofts.

Kanfer, F. H. (1971). The maintenance of behavior by self-generated stimuli and reinforcement. In A. Jacobs and L. B. Sachs (eds), *Psychology of Private Events.* New York: Academic Press.

Kanfer, F. H. (1977). The many faces of self-control, as behavior modification changes its focus. In R. B. Stuart (ed.), *Behavioral Self-Management.* New York: Brunner/Mazel.

Kanfer, F. H., and Karoly, P. (1972). Self control: A behavioristic excursion into the lion's den. *Behavior Therapy* 3:398–416.

Kant, I. (1775–80/1963). *Lectures on Ethics* (L. Infield, trans.). New York: Harper & Row.

Kant, I. (1785/1959). *Foundations of the Metaphysics of Morals* (L. W. Beck, trans.). Indianapolis: Bobbs-Merrill.

Karniol, R., and Miller, D. T. (1980). Changes in reward evaluations in two delay contexts. Unpublished manuscript, Tel Aviv University.

Karniol, R., and Miller, D. T. (1981). The development of self-control in children. In S. S. Brehm, S. M. Kassin, and F. X. Gibbons (eds), *Developmental Social Psychology*. New York: Oxford University Press.

Kelleher, R. T. (1966). Chaining and conditioned reinforcement. In W. K. Honig (ed.), *Operant Behavior: Areas of Research and Application*. New York: Appleton-Century-Crofts.

Kelman, H. C. (1958). Compliance, identification and internalization: Three processes of opinion change. *Journal of Conflict Resolution* 2:51–60.

Kerckhoff, A. C., and Back, K. W. (1968). *The June Bug: A Study of Hysterical Contagion*. New York: Appleton-Century-Crofts.

Kleinberger, A. F. (1982). The proper object of moral judgment and of moral education. *Journal of Moral Education* 11:147–58.

Kohlberg, L. (1958). The development of modes of thinking and choices in years 10 to 16. Ph.D. dissertation, University of Chicago.

Kohlberg, L. (1965). Psychosexual development: A cognitive-developmental approach. Unpublished mimeographed manuscript, University of Chicago.

Kohlberg, L. (1969/1984). Stage and sequence: The cognitive-developmental approach to socialization. In L. Kohlberg, *Essays on Moral Development. Vol. 2. The Psychology of Moral Development*. New York: Harper & Row.

Kohlberg, L. (1970). Education for justice: A modern statement of the Platonic view. In T. Sizer (ed.), *Moral Education: Five Lectures*. Cambridge, MA: Harvard University Press.

Kohlberg, L. (1971). From Is to Ought: How to commit the naturalistic fallacy and get away with it in the study of moral development. In T. Mischel (ed.), *Cognitive Development and Epistemology*. New York: Academic Press.

Kohlberg, L. (1973). The claim to moral adequacy of a highest stage of moral judgment. *Journal of Philosophy* 40:630–46.

Kohlberg, L. (1976). Moral stages and moralization: The cognitive-developmental approach. In T. Lickona (ed.), *Moral Development and Behavior: Theory, Research, and Social Issues*. New York: Holt, Rinehart & Winston.

Kohlberg, L. (1979). The young child as a philosopher: Moral development and the dilemmas of moral education. In M. Wolman (ed.), *Taking Early Childhood Seriously*. Pasadena, CA: Pacific Oaks.

Kohlberg, L. (1981/1984). The meaning and measurement of moral judgment. In L. Kohlberg, *Essays on Moral Development. Vol. 2. The Psychology of Moral Development*. New York: Harper & Row.

Kohlberg, L. (1984). The six stages of justice judgment. In L. Kohlberg, *Essays on Moral Development. Vol. 2. The Psychology of Moral Development.* New York: Harper and Row.

Kohlberg, L. (ed.) (1987). *Child Psychology and Childhood Education: A Cognitive-Developmental View.* New York: Longman.

Kohlberg, L., Boyd, D., and Levine, C. (1990). The return of Stage 6: Its principle and moral point of view. In T. Wren (ed.), *The Moral Domain: Essays in the Ongoing Discussion between Philosophy and the Social Sciences.* Cambridge, MA: MIT Press.

Kohlberg, L., and Candee, D. (1984). The relationship of moral judgment to moral action. In L. Kohlberg, *Essays on Moral Development. Vol. 2. The Psychology of Moral Development.* New York: Harper & Row.

Kohlberg, L., and Gilligan, C. (1971). The adolescent as philosopher: The discovery of the self in a postconventional world. *Daedalus* 100:1051–86.

Kohlberg, L., Levine, C., and Hewer, A. (1983/1984). Moral stages: A current statement and response to critics. In L. Kohlberg, *Essays on Moral Development. Vol. 2. The Psychology of Moral Development.* New York: Harper & Row.

Kurtines, W., and Gewirtz, J. (eds) (1984). *Morality, Moral Behavior and Moral Development: Basic Issues in Theory and Research.* New York: Wiley Interscience.

Lerner, M. J. (1970). The desire for justice and reactions to victims. In J. R. Macaulay and L. Berkowitz (eds), *Altruism and Helping Behavior.* NY: Academic Press.

Lewin, K. (1938). *The Conceptual Representation and the Measurement of Psychological Forces.* Durham, NC: Duke University Press.

Lind, G. (1985). The theory of moral-cognitive development: A socio-psychological assessment. In G. Lind, H. Hartmann, and R. Wakenhut (eds.), *Moral Development and the Social Environment.* Chicago: Precedent Publishing.

Lind, G. (1986). Parallelität von Affekt und Kognition in der moralischen Entwicklung. In F. Oser, W. Althoff, and G. Garz, *Moralische Zugäng zum Menschen.* Munich: P. Kind Verlag.

Littig, L. W., and Petty, R. M. (1971). Effects of multiply aroused motives on behavior. *Journal of Experimental Research on Personality* 5:139–44.

Loevinger, J. (1976). *Ego Development.* San Francisco: Jossey-Bass.

McClelland, D. C. (1951). *Personality.* New York: Dryden.

McClelland, D. C. (1961). *The Achieving Society.* Princeton: Van Nostrand.

MacCorquodale, K., and Meehl, P. E. (1953). Drive conditioning as a factor in latent conditioning. *Journal of Experimental Psychology* 45:20–4.

Macmurray, J. (1957). *The Self as Agent.* London: Faber & Faber.

Macmurray, J. (1961). *Persons in Relation.* London: Faber & Faber.

Maddi, S. (1972). *Personality Theories: A Comparative Analysis.* Homewood, IL: Dorsey Press.

Maller, J. B. (1934). General and specific factors in character. *Journal of Social Psychology* 5:97–102.

Mead, M. (1950). *Sex and Temperament in Three Primitive Societies.* New York: New American Library.

Meichenbaum, D. H., and Cameron, R. (1982). Cognitive-behavior therapy. In G. T. Wilson and C. M. Franks (eds), *Contemporary Behavior Therapy: Conceptual and Empirical Foundations*. New York: Guilford.

Meissner, W. W. (1981). *Internalization in Psychoanalysis* (Psychological Issues Monograph no. 50). New York: International Universities Press.

Midgley, M. (1981). *Heart and Mind*. New York: St Martin's Press.

Mill, J. S. (1838/1950). Essay on Bentham. In F. R. Leavis (ed.), *On Bentham and Coleridge*. London: Chatto & Windus.

Miller, D. R., and Swanson, G. E. (1960). *Inner Conflict and Defense*. New York: Holt.

Miller, D. T., and Karniol, R. (1976). The role of rewards in externally and self-imposed delay of gratification. *Journal of Personality and Social Psychology* 33:594–600.

Miller, N. E. (1948a). Studies of fear as an acquirable drive: I. Fear as motivation and fear-reduction as reinforcement of new responses. *Journal of Experimental Psychology* 38:89–106.

Miller, N. E. (1948b). Theory and experiment relating psychoanalytic displacement to stimulus-response generalization. *Journal of Abnormal and Social Psychology* 43:155–79.

Miller, N. E. (1951). Learnable drives and rewards. In S. S. Stevens (ed.), *Handbook of Experimental Psychology*. New York: Wiley Press.

Mischel, T. (1971). Cognitive conflict and the motivation of thought. In T. Mischel (ed.), *Cognitive Development and Epistemology*. New York: Academic Press.

Mischel, W. (1966). Theory and research of the antecedents of self-imposed delay of reward. In B. A. Maher (ed.), *Progress in Experimental Personality Research*, vol. 3. New York: Academic Press.

Mischel, W. (1968). *Personality and Assessment*. New York: Wiley.

Mischel, W. (1974). Processes in delay of gratification. In L. Berkowitz (ed.), *Advances in Social Psychology*, vol. 7. New York: Academic Press.

Mischel, W. (1976). *Introduction to Personality*. New York: Holt, Rinehart & Winston.

Mischel, W., and Mischel, H. (1976). A cognitive social-learning approach to morality and self-regulation. In T. Lickona (ed.), *Moral Development and Behavior: Theory, Research, and Social Issues*. New York: Holt, Rinehart & Winston.

Moss, M. K., and Page, R. A. (1972). Reinforcement and helping behavior. *Journal of Applied Social Psychology* 2:360–371.

Nagel, T. (1970). *The Possibility of Altruism*. Oxford: Clarendon Press.

Nagel, T. (1986). *The View from Nowhere*. Oxford: Oxford University Press.

Noam, G. (1990). Beyond Freud and Piaget: Biographical worlds – interpersonal self. In T. Wren (ed.), *The Moral Domain: Essays in the Ongoing Discussion between Philosophy and the Social Sciences*. Cambridge, MA: MIT Press.

Noam, G. (In press). The clinical-developmental contribution to self and morality. In G. Noam and T. Wren, *Morality and the Self*. Cambridge, MA: MIT Press.

Olds, J., and Milner, P. (1954). Positive reinforcement produced by electrical stimulation of septal area and other regions of rat brain. *Journal of Comparative and Physiological Psychology* 47:419–27.

Parfit, D. (1984). *Reasons and Persons.* Oxford: Clarendon Press.

Peck, R. F., and Havighurst, R. J. (1960). *The Psychology of Character Development.* New York: Wiley.

Peters, R. S. (1958). *The Concept of Motivation.* London: Routledge & Kegan Paul.

Piaget, J. (1951). *Play, Dreams, and Imitation in Childhood.* New York: Norton.

Piaget, J. (1952). *The Origin of Intelligence in Children.* New York: International Universities Press.

Piaget, J. (1954/1981). *Intelligence and Affectivity: Their Relationship during Child Development.* Palo Alto, CA: Annual Reviews.

Piaget, J. (1960). Equilibration and development of logical structures. In J. M. Tanner and B. Inhelder (eds), *Discussions on Child Development,* vol. 4. New York: International Universities Press.

Piaget, J. (1962). Three lectures presented to the Menninger School of Psychiatry: 1. The stages of the intellectual development of the child. 2. The relation of affectivity to intelligence in the mental development of the child. 3. Will and action. *Bulletin of the Menninger Clinic* 26:120–45.

Piaget, J. (1932/1965). *The Moral Judgment of the Child.* (M. Gabain, trans.). New York: The Free Press.

Piaget, J. (1967). *Six Psychological Studies.* New York: Random House.

Piaget, J. (1970). *Structuralism.* New York: Basic Books.

Piaget, J. (1971). *Biology and Knowledge: An Essay on the Relations between Organic Regulations and Cognitive Processes.* Chicago: University of Chicago Press.

Pribram, K. (1962). The neuropsychology of Sigmund Freud. In A. J. Bachrach (ed.), *Experimental Foundations of Clinical Psychology.* New York: Basic Books.

Puka, B. (1990). The magic and mystery of Kohlberg's Stage 6. In T. Wren (ed.), *The Moral Domain: Essays in the Ongoing Discussion between Philosophy and the Social Sciences.* Cambridge, MA: MIT Press.

Putnam, H. (1975). The meaning of 'meaning.' In H. Putnam, *Mind, Language and Reality: Philosophical Papers,* vol. 2. Cambridge: Cambridge University Press.

Rapaport, D. (1951). The autonomy of the ego. *Bulletin of the Menninger Foundation* 15:113–23.

Rapaport, D. (1960). The structure of psychoanalytic theory. *Psychological Issues* 2 (2, Whole no. 6).

Rawls, J. (1971). *A Theory of Justice.* Cambridge, MA: Harvard University Press.

Raynor, J. (1974). Future orientation in the study of achievement motivation. In J. W. Atkinson and J. Raynor (eds), *Motivation and Achievement.* New York: Wiley.

Rest, J. (1969). Hierarchies of comprehension and preference in a developmental stage model of moral judgment. Unpublished Ph.D. dissertation, University of Chicago.

Richards, D. A. J. (1971). *A Theory of Reasons for Action*. Oxford: Clarendon Press.

Rosenhan, D. L. (1972). Learning theory and prosocial behavior. *The Journal of Social Issues* 28:151–63.

Rushton, J. P. (1980). *Altruism, Socialization, and Society*. Englewood Cliffs, NJ: Prentice-Hall.

Russell, B. (1905/1956). On denoting. *Mind* (1905) 14:479–93. (Reprinted in R. C. Marsh (ed.), *Logic and Knowledge*. London: Allen & Unwin, 1956.)

Russell, B. (1921). *The Analysis of Mind*. London: Allen & Unwin.

Ryle, G. (1949). *The Concept of Mind*. London: Hutchinson's University Library.

Sears, R. D., Rau, L., and Alpert, R. (1965). *Identification and Child Rearing*. Stanford, CA: Stanford University Press.

Sharp, F. C. (1928). *Ethics*. New York: Century.

Sidgwick, H. (1907/1962). *The Methods of Ethics* (7th ed.). London: Macmillan.

Skinner, B. F. (1938). *The Behavior of Organisms: An Experimental Analysis*. New York: Appleton-Century-Crofts.

Skinner, B. F. (1948). Superstition in the pigeon. *Journal of Experimental Psychology* 38:168–72.

Skinner, B. F. (1953). *Science and Human Behavior*. New York: Macmillan.

Skinner, B. F. (1963). Behaviorism at fifty. *Science* 140:951–8.

Skinner, B. F. (1971). *Beyond Freedom and Dignity*. New York: Alfred A. Knopf.

Snarey, J., Kohlberg, L., and Noam, G. (1987). Ego development and education: A structural perspective. In L. Kohlberg (ed.), *Child Psychology and Childhood Education: A Cognitive-Developmental View*. New York: Longman.

Solomon, R. C. (1974). Freud's neurological theory of mind. In R. Wollheim (ed.), *Freud: A Collection of Critical Essays*. New York: Anchor Books.

Solomon, R. L., Turner, L. H., and Lessac, M. S. (1968). Some effects of delay of punishment on resistance to temptation in dogs. *Journal of Personality and Social Psychology* 8:233–8.

Sprintall, N. (1986). Affective processes. In G. Sapp (ed.), *Handbook of Moral Development: Models, Processes, Techniques, and Research*. Birmingham, AL: Religious Education Press.

Stevenson, C. L. (1944). *Ethics and Language*. New Haven: Yale University Press.

Strickland, L. H., and Grote, F. W. (1967). Temporal presentation of winning symbols and slot-machine playing. *Journal of Experimental Psychology* 74:10–13.

Sytsma, S. (1990). Internalism and externalism in ethics. Ph.D. dissertation, Loyola University of Chicago.

Tappan, M., Kohlberg, L., Schrader, D., and Higgins, A. (1987). Assessing autonomous and heteronomous morality: From substages to moral types. In A. Colby and L. Kohlberg, *The Measurement of Moral Judgment. Vol. 1: Theoretical Foundations and Research Validation*. New York: Cambridge University Press.

Taylor, C. (1971). Interpretation and the sciences of man. *Review of Metaphysics* 25:3–51.

Taylor, C. (1976). Responsibility for self. In A. Rorty (ed.), *The Identities of Persons*. Berkeley: University of California Press.

Taylor, C. (1977). What is human agency? In T. Mischel (ed.), *The Self: Psychological and Philosophical Issues*. Totowa, NJ: Rowman & Littlefield.

Taylor, C. (1983). The significance of significance: The case of cognitive psychology. In S. Mitchell and M. Rosen (eds), *The Need for Interpretation*. London: Athlone Press.

Taylor, C. (1989). *Sources of the Self: The Making of the Modern Identity*. Cambridge, MA: Harvard University Press.

Taylor, G. (1985). *Pride, Shame, and Guilt: Emotions of Self-Assessment*. Oxford: Clarendon Press.

Thorndike, E. L. (1932). *The Fundamentals of Learning*. New York: Teachers College Press.

Tolman, E. C. (1945). A stimulus-expectancy need-cathexis psychology. *Science* 101:160–6.

Tolman, E. C. (1949). There is more than one kind of learning. *Psychological Review* 56:144–55.

Tolman, E. C. (1951). A psychological model. In T. Parsons and E. A. Shils (eds), *Toward a General Theory of Action*. Cambridge, MA: Harvard University Press.

Tugendhat, E. (In press). The role of identity in the constitution of morality. In G. Noam and T. Wren (eds), *Morality and the Self*. Cambridge, MA: MIT Press.

Walster, E., Walster, G. W., and Berscheid, E. (1978). *Equity, Theory and Research*. Boston: Allyn & Bacon.

Watson, J. B. (1919). *Psychology from the Standpoint of a Behaviorist*. New York: J. B. Lippincott.

Weber, M. (1949). *The Methodology of the Social Sciences*. New York: Free Press.

Weissbrod, C. (1975). Noncontingent warmth induction, cognitive style and children's imitative donation and rescue effort behaviors. *Journal of Personality and Social Psychology* 34:274–81.

Wheeler, L. (1966). Toward a theory of behavioral contagion. *Psychological Review* 73:179–92.

Wheeler, L., and Caggiula, A. R. (1966). The contagion of aggression. *Journal of Experimental Social Psychology* 2:1–10.

White, R. (1959). Motivation reconsidered: The concept of competence. *Psychological Review* 66:297–334.

Whiting, J. W. M., and Child, I. L. (1953). *Child Training and Personality: A Cross-Cultural Study*. New Haven: Yale University Press.

Williams, B. (1973). *Problems of the Self*. Cambridge: Cambridge University Press.

REFERENCES

Williams, B. (1976). Persons, character and morality. In A. Rorty (ed.), *The Identity of Persons*. Berkeley: University of California Press.

Williams, B. (1982). The point of view of the universe: Sidgwick and the ambitions of ethics. *Cambridge Review* 103:183–91.

Williams, B. (1985). *Ethics and the Limits of Philosophy*. Cambridge, Mass.: Harvard University Press.

Wollheim, R. (1971). *Sigmund Freud*. London: Collins.

Wollheim, R. (1984). *The Thread of Life*. Cambridge, MA: Harvard University Press.

Wren, T. (1974). *Agency and Urgency: The Origin of Moral Obligation*. New York: Precedent.

Wren, T. (1982). Social learning theory, self-regulation, and morality. *Ethics* 82:409–24.

Wren, T. (1990). The possibility of convergence between moral psychology and metaethics. In T. Wren (ed.), *The Moral Domain: Essays in the Ongoing Discussion between Philosophy and the Social Sciences*. Cambridge, MA: MIT Press.

Yarrow, L. J., McQuiston, S., MacTurk, R., McCarthy, M., Klein, R., and Vietze, P. (1983). Assessment of mastery motivation during the first year of life: Contemporaneous and cross-age relationships. *Developmental Psychology* 19:159–71.

Young, P. T. (1961). *Motivation and Emotion: A Survey of the Determinants of Human and Animal Activity*. New York: Wiley.

Youniss, J. (1980). *Parents and Peers in Social Development*. Chicago: University of Chicago Press.

Youniss, J. (1984). Moral, kommunikative Beziehungen und die Entwicklickung der Reziprozität. In W. Edelstein and J. Habermas (eds), *Soziale Interaktion und soziales Verstehen*. Frankfurt: Suhrkamp.

INDEX